Opportunities and Challenges at Historically
Black Colleges and Universities

Opportunities and Challenges at Historically Black Colleges and Universities

Edited by
Marybeth Gasman
and
Felecia Commodore

OPPORTUNITIES AND CHALLENGES AT HISTORICALLY BLACK COLLEGES AND UNIVERSITIES
Copyright © Marybeth Gasman and Felecia Commodore, 2014.

Softcover reprint of the hardcover 1st edition 2014 978-1-137-48040-8

All rights reserved.

First published in 2014 by
PALGRAVE MACMILLAN®
in the United States—a division of St. Martin's Press LLC,
175 Fifth Avenue, New York, NY 10010.

Where this book is distributed in the UK, Europe and the rest of the world, this is by Palgrave Macmillan, a division of Macmillan Publishers Limited, registered in England, company number 785998, of Houndmills, Basingstoke, Hampshire RG21 6XS.

Palgrave Macmillan is the global academic imprint of the above companies and has companies and representatives throughout the world.

Palgrave® and Macmillan® are registered trademarks in the United States, the United Kingdom, Europe and other countries.

ISBN 978-1-349-50267-7   ISBN 978-1-137-48041-5 (eBook)
DOI 10.1057/9781137480415

Library of Congress Cataloging-in-Publication Data

Gasman, Marybeth.
    Opportunities and challenges at historically black colleges and universities / Marybeth Gasman and Felecia Commodore.
        pages cm
    Includes bibliographical references and index.

    1. African American universities and colleges. 2. African Americans—Education (Higher) I. Commodore, Felecia. II. Title.
LC278.G37 2014
378.7308996073—dc23   2014023454

A catalogue record of the book is available from the British Library.

Design by Newgen Knowledge Works (P) Ltd., Chennai, India.

First edition: November 2014

10 9 8 7 6 5 4 3 2 1

Transferred to Digital Printing in 2015

Dedicated to the students, faculty, and staff at Historically Black Colleges and Universities across the nation.

CONTENTS

Acknowledgments ix

Introduction 1
Marybeth Gasman and Felecia Commodore

Part I Pipelines and Plans

One   Black Colleges, Media, and the Power of Storytelling   11
Quinton Stroud

Two   Spelman College: A Case Study of Student Retention Strategies   27
Sakinah I. Rahman

Three   The Crisis: Decreasing Male Enrollment at HBCUs   39
Matthew Nelson and Phillip Scotton

Four   Three Layers of Underrepresentation: Academic Pipeline Issues for African Americans   57
Ufuoma Abiola

Five   White Faces in Black Places: HBCUs and the White Faculty Experience   75
Atiya Strothers

Six   HBCU Young Alumni: Paying It Forward   89
Brandy Jackson and Jacqueline Amparo

Part II People and Programs

Seven   Expanding the HBCU Legacy: Enrolling and Supporting the Rising Latino Population   107
Paola Esmieu and Andrew Martinez

Eight	Beyond the Fifth Quarter: The Influence of HBCU Marching Bands *Yulanda Essoka*	129
Nine	Study Abroad at HBCUs: Challenges, Trends, and Best Practices *Sarah Mullen*	139
Ten	LGBT Centers on HBCU Campuses: Bowie State University *Joseph Barone*	165
Eleven	Leveraging Honors Programs at HBCUs *Channing Johnson and Tyree Williams*	181
Twelve	Black Greek Fraternity Experiences on Predominantly White and Historically Black Campuses: A Comparison *Dennis Daly*	201

Part III Purpose and Philosophy

Thirteen	Black Lesbian Identity at HBCUs *Alexandra Iannucci*	219
Fourteen	Not in My Backyard: Puritan Morality versus Puritan Mercantilism and Its Impact on HBCUs *Tiffany N. Decker*	235
Fifteen	Searching for Whitley Gilbert: Pluralism, Belles, Bourgeoisie Activism, and HBCUs *Christian Edge*	253
Sixteen	A Place at the Table: Etiquette and Invalidation in the Quest for Cultural Capital at Spelman College *Tiffany N. Decker*	269

List of Contributors	295
Index	297

ACKNOWLEDGMENTS

I am grateful and in awe of the students that participated in our Black college seminar. They worked hard to understand the issues surrounding Black colleges and to create new knowledge. It is because of them that Felecia and I were able to bring this book together.

I would also like to thank Felecia for being an excellent coeditor. I look forward to seeing Felecia develop as a scholar, professor, and eventually president of a Black college. She has tremendous skills.

Many people helped with putting this book together including Melanie Wolff, Audrey Wilson, Thai-Huy Nguyen, and Tope Ligali. I am thankful to each of them for their hard work. I am also grateful to the entire staff at the Penn Center for Minority Serving Institutions as they provide support across every dimension.

Last, I want to thank my best friend Nelson Bowman for his support during the editing of this book and my daughter Chloe who thinks that I can do only great things in life. What a motivation!

MARYBETH GASMAN
Philadelphia, PA

All of the students who contributed chapters have pushed my thinking about various HBCU subjects, and have made me a better scholar by being awesome scholars themselves. This has been a great experience and I am excited about the conversations this book will spark.

I want to thank Marybeth Gasman for giving me the opportunity to be a coeditor with her on this project. She continues to be a great mentor, guide, and example of greatness in higher education. I would also like to acknowledge my parents, Bedelia and Franklin Commodore Jr., my sisters, Angie and Yura, my niece, Michaela, nephews, Michael and Brian, and Godchildren, C.J. and Sydnee, who I work hard to make proud everyday. And finally, to my grandmother, Queenie Coleman, who only had a sixth grade education, loved HBCUs, and always wanted to write a book. Her spirit and dreams live through me and I hope that I honor her memory and life in all that I do.

FELECIA COMMODORE
Philadelphia, PA

Introduction

MARYBETH GASMAN AND
FELECIA COMMODORE

Historically Black Colleges and Universities (HBCUs) are institutions with a unique mission—to aid a significant number of minority, low-income, and first-generation college students attain degrees. In this book, we discuss topics and issues about HBCUs that rarely make their way into the common conversation pertaining to these institutions. However, prior to this discussion let us explore what we do know already.

When envisioning HBCU campuses, monolithic student bodies come to mind. Many HBCU campuses comprise majority Black students, but there is much diversity as well. HBCU campuses serve various communities and the enrollment breakdown is as follows: 76% African American/Black, 3% Hispanic/Latino, 13% White, 1% two or more races, 5% Race/Ethnicity Unknown, 1% Resident Alien (Gasman et al., 2013).

The student bodies at HBCUs are diverse in ways other than their race. One way is class or socioeconomic status. HBCUs overwhelmingly serve more Pell Grant recipients and first-generation students than their HWI (Historically White Institutions) counterparts. The diversity of HBCU campuses does not end with the students. HBCUs have had a long-standing tradition of diverse faculty. In 2011, HBCU faculty was 64% Black, 25% White, 8.3% Asian American, and 3% Hispanic (Gasman et al., 2013). HBCUs not only increase access to degrees but also to the professoriate for scholars of color.

The Obama administration set forth their 2020 college attendance and degree attainment goals and as a result higher education, its value and accountability, has increasingly been featured in national conversation. Areas such as funding, student success, and leadership have become important in understanding how the higher education community will be able to reach the 2020 goals. Furthermore, institutional types such as HBCUs are being examined and questioned on how they will perform and contribute.

Student success has been discussed in various ways, but mostly in terms of graduation rates. Education research for many years has touted quantitative data as the golden standard of measurement. Often the sentiment is that qualitative data is not reliable, subjective and anecdotal. This sentiment is what leads to the understanding of student success through the narrow lens of graduation rates and retention rates. This is not to imply that graduation and retention rates are not extremely important in evaluating and assessing the performance of higher education institutions. Rather, it is to bring to light that only part of the story is being told—there is more to understand regarding student success. Qualitative and mixed methods approaches have increased in education research. Many researchers understand that qualitative data aids in the understanding of quantitative data and creates a context that allows for recommendations, policies, and programming that better fits institutions' and groups' particular needs.

HBCUs have often found themselves under the microscope being examined through this context free lens, often to their detriment. Without the context that qualitative data provides, some of these institutions' performances and efficiencies are called into question. In the ongoing debate as to whether HBCUs are still relevant, statistics such as enrollment, retention rates, and graduation rates at HBCUs are being scrutinized. These numbers bring pause to some, but they do not tell the full story of the work that HBCUs are doing and what they are achieving. More stories of HBCU student successes are beginning to emerge with examples such as recent reports from the Center for the Study of MSIs. This emerging research begs the following questions: Are HBCUs given a fair measure of student success? Does student success look differently at HBCUs than at PWIs (Predominantly White Institutions)? If this is the case, how exactly is that difference captured? One way to spotlight these differences is to recount more of the stories of HBCUs; not just the historical significance and contributions to higher education, but how they are currently building upon the rich legacy they have created. Though emerging research should do its best to provide a better understanding of the work that HBCUs are doing in the area of student success, it should not shy away from making a critical analysis. However, this critical analysis must be approached with an ethic of care and within the proper context. Getting a full understanding not only of what HBCUs are achieving in student success but also of some areas in which HBCUs may be able to improve will prove beneficial for their sustainability.

Funding is another topic that is heavily discussed in higher education and policy circles. Currently the United States has found itself in an economic crisis. This being the case funding across all areas of education has come into question. Gone are the days of schools receiving money simply because an institution provided higher education to the state or to persons in general. Though accreditation has long been a stipulation for federal funding, there has been a move toward performance-based funding at the state government level. Also foundations and philanthropists who can provide funding from the private sector want more assurances that they are funding projects, programs, and institutions that have already proven successful.

Funding challenges are not new for HBCUs. Historically HBCUs have always been underfunded in comparison to their PWI counterparts. When comparing the average HBCU endowment to the average PWI endowment, the difference is drastic (Gasmen et al., 2013). Further, performance-based funding is often based on measurements that unfairly place HBCUs in jeopardy. For quite some time HBCUs have been producing graduates and providing quality education to students with resources that were beyond strained. However, the current economic scenario has placed some HBCUs in a dangerous financial situation. We have begun to lose some HBCUs due to financial constraints, and a number of their fellow institutions find themselves with dangerously low endowments. Given that the country is just emerging from a recession and government funding is shrinking, HBCUs must begin to think about how they will be financially sustainable. From alumni giving to innovative streams of funding, how HBCUs attain financial stability and attain and use resources is a pertinent topic for discussion.

As higher education becomes more like a business model, leadership finds itself coming under more scrutiny. Who is the leader of an institution and how they lead is becoming a topic researchers are increasingly exploring. HBCU leaders are considered the face of their institutions—a living logo. HBCUs have also found their leadership to be the victim of stereotyping. The constructed narrative around HBCU leadership is that it is autocratic, rampant with money mismanagement, and ill equipped to navigate the spaces of those that create policy. A need for increased research on leadership, and HBCU leadership in particular, can aid in debunking some of these myths as well as in understanding the unique challenges of leadership within the HBCU context. There is much to learn about what is currently occurring with HBCU leadership. We now have more presidents that do not have HBCU backgrounds than before, HBCU presidents that come from varied backgrounds (i.e., student affairs, industry), and more women than before, but still more men than women. With the seemingly rapid removing and resigning of presidencies the state of HBCU leadership is a hot topic. There is also interest as to where future HBCU leadership should emerge. Should it be from academia, industry, law, etc.?

With all the varied discussions about HBCUs it must be understood that they are a very vital part of the higher education community. As we look into the future of higher education we can see that there are various opportunities available for HBCUs to continue to thrive and flourish. This book will discuss the current issues, challenges, and strengths of HBCUs. It will also point out the prime opportunities for success available to HBCUs due to their unique skills and contexts.

Challenges

HBCUs are great contributors to the higher education community. This being the case, these institutions as do many others have challenges that they must address as they move forward into the next phase of global education. One of those challenges, as mentioned earlier, is the area of funding. HBCUs must figure out ways in which to wisely manage and grow their current endowments as well as seek out new avenues and streams of income. Historically it has been made clear that government funding for HBCUs is not reliable. With governmental funding dwindling and HBCU relevancy being called into question, the latter must be entrepreneurial in their approach to funding.

Another area that HBCUs will need to address is their dwindling Black male enrollment. Black male enrollment in all institutions is alarmingly low. At HBCUs, where there has historically been a strong male presence, there is an as equally if not more alarming shrinking in the Black male population. With missions of access and uplift HBCUs must figure out a way to address this issue. This is an opportunity to aid in educating a population that is much lower in degree attainment then other minority groups. This will also aid in bolstering the enrollment at many HBCUs.

There are other avenues that HBCUs must explore if they want to sustain their institutions. With ethnic demographic changes in the United States, HBCUs will need to begin recruiting the Latino student population with intent, particularly in institutions located in border states; further, HBCUs will need to be strategic and deliberate in creating campus environments that are supportive of Latino students. Not only do these campuses need to be structurally supportive for Latino students, but also of students who have multiple identities (i.e., gender, LGBT, International, etc.). Building upon their already supportive campuses will lead to positive developments in these institutions.

Strengths

Much of research focuses on HBCUs' challenges, but there are many strengths to be found as well. HBCUs are often touted for their nurturing environments for African American students. But, what is often grossly overlooked is how these institutions succeed with other student populations. The work that many HBCUs do with developmental students is impressive. In many other institutional types these students would find themselves caught in a costly pipeline of developmental coursework, assuming they would even be accepted into the institution. At many HBCUs one will find faculty, administration, and staff working to ensure that students are progressing successfully through their developmental courses and doing so in a timely manner. They are doing a lot of the heavy lifting that many other institutions find to be too costly, both for their finances and in their race for prestige. HBCUs are not only providing access to these students but are also working very hard to turn that access into retention, persistence, and ultimately, graduation. Keeping true to the mission of access many HBCUs hold at their core, the support they supply for first generation students also creates environment for these students' successes. First generation students often have challenges that that are more social rather than academic in nature. Without much support, navigating college and campus culture and practices can be challenging—a constant state of feeling lost. HBCUs having had much experience with such groups of students and are very steadfast in providing the information and services needed, both formally and informally, to equal the playing field.

Apart from student services and campus climate created for students, the curriculum at HBCUs often plays a role in ensuring success for many students of color. The cultural lens and awareness often found in

HBCU curriculum empowers many students of color and aids in their increased comprehension of coursework. This culturally aware curriculum also proves beneficial for the White students at HBCUs as they are able to learn and experience a curriculum that often is not found or practiced in the K-12 sector. This approach creates an increased appreciation and understanding of culture for all students. Students are also educated about diversity in what they see and not just in what they are taught. HBCUs can boast of having very diverse faculty. If it were not for HBCUs we may not have as many employed or tenured faculty of color or women faculty as we do now. HBCUs are spaces where these often marginalized groups can find communities that offer them opportunity. This is beneficial for students as many are able to see professors who look like them and share similar backgrounds. This is something many students of color would not readily experience at a PWI, and certainly not in abundance.

We are aware of the challenges and strengths of HBCUs. However, there is still very little research on these historic institutions. With this book, we seek to bolster the literature by presenting new research that spans the landscape of HBCUs and informs new areas of interest and research. We hope that this book will spur debate and serve as the impetus for better practices at HBCUs and for more rigorous research.

We've divided the book into three parts: "Pipelines and Plans," which focuses on solving looming problems in the pipeline for faculty, students, and administrators and laying plans for the future of HBCUs; "People and Programs," which focuses specifically on students and the programs and organizations in which they operate; "Purpose and Philosophy," which asks questions about the history and relevance of HBCUs.

In Part 1, Quinton Stroud discusses Black colleges, the media, and the power of storytelling in demonstrating the importance of HBCUs. Sakinah I. Rahman writes about the retention success at Spelman College, arguably the strongest HBCU in the nation. Also concerned with retention as well as access, Matt Nelson and Phillip Scotton write about Black male enrollment across HBCUs. Ufuoma Abiola moves the conversation to the production of African American faculty and leaders and the pathways to increasing this production. Atiya Strothers spotlighs the White faculty who choose to teach at HBCUs. The last chapter in this section by Brandy Jackson and Jacqueline Amparo focuses on young alumni and their potential contributions to HBCUs.

In Part 2—People and Programs—Paola Esmieu and Andrew Martinez explore the fastest growing student population in the nation and also in HBCUs: Latinos. Yulanda Essoka contributes a chapter that examines the historical and current influence of membership in marching bands at HBCUs. Although membership in marching bands may seem inconsequential, at HBCUs membership is a powerful force. Sarah Mullen contributes a chapter pertaining to study abroad programs at HBCUs. Her research is particularly important as more African American students must embrace study abroad in order to be competitive in a global economy. Joseph Barone adds to the book with a chapter related to Lesbian, Gay, Bisexual, and Transgender (LGBT) Centers on HBCU campuses. Although a taboo subject for decades, a handful of HBCUs are embracing LGBT students and their needs. Channing Johnson and Tyree Williams contribute a chapter that explores the experiences of students in honors programs at HBCUs. Alexandra Iannucci, like Joeseph Barone, explores lesbian identity at HBCUs while also challenging her own assumptions as a White lesbian. The last chapter in this section by Dennis Daley provides a comparison of experiences between Black Greek letter organizations with the Black fraternities operating in both Black and White institutions.

In Part 3—Purpose and Philosophy—Tiffany Decker writes about the origins of the Puritanical culture that exists at some HBCUs to this day. Christian Edge asks us to contemplate the diversity of African Americans at HBCUs through the lens of Whitley Gilbert, a popular character on television's A Different World. This section also includes a second chapter by Tiffany Decker, which focusses on etiquette and the expectations of women at Spelman College.

Reference

Gasman, M., Nguyen, T., Castro Samayoa, A., Commodore, F., Abiola. U., Hyde-Carter, Y., & Carter, C. (2013). *The changing face of historically black colleges and universities.* Philadelphia, PA: University of Pennsylvania, Center for Minority Serving Institutions.

PART I

Pipelines and Plans

CHAPTER ONE

Black Colleges, Media, and the Power of Storytelling

Quinton Stroud

In their article titled "How to paint a better portrait of HBCUs," Gasman and Bowman (2011) interrogate current media portrayals of Historically Black Colleges and Universities (HBCUs) as well as highlight a variety of potential factors affecting current perceptions of these institutions in the media. Through an examination of the history of media relations with HBCUs, they have uncovered what they deem to be a "pattern of unfair news accounts" and suggest that HBCUs have been at the center of intense scrutiny since their inception. They assert that one of the major issues that perpetuates unfair coverage is the propensity for media outlets to report the most desperate and turbulent situations occurring at HBCUs as being the norm.

This normalizing of turmoil across HBCUs is supported by the underrepresentation of HBCU stories in media and national education publications. The low levels of mainstream coverage received by these institutions allow for single stories to be held as representative of all HBCUs. This practice supports the construction of narrowly framed stories of HBCUs, which are noted as often lacking context, ignoring the diversity that is represented among the current 105 HBCUs, and diminishing the accomplishments and contributions of HBCUs to American higher education.

The threat of these narrowly framed stories lies in the potential for wide generalizations and stereotypes to negatively impact HBCUs.

These generalizations and stereotypes affect HBCUs' ability to recruit students and faculty, funding, accreditation, and the policymaking process at state and national levels with regard to the viability and persistence of this particular set of institutions.

After noting the tendency of the media to support generalizations of HBCUs, Gasman and Bowman consider strategies that the media might implement in order to create more balanced and accurate depictions of HBCUs. They suggest that one such strategy is to provide context when penning stories regarding HBCUs and through the use of stories garnered from a variety of HBCUs. Too often the accomplishments of HBCUs in the mainstream are drawn from only a few select schools—most often Morehouse, Spelman, and Howard—and ignore the diversity of the 105 institutions. The authors also highlight the use of unfair comparisons in media that juxtaposes HBCUs with elite wealthy institutions such as Ivy League schools, which have much larger endowments and have not experienced the history of racial discrimination experienced by HBCUs.

The authors go on to suggest potential areas of growth for HBCU administrators and leaders in the process of crafting better portrayals and stories regarding the institutions that they head. Though the authors acknowledge that HBCU leaders may often decide to shy away from reporters and media as a result of past mistreatments, they suggest that the tendency to disengage with media allows for stories lacking the authentic voice of HBCU leadership, which are needed for providing more nuanced articles regarding these institutions. Choosing to disengage with media does more harm than good as it allows those outside of the schools, who often lack genuine experience and interaction with these institutions, to dictate the direction of discussion.

Honestly and thoughtfully engaging with media will allow HBCUs to have a larger share of control in shaping their own public image and will provide leadership the opportunity to dispel inaccurate generalizations and stereotypes that may exist surrounding their schools. The most critical suggestion made by the authors is the need for HBCU leaders to be intentional in their efforts to tell their own stories. They recommend the need for HBCUs to vigorously engage media by providing stories that will support and uplift their institutions and combat damaging generalizations. For the purposes of this review, I will focus my attention on the potential of storytelling to serve as a tool for HBCU leadership to support and preserve the legacy of their respective institutions and promote the viability of the entire HBCU system.

Methods

In order to develop a framework for the power of storytelling, I will review the concept of the counter-story as developed by critical race theorists. Then using analysis of media narratives produced by HBCU leaders, I will highlight the means by which several HBCU leaders have used storytelling to develop better images of their institutions, challenge preconceived notions, and support the communities in which their schools are located. I conclude with recommendations on ways in which HBCUs can craft better stories and develop more positive images for themselves in mainstream media.

The Power of Storytelling

Solórzano and Yosso (2002) have provided a useful conception of storytelling through their development and discussion of the counter-story.[1] The counter-story has been described as a story that yields the power and potential to build community, challenge perceived wisdom, open new realities for those often found voiceless in dominant discourse, and teach others the possibility of creating a richer, more complex narrative than the ones that dominate the dialogue surrounding a particular topic. The counter-story is created through the process of combining data-based research with the existing knowledge surrounding a topic, along with the professional and personal experiences of the people responsible for the storytelling. I suggest that the counter-story, to a large extent, relies on proven data and research as a means of directly deflating dominant stories and generalizations.

Though the counter-story has been noted to be useful in combating generalizations, competing with stereotypes is not its sole purpose. Focusing only on this purpose, that is, competing with stereotypes and generalizations, is seen as having the potential to strengthen the stereotype by allowing it to continually dominate public discourse. The notion of the counter-story relies on a method of discourse that highlights and supports groups whose authentic voices and experiences may often be missing in dominant discourse surrounding a particular topic. The underrepresentation of articles in the media dedicated to discussing HBCUs is noted in Gasman and Bowman's (2011) article, and as such I suggest that this type of storytelling may prove to be an effective tool in the arsenal of HBCU administrators for supporting the development of their various institutions. The counter-story has the three-pronged ability to "shatter complacency, challenge dominant discourse, and further the struggle for reform" (Solórzano & Yosso, 2002, p. 32).

In the following sections I will draw on analysis of HBCU leaders using media in order to tell stories representative of the method of counter-storytelling in ways that support their respective institutions and HBCUs in general.

Combating Complacency

The first qualifier of the counter-story, its ability to stir consciousness or combat complacency, can be noted in an article penned by Walter Kimbrough, president of Dillard University. In an article in the *LA Times* titled, "Why USC and not a Black College, Dr. Dre?" Kimbrough (2013) contemplates the donation of $70 million to USC by music moguls Dr. Dre and Jimmy Iovine. The money was given to the university to develop a program combining "liberal arts, graphic and product design, business and technology" in order to build the type of talented applicants needed to further the aims of the music moguls' thriving music technology business. Kimbrough goes on to discuss the various reasons the duo may have chosen to support USC over other schools including its proximity to Compton—the area where Dr. Dre was raised—coupled with the fact that Iovines' daughter is an alumna of the university.

Though Kimbrough acknowledges that these artists are allowed to use their money as they please, he uses this article to suggest the transformative possibilities of such a sizeable donation if given to a Black college. While affirming the respectability and prestige of USC, Kimbrough notes that the $3.5 billion dollar endowment while impressive—Dr. Dre's $35 million donation being the largest by a Black man to an institution of higher learning—is "gravy" to such well-resourced institutions where the yearly tuition alone is $45,602. He notes that such a gift to an HBCU would not only support multiple scholarships for the same price but also be instrumental in supporting entire communities of color.

Continuing his interrogation of Dr. Dre's decision to donate to USC instead of an HBCU, Kimbrough addresses the notion that HBCUs might lack the capacity and expertise to undertake and support such an innovative technological program. To prove that this notion is inaccurate, Kimbrough relies on the use of data and research. Citing research from the National Science Foundation, which highlights the importance of Black colleges in the production of Black scientists and engineers, he presents data stating, "the top five producers of Blacks who go on to earn science, technology, engineering and math graduate degrees are Black colleges, as are 20 of the top 50." He further asserts that the legacy of musical tradition associated with HBCUs would have made a Black college an optimal site for such a historic donation.

Kimbrough's article meets the potential of the counter-story to "shatter complacency" as it is not simply an attempt to chastise Dr. Dre for his personal decision, but a call to action, which can be used to challenge and ignite philanthropic support of HBCUs by prominent Black figures. Kimbrough is careful to note that these institutions provide opportunities to students who play significant roles in supporting the careers of many current Black entertainers. Kimbrough's use of data and research to support his claim that HBCUs are indeed a "quality product" also support my selection of his article as a manifestation of the counter-story.

The value of Kimbrough's article lies in its potential to stir the conscious of philanthropists who may have never considered HBCUs as sites for giving as well as challenging notions regarding the HBCUs' abilities to manage new and innovative programming. Kimbrough was also able to present the accomplishments of HBCUs in a larger context, a tactic for displaying HBCU successes presented in Gasman and Bowman's article. By presenting data on the capacity of HBCUs and its involvement in the production and preparation of Black scientists, Kimbrough is able to ensure that readers of his article become more educated on the capacity of HBCUs. Thus, I suggest that Kimbrough's article is important and representative of how HBCU leadership must engage in the art of storytelling as a means of supporting their respective universities.

Challenging Dominant Discourse

The counter-story has the ability to "challenge dominant discourse." This type of storytelling is showcased by op-eds penned by HBCU leader Dr. Larry Robinson, who served as the interim president of Florida A&M University (FAMU). In 2011, FAMU found itself in the center of a media maelstrom surrounding the hazing death of Robert Champion, member of the university Marching 100 band. Reports affirm that Champion's death was the result of a hazing-related practice, which band members participated in as an attempt to gain respect and position within the organization. In presenting the facts surrounding the death of Mr. Champion, the ability of the university to protect its student body was brought into question not only by media but also by prospective students (Bennett, 2012). Amanda Wilson, an incoming freshman the year following the incident, spoke of her angst regarding enrolling at the university. She mentioned the decisions of many of her friends to go elsewhere following the death of Mr. Champion, and even her own doubts prior to deciding FAMU was the right choice for her (Bennett, 2012). This type of questioning of the university became evident when the fall enrollment of incoming students dramatically decreased from 3,778 in 2011, the year of the incident, to 2,508 in 2012 (Enrollment, 2013).

Though the image of the university may have been tarnished, interim president Dr. Larry Robinson has reached out to state media outlets in order to tell a different story. Robinson's articles are crucial to moving the university beyond the stigma of hazing, surrounding and complicating the image of FAMU, by highlighting the various successes and contributions the university has made to the state of Florida and the nation.

Robinson has used various news outlets throughout the state including the *Tallahassee Democrat*, the *Ft. Lauderdale Sun Sentinel*, and the *Tampa Bay Times* in his attempts to redirect the dialogue surrounding FAMU. In these articles, he acknowledges the university's shortcomings as a means of addressing prior potential critiques of the institution. He then uses data to highlight the value of FAMU to the current student body, the state of Florida, and the nation (Robinson, 2013a, b). Robinson notes that the turmoil surrounding the university has supported the media in "repeatedly asking what went wrong with FAMU and focused on unflattering news stories" and may have caused the "general public to miss more prominent yet less told stories of what goes right at FAMU" (2013b, p. 1). Robinson (2013b) states that the often "myopic snapshots" that showcase the university in turmoil miss the "intricate collage of great things" that are happening at the university on a regular basis.

The stories Robinson crafts in his articles are used to create a more nuanced image of the university, one that has received 21 patents in pharmaceutical research in recent years and has developed innovations and technological advancements in agriculture that are beneficial to the state at large. Robinson highlights the work of the university viticulture center in supporting the efforts of Florida grape farmers and wine manufacturers through outreach programming and the production of innovative agricultural biotechnology. Like Kimbrough, Robinson utilizes specific data and research to support his claims, noting that the university has assisted in increasing vineyard acreage throughout the state by more than 16% and has been instrumental in increasing the production and sale of Florida wines by approximately 35%. The school's College of Agriculture and Food Sciences has recently "developed a new disease-resistant Muscadine grape known as Majesty," which has been highlighted for its superior size and taste (Robinson, 2013a).

Beyond supporting agricultural initiatives in the state of Florida, Robinson tells stories of FAMU that highlight the development of a new lightweight material that has been proved useful for aircraft assembly and has gained the attention of the National Football League for its potential in producing protective headgear for athletes. Robinson (2013b) notes that the university remains one of the nation's largest producers of African Americans with bachelor's degrees, and continues to produce nearly one-fifth of the African Americans with doctorate degrees in environmental and pharmaceutical sciences as reminders of the capabilities of the university. The stories Robinson crafts are of highly trained faculty, chemists, and pharmacists on the verge of breakthroughs in cancer, HIV/AIDS, and obesity, and physicists and engineers on the cutting edge of research.

While Robinson's articles discuss the accomplishments and contributions of FAMU, he also makes sure to include the administration's ongoing work, which is geared toward increasing efficiency and productivity by ensuring to "take stock of our challenges in order to avoid these same problems in the future and continue to improve." Dr. Robinson's engaging of the media is representative of the art of counter-storytelling through his intentional use of story to complicate what he deemed "myopic snapshots" and provision of nuanced articles supported by data and research that portray the university's successes, accomplishments, and contributions. The articles compete with stories of challenges and complications, which have recently dominated news surrounding the institution, to build and reinforce the university's positive image (Robinson, 2013a,b).

Though it is not the sole function of the counter-story to compete with dominant discourse (Solórzano & Yosso, 2011), the presence of different stories combats stereotypes. In attempting to challenge overly narrow depictions, the counter-story provides broader images that may be missing in dominant discussions. The narratives Robinson crafts provide information on the university that the general population of

Florida may be unaware of, and thus dispels the notion that FAMU is known only for its band culture in general and the hazing death of fallen Rattler, Robert Champion, in particular. While acknowledging the need for change, Robinson is able to craft stories that move FAMU from past mistakes and challenges and into what he sees to be a promising future.

Though it is understandable that the articles Robinson penned are routed through media outlets in the state of Florida, I suggest that Robinson should begin focusing his attention on reshaping the public image of the university on a larger scale. As the hazing death of Mr. Champion garnered national attention, it is crucial that his message in publications should reach beyond the limits of the state of Florida. I suggest that this expansion of the storytelling regarding FAMU will likely be useful in a variety of areas, but particularly in the recruitment of students from outside the state.

The Potential for Reform

To represent the ability of the counter-story to "further the struggle for reform" (Solórzano & Yosso, 2002, p. 32), I have selected media narratives constructed by Michael J. Sorrell, the current president of Paul Quinn College. I have selected Sorrell specifically for his engaging the media with a sort of storytelling that goes beyond simply calling for change and support for the university he leads, for his challenge to the actual socioeconomic structure of the city of Dallas in which Paul Quinn is located. In an article titled "A tale of two cities," Sorrell (2011) describes the existence of two distinct sections of the Dallas community, which he suggests are divided along lines of economic status, or a manifestation of a have versus the have not's scenario.

The city, as described by Sorrell, is divided into north and south with northern Dallas being described as a place where the convergence of power and wealth have allowed for the development of a beautiful community with access to the resources necessary to support thriving families. In contrast south Dallas is described in much more despondent tones. The area in which Paul Quinn is located is described as one where "security bars protect the windows and doors of affordable housing, where the only cranes erect bland government buildings funded mostly by the taxes of the rich and the powerful" (Sorrell, 2011, p. 1). His portrayal of the southern section of the city continues to describe in detail the way that "environmental hazards such as garbage dumps and metal scrapyards qualify as economic development for its neighborhoods" and note the reality of the area as a food desert in which residents even lack access to quality and nutritious sources of food within their own community (Sorrell, 2011).

Sorrell highlights that the current condition of southern Dallas has historically been blamed on "inadequate infrastructure, fiscal challenges and an undereducated citizenry" (p. 1), but suggests that the true crux of the problem may lie in the fact that Dallas has "become comfortable with its dysfunctional two-city arrangement" (p. 1). In this way not only does Sorrell use the power of story to push for reform and change in Dallas, but also harnesses the power of the counter-story to "shatter complacency" (Solorzano & Yosso, 2002, p. 32) as he address the inequitable status quo existing in his community and issues a call for reform.

Sorrell has even taken to combining his position as president of Paul Quinn with the status of other local community leaders in order to tell the story of Dallas as viewed from residents inhabiting the southern section of the city. In an article penned with area pastor Gerald Britt, the pair narrates the existing inequity present in the restructuring of Dallas education. They begin their article by acknowledging the ongoing efforts of reform-minded individuals to bring change to the Dallas school system but assert that these efforts will remain fruitless until the persistence of highly concentrated poverty in the south side of Dallas is addressed and actively combated. In a direct call for change and economic resources in south Dallas they state:

> We all know what it takes to create an ideal environment for a great education: nurturing adults at home and in the community, access to affordable health care and quality food, exposure to great literature, art and music, and safe neighborhoods teeming with adults living productive lives. However, we have become comfortable ignoring the fact that some neighborhoods lack most if not all of what inspires student achievement. Additionally, many of the schools in these neighborhoods do not have the resources to adequately facilitate such achievement. (Sorrell & Britt, 2013, p. 1)

Sorrell's method of engaging the media is representative of counter-storytelling as it attempts to focus on igniting change and reform amid the inequitable conditions in Dallas. This sort of engaging with and advocating on behalf of the communities in which they are located is an issue highlighted by Andrea Harris, president of the NC Institute of Minority Economic Development. Harris presents the ties that have long existed between HBCUs and the communities, and highlights the fact that often times these institutions' development and progression has been due in large part to the efforts of the communities in which they find themselves situated. Directly relating HBCUs to their host communities, Harris states:

> They are not silos that sit separate and apart from the rest of those living on the same dirt in and around the institutions. Nor are they separate and apart from the very network of people who share or uphold their mission, interests, or with whom they collaborate on ideas, resources, and who identify with the institutions as a part of who they are as a community or a people or a neighborhood. (2011, p. 2)

Harris notes that the physical location of most HBCUs is in the midst of the lower-income tracks of their respective cities. "Most are surrounded by deteriorating housing stock and limited private sector investment. Public sector investment in and around most HBCUs is disproportionately low as compared with other geographic areas of the respective host city that bring the same or less economic value than the HBCU" (Harris, 2011, p. 4). As such Harris calls on HBCUs to reexamine the way in which they view themselves in relationship to their surroundings, as they provide major sources of employment opportunities for their host communities. She further suggests that these schools should be intentional to invigorate partnerships between their host neighborhoods and community organizations geared toward the needs and concerns of low-income and minority communities.

Harris goes on to highlight the ways in which "economic stratification of neighborhoods, gentrification, classism, and to some extent elitism (p. 4)" have diminished the strength of the bonds between many HBCUs, working-class Blacks, the neighborhoods in which they are situated, and many of the civil rights and political organizations that were once viewed as sources of support for Black communities. Harris points directly to the need for determined and deliberate action on the part of HBCUs in engaging the needs of their host communities.

However, Harris warns against the sort of partnership that may situate the college or university as superior to the community in which they serve, as though the collaboration represents charity on the part of the university. Efforts to engage host communities must not "be seen as the pristine scholarly space" (p. 1) attempting to provide breadcrumbs or favors to the unfortunate Black community around it. A relationship in which one party is viewed as less than or more than the other will serve to further separate the parties involved. Harris suggests the imperative of HBCUs reconnecting not only with their communities and neighborhoods but also to other HBCUs is necessary as the future of each is inextricably linked to the other. Through engaging with the community and creating partnerships the entire community will be lifted. Drawing on Harris's prescription for communal engagement on the part of HBCUs and on the stories and advocacy of President Sorrell on the behalf of southern Dallas are crucial for effectively building and maintaining relationships with host communities that are mutually beneficial to both the school and neighborhoods in which they are located.

The Story and the Stereotype

In the preceding sections I have presented examples of HBCU leaders using their platforms in order to engage the media in the process of counter-storytelling. The counter-story is not useful solely for the process of combating negative stereotypes as this sort of reactionary response further supports the existence and proliferation of negative stereotypes by allowing them to shape the direction of discourse surrounding the topic at hand (Solórzano & Yosso, 2002). I suggest then that the power of the counter-story may lie in its ability to generate and craft new and potentially edifying generalizations and stereotypes. The term stereotype carries with it a negative connotation but I suggest that negativity is not a central element of the stereotype. Simply put, a stereotype is a wide-reaching generalization about a group that typically ignores the diversity of the group being stereotyped.

Stereotypes themselves are neutral but provide positive or negative direction through the stories that support their existence. For example, the American Ivy Leagues carry with them the positive generalization of high levels of academic rigor, technological and intellectual innovation, and producers of the nation's best and brightest students. I do not highlight the Ivy League in an attempt to diminish their respectability and prestige among institutions of higher learning or to draw comparisons between them and HBCUs, but in order to highlight the potential for stereotypes and generalizations to be uplifting and even beneficial when they center on positive and edifying beliefs and stories. HBCU leaders can begin the process of building more positive images and generalizations surrounding their institutions by ensuring the constant production of uplifting and positive stories highlighting their accomplishments, successes, and contributions (Gasman & Bowman, 2011).

As stated earlier, HBCUs stand at risk of being negatively impacted by wide-reaching generalizations informed by media representations that more often highlight negative instances in these institutions (Gasman & Bowman, 2011). I suggest that this undermining of performance due to negative generalizations is akin to the concept of "stereotype threat" as developed by social psychologists Steele and Aronson. In a series of experiments testing the effect of stereotypes on the cognitive ability of African Americans students, they discovered that the actual cognitive performance of African American students could be affected negatively by the perceived existence and risk of confirming a negative stereotype surrounding them, in this instance the idea that Black students may not be as smart as their White counterparts (Steele & Aronson, 1995).

Though Steele and Aronson's experiments focus on the cognitive ability of African American students, the potential for stereotypes is presented as one that can be potentially damaging to any group identity to which a particular stereotype pertains. Drawing on this ability of stereotypes to serve as detrimental to performance, I suggest that the concept of stereotype threat might be extended to the institutional level, and in this case to HBCUs, which represent a group identity among American institutions of higher education. I posit that similar to the students in Steele and Aronson's experiments, HBCUs are consistently at risk for the potential of stereotypes to undermine and impact performance. In the case of HBCUs as in the case of the students it is the existence of a group identity that allows for the collective damage experienced by this set of schools due to generalizations and stereotypes.

Though I recognize the potential for group identity to be damaging, I do not suggest that HBCUs should somehow disassociate themselves from their group identity in an attempt to be viewed as individual schools, but advocate just the opposite. I suggest instead that HBCUs should harness the power of their collective group identity to intentionally craft more positives stereotypes that will serve as an advantage and support these institutions. In the same way that negative generalizations can be damaging to HBCUs, it is logical to believe that positive generalizations will be useful in developing the opposite responses, which would include increases in funding, student and faculty recruitment, and would likely produce positive effects on the overall respectability afforded to the HBCU system.

For HBCUs to fully use storytelling, a collaborative effort among all institutions and their leadership will be required to consistently present uplifting stories. I suggest that this sort of collective storytelling must not focus solely on individual institutions but on the wellbeing of HBCUs in general, like the earlier example of Dr. Kimbrough's article (2013) in the *LA Times*. The intentional, consistent, and strategic presentation of well-crafted stories showcasing the collective benefit of HBCUs to the nation in local and national media outlets as well as educational journals is likely to begin a shift in the current depiction of HBCUs in the media (Gasman & Bowman, 2011).

Recommendations

Returning to the suggestions made in Gasman and Bowman's (2011) article, I support their prescription for the necessity of HBCUs to engage media with vigorous and strategic methods of storytelling as a means of preserving the legitimacy of this set of institutions. I find their urging of HBCUs leaders to directly involve themselves with the task of engaging the media to be crucial if HBCUs are to begin the process of defining themselves in the media. Not doing so will only allow reporters, who often lack meaningful interaction with these universities, to shape the direction of the surrounding dialogue. I suggest that the collaborative effort of HBCUs to focus on defining themselves in the media through the process of storytelling will serve to debunk generalizations and stereotypes currently surrounding these institutions (Gasman & Bowman, 2011).

Though engaging media will not eliminate the stories of struggles and downfalls of HBCUs, it will ensure that these stories are not the only representations of HBCUs in the media and will likely assist in influencing more fair and complex depictions of HBCU. Consistent portrayals of HBCUs in the media that are edifying and uplifting are often lacking in the mainstream media and this is where HBCU leaders must step in, ensuring that the media has access to stories that showcase the many accomplishments of HBCUs. Often those associated with the media have highlighted the fact that HBCU administrative members do not return calls from media personnel. Though it might be tempting to disengage and create distance from media due to past misrepresentations, this will continually serve more harm than good for HBCUs as it places the direction and power of the story in the hands of reporters and persons outside the actual institution (Gasman & Bowman, 2011).

Second, those engaged in the storytelling process at HBCUs can assist "by couching their institutions' accomplishments within a larger context whenever possible" (Gasman & Bowman, 2011). This sort of intentional provision of accomplishments can be noted in the articles of both Walter Kimbrough (2013) and Larry Robinson (2013a, b) and is representative of the type of storytelling that I suggest will be useful in building better perceptions of HBCUs in the media. Leaders of HBCUs must also ensure that they are vocal in speaking on the issues and challenges that face their institutions (Gasman & Bowman, 2011). This sort of speaking on issues that effect and challenge HBCUs is notable in the articles of President Michael J. Sorrell as he uses the power of story to support and advocate on the behalf of the community in which his institution is located. Being mindful that HBCUs and the communities in which they are located have long been connected with one another in supportive and meaningful ways reminds us that the issues of their respective communities are often issues that deeply impact the universities themselves (Harris, 2011).

Being intentional about speaking out on issues that impact their host communities is likely to develop and maintain support for these institutions locally, and a pathway for HBCUs to harness their power to positively impact their surrounding communities. The sort of communal engagement highlighted by President Sorrell and advocated by Andrea Harris is mutually beneficial for both university and community, and is crucial to ensuring the relationship between HBCUs and their host communities is strong, productive, and mutually beneficial.

Finally, I suggest that when crafting stories to engage the media HBCU leadership should be sure to include the voices of their most valuable resource, their students. Engaging students will be an effective way to increase the capacity of HBCU leaders to craft diverse and insightful stories regarding their respective institutions. These stories may be useful in consistently highlighting the production power of HBCUs and the caliber of students matriculating from these universities, as was done in Dr. Kimbrough's article. HBCU leaders engaging with students' stories will lead to a powerful way to tell stories that will be useful in shaping perceptions of the university. This process of story sharing, from the student's viewpoint, will aid the perceptions of the university held by administration and leadership. I suggest that this sort of story sharing from student to administrators will be useful in developing innovative programming that is based on the authentic needs of the student body, which will be useful for the development of these institutions.

Conclusion

I have discussed the ways in which media perceptions of HBCUs have assisted in the production of stories and generalizations that have often presented HBCUs in monolithic terms. I have presented suggestions for media persons as well as HBCUs administrators for crafting more complex portrayals of these institutions and have introduced the concept of the counter-story as a potentially effective tool for HBCU leaders attempting to shape and influence the discourse on the institutions they lead. I attempted to present depictions of the type of storytelling I deem to be necessary for the future success of HBCUs through the voices of such HBCU leaders as Dr. Walter Kimbrough, Dr. Larry Robinson, and Michael J. Sorrell.

The selection of these three presidents in particular is not meant to overshadow the stories being told by HBCU administrators throughout the nation but simply as a sample of the type of storytelling I find to be of importance for the progression of this set of institutions. I presented ways in which leadership might begin the process of crafting stories, which will be useful in creating better representations of HBCUs in the media, and provided direction recommendations on useful ways to begin the process of storytelling. In short, I find that if HBCUs are to remain strong entities for the preparation of the students they serve it is time that they begin telling better stories (Gasman & Bowman, 2011).

Note

1. Unless indicated otherwise, this entire section is based on Solórzano and Yosso (2002).

References

Bennet, L. (Performer) (2012). Freshmen move into dorms; fewer students on FAMU's campus [Television series episode]. Tallahassee, FL: WCTV. Retrieved from http://www.wctv.tv/news/headlines/Freshmen-Move-Into-Dorms-Fewer-Students-on-FAMUs-Campus-167251015.html.

Enrollment (2013). Master's thesis. Florida A&M University. Retrieved from http://www.famu.edu/index.cfm?oir&enrollment.

Gasman, M. & Bowman, N. (2011). How to paint a better portrait of HBCUs. *Academe*. Retrieved from http://www.aaup.org/article/how-paint-better-portrait-hbcus.

Harris, A. (2010, June). *Community engagement*. NCCUs centennial symposium: Setting the agenda for historically black colleges and universities.
Kimbrough, W. (2013, May 21). Why USC and not a black college, Dr. Dre? *Los Angeles Times*. Retrieved from http://articles.latimes.com/2013/may/21/opinion/la-oe-kimbrough-usc-dre-20130521.
Robinson, L (2013a, April 27). FAMU marches toward innovation, improvement. *Tampa Bay Times*. Retrieved from http://www.tampabay.com/opinion/columns/column-famu-marches-toward-innovation-improvement/2117561.
——— (2013b, May 14). Florida A&M University's legacy is one of improving lives, community. *Sun Sentinel*. Retrieved from http://articles.sun-sentinel.com/2013-05-14/news/sfl-florida-am-universitys-legacy-is-one-of-improving-lives-community-20130514_1_famu-faculty-improving-lives.
Solórzano, D. & Yosso, T. (2002). Critical race methodology: Counter-storytelling as an analytical framework for education research. *Qualitative Inquiry*, 8(23), 23–44.
Sorrell, M. (2011, August 10). Here in Dallas, we truly have a tale of two cities. *Dallas News*. Retrieved from http://www.dallasnews.com/opinion/latest-columns/20110810-michael-sorrell-here-in-dallas-we-truly-have-a-tale-of-two-cities.ece.
Sorrell, M. & Britt, G. (2013, May 28). Confront poverty or Dallas schools are stuck in place. *Dallas News*. Retrieved from http://www.dallasnews.com/opinion/latest-columns/20130528-michael-sorrell-and-gerald-britt-confront-poverty-or-dallas-schools-are-stuck-in-place.ece.
Steele, C. & Aronson, J. (1995). Stereotype threat and the intellectual test performance of African Americans. *Journal of Personality and Social Psychology*, 69(5), 797–811.

CHAPTER TWO

Spelman College: A Case Study of Student Retention Strategies

SAKINAH I. RAHMAN

Are freshmen retention rates and graduation rates above national and/or peer group averages solely reflective of the respective college or university's selectivity? I venture the answer just may be an overwhelming "No." As support for my assertion, The College Board released in 2009 its initial report titled "How Colleges Organize Themselves to Increase Student Persistence: Four-Year Institutions" addressing the influence of colleges and universities on student persistence. The report specifically summarized six institutional initiatives, such as academic advising and freshmen orientation programs, to assess the level of an institution's resolve to increase student persistence as well as to compare the performance of comparable colleges and universities. Based upon this report and the referenced literature within, I proceed under the presumption that administrators, faculty, policy analysts, graduate students, and other academic scholars most likely agree that an organization's outcome is not the result of any single institutional attribute. If this is true, and assuming so, what are the contributory factors other than institutional selectivity? Specifically, from the vantage point of one particular institution, what are the successful student retention practices employed at existing colleges that can be institutionalized by any postsecondary institution concerned with increasing or stabilizing tuition revenue through improvements in attainment rates? To answer this question I turned to Spelman College in Atlanta, Georgia.

Spelman, founded in 1881 by Christian missionaries, is a private, not-for-profit college and is the oldest surviving Historically Black College and University (HBCU) for women in the United States. Spelman continues to cultivate a niche in developing socially conscious leaders. The mission statement of Spelman is as follows:

> Spelman College, a historically Black College and a global leader in the education of women of African descent, is dedicated to academic excellence in the liberal arts and sciences and the intellectual, creative, ethical, and leadership development of its students. Spelman empowers the whole person to engage the many cultures of the world and inspires a commitment to positive social change.

The commitment to developing more than the intellectual growth of students started with Sophia B. Packard and Harriet E. Giles, Spelman's founders, and continues to be evident through the College's student services and new and integrated curriculum—the Spelman MILE. Since its origin, Spelman's curriculum transformed from vocational and intellectual coursework to its current offering of an undergraduate, liberal arts education with Bachelor of Arts or Bachelor of Science degrees offered in the Fine Arts, Humanities, Social Sciences, and Natural Sciences. Spelman currently serves 2,100 students hailing from 41 states and 15 countries. Spelman is also one of the more selective HBCUs reflected by its Fall 2011 acceptance rate of 37.6%. Spelman's matriculating class of 2011 had an average Grade Point Average of 3.64, average SAT composite score of 1,039, 28 points above the national average, and 30% were ranked in the top 10% of their graduating high school class.

Spelman offers small classes with a student-to-faculty ratio of 11:1. Per the College's Strategic Plan Report dated April 17, 2009, the target student-to-faculty ratio is 10:1, comparable to the College's regional competitors. Eighty percent of Spelman's faculty has a doctorate or other terminal degree. The Southern Association of Colleges and School Commission on Colleges accredits the College. Important to my research, according to the *U.S. News & World Report* 2013 ranking data, Spelman College is the top ranked HBCU with a freshmen retention rate of 88%. Equally as notable, if not more so, is Spelman's lead of HBCUs in six-year graduation rates with 77%. I should note that a common critique of HBCUs is their comparatively low graduation rates. This critique masks the differentiation amongst HBCUs and the success of some HBCUs at retaining and graduating future participants in the global workforce. One such institution is Spelman College. As will be discussed further in the next section, there is existing literature providing insight into Spelman's maintenance of above national average of freshmen retention and six-year graduation rates. I continued my research for two reasons. The first is that any solution regarding student retention is not static in an environment of changing student demographics and labor market demands. Second, the existing literature provides general principles or the framework for effective strategies, such as the role of curriculum and faculty. I sought to examine the details—the specific programs, rituals, training that support the framework offered by current literature. There is not a lot of existing literature on the specific programmatic activities being implemented by colleges and universities. In examining the student retention strategies employed by Spelman, I hope to not only gain insight into practices applicable for other HBCUs but also other women colleges and private and/or public institutions increasingly dependent on student tuition revenue.

Review of Literature

According to a senior Spelman administrator, during 2017, implementation of Spelman's new four-year liberal arts curriculum—the Spelman MILE or My Integrated Learning Experience—will be complete (D. Pedescleaux, personal communication, March 11, 2013). In 2005, Butler commissioned an evaluation of Spelman's curriculum. The first phase of the new curriculum, under the academic leadership of the College's ninth President, Beverly Daniel Tatum, and Provost, Johnnella Butler, was launched in 2011. The Spelman MILE, as described in the Spelman College Strategic Plan Report dated April 17, 2009, articulates the College's value proposition or expected student experience over a four-year term. The Spelman MILE is the College's coordination of students' academic and extracurricular experiences on campus. Toward this end, some of the goals of the new curriculum when fully launched are 100% student participation in undergraduate research or major-related internship, 100% participation in the alumnae mentorship program, increased number of learning communities from the existing two on campus to ten, and each Freshman's development of a leadership plan. The coordination of these services involves collaboration of the College's Provost, Enrollment Management,

Student Affairs, Alumnae Affairs, and Undergraduate Studies offices. Consequently, the College's entire senior team is accountable for the implementation of the Spelman MILE. The revised curriculum is recognition of the need for different learning methods for the Millennial student in the twenty-first century, particularly interactive instruction, versus traditional lecture, and curriculum infused with global context. The curriculum was also last modified approximately 16 years prior to Butler's commission. The objectives of Spelman's new curriculum provide the quintessential case study of the student retention principles advocated by Vincent Tinto, a professor at Syracuse University and scholar of student retention strategies, as well as a continued demonstration of the College's focus on providing a comprehensive education, as communicated by Spelman academics and past presidents.

While acknowledging that there are unique characteristics in every higher education institution affecting baccalaureate attainment, such as the degree of selectivity of an institution, which has been shown to reduce first year attrition rates for full-time students, Vincent Tinto offers general principles for the development and implementation of student retention strategies in the 1993 second edition of his book titled *Leaving College: Rethinking the Causes and Cures of Student Attrition*. Tinto's inaugural article on student retention—"Dropout from Higher Education: A Theoretical Synthesis of Recent Research"—was published in 1975. Per Mertz's "Challenges and Changes to Tinto's Persistence Theory," criticism of Tinto's 1975 article include his consideration of only traditional students (residential students at four-year institutions) and an anthropological critique that social integration theory does not acknowledge and consequently does not provide guidance to address student retention on a campus representative of multiple cultures (as cited in Tierney, 1992). To Tierney, integration is synonymous with assimilation. Cultivating a campus culture, often the culture of the dominant or mainstream society, is important but there needs to be recognition that the campus culture may be foreign or jarring to some matriculating students; thereby, requiring additional considerations when integrating underrepresented minorities into campus life. The absence of such recognition could result in social isolation of certain students and distortion of the institution's underlying causes of student departure.

Having said that, I believe Tinto (1993) presents a general framework for all institutions to consider, leaving flexibility to the college to tailor specific action based upon its respective student demographics. Tinto asserts colleges should not focus on retention strategies but on the intellectual and social growth of students. If this is accomplished, retention will be a natural byproduct. Therefore, the foundation of any successful retention program must include the "principles of effective retention." The common theme underlying the principles is commitment. These fundamental principles are: (i) commitment to a student-centered organization, (ii) commitment to student education, and (iii) commitment to establishing a community among students and between students, faculty, and staff. All three principles recognize that the campus experience is a significant determinant of persistence. The principles further underscore that faculty is core to student integration into the intellectual life on a campus, and personal ties with other students and staff are critical for a student's integration into the informal or social experiences offered by the campus. Development of a retention program is the first step. Implementation completes a program. Two of the seven guidelines provided are increase, through incentives, the departments or number of staff and faculty focused on student retention and concentrate retention efforts to the first year of college. Spelman has taken this to heart with an increased focus on trained faculty for advising and mentoring during students' first year experience.

In *Daring to Educate: The Legacy of the Early Spelman College Presidents* (2005), Yolanda Watson and Sheila Gregory document the advancement of Spelman's curriculum during the tenure of the College's first four Presidents and the influence of the curriculum (formal and informal) on Spelman's culture and socialization of the student body. From President Sophia Packard to President Florence Read, Spelman's formal curriculum evolved from an "ungraded" school offering basic reading, writing, and arithmetic instruction to a practical or industrial collegiate curriculum to eventually the liberal arts curriculum we associate with the College today. Spelman's curriculum changed under the leadership of the first four presidents, resultant changes to the vocational opportunities available to African American women, beliefs held by the individual presidents, societal expectations as well as philanthropist' expectations. During this 72-year period, extracurricular activities included Bible study, athletic games, social hours, performances by renowned musicians, and guest lecturers consisting of politicians, philanthropists, and actors. The authors conclude based upon their analysis of the College's first 72 years of existence that Spelman's success at graduating African American women is attributable to the provision of a comprehensive education focusing on the "training of the heads," "training of the hands," and "training of the hearts" of Spelmanites, meaning the simultaneous focus on college instruction, activism or community involvement, and Christian faith and sisterhood.

Intellectual and personal growth of students has been the intentional core of Spelman instruction since the College's founding. Two key takeaways for my research—Spelman has a history of administrators (and in this case campus presidents) serving as role models and also that Spelman's curriculum has evolved over time based upon the interests of the current presidents and also to accommodate changes within the nation as well as global community. This book details this precedent established with Presidents Packard and Giles, the College's cofounders. The Spelman MILE continues the tradition of the College employing curriculum to shape Spelman's culture and student experience. The legacy established by the early presidents was that a Spelman education should be practical; thereby, having professional and personal application and also be used for the general benefit of African Americans.

Johnnetta Cole concludes her autobiography with the lessons she learned about Spelman's success during her tenure as the College's seventh president (Cole, 1993). Four of the six lessons gleaned from her tenure at Spelman focused on staff, faculty, and curriculum. Student success was dependent upon high expectations, quality faculty, positive role models, and a curriculum reflective of the contributions of the members of the class. Cole's words beautifully summarize the secret of Spelman's success of undergraduate persistence:

> In an atmosphere relatively free of racism and sexism, where teachers care and expect the very best, parents and kinfolk are involved, and the curriculum and those around the students reflect in positive ways who the students are—there are no limits to what individuals can learn and who they can become.

Spelman undertook its own research into increasing student retention with a grant provided by the Pew Charitable Trust (Nettles et al., 1999). The Pew Charitable Trust provided grants to ten HBCUs between 1994 and 1998 under the Trust's Third Black Colleges Program. The proceeds of the grants were to be used to implement programs, initiatives, or services specific to the needs of the participating campuses. The focus of Spelman's grant was the Learning Resources Center (soon to be renamed the Student Success Center) and the dual role of faculty at Spelman as instructor and advisor. The Learning Resources Center provides academic advising, assistance with study strategies, and peer tutoring. Student services complement faculty retention initiatives.

Methods

I used the case study method to research the services, practices, and personnel employed by Spelman to increase student retention. A single-institution case study afforded a comprehensive approach best suited to address the question of how the College has attained its level of student persistence. Information was collected via primary and secondary research with the objective of gaining insight into the role of faculty in retaining students, available academic support, and the College's efforts to develop a well-rounded individual. Regarding secondary research, I reviewed the College's website for published retention strategies as well as the available literature on student retention policies, generally, and at Spelman, specifically. This secondary research was supplemented with two phone interviews with senior Spelman administrators as well as surveys of Spelman alumnae. My primary point of contact at Spelman College was the Dean of Undergraduate Studies. I developed a ten-question online survey for Spelman alumnae. The online survey allowed former students to discuss the experience, faculty, traditions, events, and resources, if any, that enabled them to persist in their undergraduate studies. The survey also served as a cross-reference for the effectiveness of campus retention services communicated by Spelman administrators. The survey was distributed via email, networking sites, and social media.

Findings and Discussions

Spelman's answer to the student retention question is dedicated faculty and student services. The underlying structure coordinating or integrating academic instruction, faculty engagement, and student services is the Spelman MILE. Spelman College has institutionalized its mission statement through the Spelman MILE. The goal of the Spelman MILE is not only integrating freshmen with college instruction and life but also creating an experience for students.

Faculty Engagement. The changes made to Spelman's advising program and the creation of first-year experiences commenced pursuant to development of Spelman's new curriculum, both of which center on the dual role of faculty as instructor and advisor. Along with the review of Spelman's curriculum, an advising taskforce was formed in 2006 to review the College's existing advising system and provide any recommendations for improvement. The Office of Assessment and Student

Learning annually surveys freshmen and seniors to evaluate the effectiveness of campus advising. During 2004 and 2007, the survey results revealed that the existing advising system was simply a registration tool for students. Based on this feedback Spelman's faculty advising program began transitioning to an advising mentoring program in 2008 with faculty incorporating informal, social meetings with students, such as on-campus pizza parties. A goal of Spelman's advising program is for faculty mentoring to facilitate student development of educational and professional goals. As part of the advising process, all freshmen are required to create a leadership plan. The leadership plan coordinates a student's academic activities each year of her tenure at Spelman with her identified professional objectives. In addition to informal interactions, the frequency of advisor/student meetings has been increased. Freshmen meet with their advisors twice a week starting during new student orientation. Participation in the freshmen advising program is a requirement for freshmen.

There are 42 trained first-year facilitators or advisors. There is a mandatory one- to two-day training workshop for advisors. The workshop includes an overview of academic policies and procedures, best practices in advising, course sequence for various degrees, and the importance of a liberal arts education. The workshop is typically facilitated by the Dean of Undergraduate Studies' office. All advisors are equipped with a First-Year Advising Handbook and Course Sequence Handbook for all majors and minors offered at the College. The First-Year Advising Handbook covers the material provided in the training workshop and includes the College's academic support services and academic policies. Each advisor, on average, has between 16 and 18 advisees. The administration of the freshman advising program is shared between the Office of Undergraduate Studies and the academic departments. Once a student declares a major, her advisor becomes a faculty member in her selected academic department. The respective department chair advises all seniors.

Advising and mentoring is prioritized for early detection of problems a student may have acclimating to college life. Regarding academics, faculty, as the first line of defense, participate in the Early Alert Program. Prior to midterms, all faculty members will receive a professor's notice that a student is having academic difficulty, evidenced by a "C" grade. This notice will prompt the discussion of the student's need for additional resources, tutoring, or recommendations to drop the class. Administrators are also involved in the retention efforts. The Office of Enrollment Management conducts 60-second interviews with freshmen each semester as a quick gauge of their experience.

Student Services

Spelman offers a variety of student services, such as a math lab, writing center, and Learning Resources Center. The academic support services provided by the Learning Resources Center include academic workshops regarding strategies for reading textbooks and taking notes and exams. Not all of the College's available student services relate to academic preparation, such as the Bonner Office of Community Service and Student Development and the Gordon-Zeto Center for Global Education. The Bonner Office of Community Service and Student Development programs are designed to provide opportunities for community service, such as the campus-wide service initiatives organized on the weekends throughout Atlanta. The Gordon-Zeto Center for Global Education responsibilities include, but are not limited to, coordination of study abroad opportunities for students. The available student services and extracurricular activities reinforce the mission of the College—academic excellence, leadership, civic engagement, and global awareness.

To a lesser extent convocations, such as the New Student Orientation Induction ceremony, utilize tradition, alumnae, and institutional history to bind students with each other and the institution. Alumnae come to campus to participate in the induction ceremony, held the Sunday following the first week of class, to welcome the freshmen into Spelman's sisterhood. Students committed to graduating from a particular institution are more willing to persist (Tinto, 1993). The combination of a rigorous curriculum taught by dedicated faculty and coordinated with student services for academic need, community service, and leadership creates a niche for the College to further differentiate itself and its value to students from competitors.

Alumnae Feedback

President Florence Matilda Read asked in *The Story of Spelman College*:

> Yet when all that is said, the real test, the fruit of the undertaking, is the alumnae, the women whom it has trained. What of them?

In response to this question, I created a ten-question online survey to obtain feedback from Spelman's alumnae regarding their selection of the College and sources of motivation for persisting at Spelman.

Additionally, I sought the alumnae feedback for affirmation of research via literature review and my interview with a senior administrator as well as illumination of new perspectives. Spelman's alumnae conveyed better than any book or interview the College's success in creating a sense of community on campus. Spelman's conscious effort to utilize faculty engagement in its student retention has not been in vain. A consistent theme from the alumnae surveys was the influence of the small classes, faculty, and staff expectations and availability as well as the encouragement of equally motivated peers on their persistence at Spelman. According to a 2000 graduate:

> At Spelman both the faculty/staff and students valued education. So we held each other accountable. You were expected to do your best. The school made a point to expose us to a variety of opportunities—travel/study abroad, lectures, internships. For example, I was a member of the Spelman Jazz Ensemble, which gave me the opportunity to tour to various parts of the country throughout the year. We also, met and were able to learn from established musicians. Also, community service was expected, so we all dedicated a good portion of our time to giving back to our community in some way. When you attend Spelman you automatically become a part of a lifelong sisterhood. This sisterhood has helped me further my career as well as help others. Attending Spelman was one of the best choices I have ever made in my life.

One of the survey questions requested respondents to check the factors that contributed to the successful completion of their undergraduate studies. Seventy-seven percent or 30 of the 39 respondents acknowledged the influence of faculty. Peer effects are also high at Spelman. Faculty was topped only by the academic aptitude and encouragement of "classmates" as a motivation for persistence. Secondary sources of support included community service opportunities, classroom sizes, and academic offering, particularly the dual-degree engineering program. Spelman's academic reputation and success with medical and law school placement were also important considerations. Regarding the respondents—this alumnae group represented classes between 1976 and 2012, graduated between two and five and a half years, with an average of four years, and approximately one-third were related to Spelman alumnae. The majority of respondents received some form of financial aid from Spelman, primarily in the form of partial academic scholarships or work-study. The majority also applied to both majority (73%)

and historically Black colleges. This sample alumnae group includes 40 graduates.

Conclusions

College completion in the United States is a function of the affordability of postsecondary education, parental characteristics, and academic preparation of high school graduates, some of which are outside of the control of colleges. Therefore, this chapter focused on the initiatives within the control and employed by a US college to improve undergraduate completion. I hope the primary takeaway from my research is that student success at a college or university does not occur by chance but reflects the actions of an intentional college. Toward this end and in support of quantifying the role of postsecondary institutions in increasing student retention, follow-up research on Spelman College in 2015 and 2017 should be conducted to monitor the College's progress with attainment of curriculum goals communicated in the College's 2009 Strategic Plan Report. This research of comparing stated objectives to actual performance could be expanded to other HBCUs that have published strategies and goals, assuming an institution's Institutional Research department does not provide progress updates. This increased transparency could aid in furthering the College and this sector's accountability with parents, alumnae, legislators, and other funders. Since the increase of learning communities was one stated goal of Spelman, a study of the use, success, and challenges, if any, of learning communities at HBCUs is a related topic for expanded research.

A tertiary objective of this study is reframing the discussion of the relevancy of HBCUs and the marketing of these institutions in the twenty-first century. In my survey I asked alumnae why they chose Spelman knowing their responses would be helpful in informing the marketing of the College. Perhaps the available academic and extra-curriculum programs, commitment of administrators and faculty, and testimony of alumnae suggest that Spelman is an example of a private college that is an option for *academically prepared* female students interested in a rigorous liberal arts curriculum focused on student research, leadership development, and international issues, with a particular emphasis on women's role in resolving conflict where present throughout the African Diaspora. An intimate campus, a liberal arts curriculum with a leadership and international niche, all at an institution with a proven track record of timely degree completion—it is enough to make one spellbound.

References

Cole, Johnnetta (1993). *Conversations: Straight talk with America's sister president Johnnetta B. Cole*. New York: Doubleday.

The College Board (2009). How colleges organize themselves to increase student persistence: Four-year institutions. Retrieved on July 12, 2013 from http://professionals.collegeboard.com/profdownload/college-retention.pdf.

Nettles, M. T., Wagener, U. Millett, C., & Killenbeck, A. (1999). Student retention and progression: A special challenge for private historically Black colleges and universities. *New Directions for Higher Education, 27*(4), 51–67.

Pedescleaux, D., Baxter, G., & Sidbury, C. (2008). Transforming learning: Academic advising at Spelman College. *Peer Review, 10*(1), 24–26.

Perna, Laura W., Lundy-Wagner, Valerie C., Drezner, Noah D., Gasman, Marybeth, Yoon, Susan, Bose, Enakshi, & Gary, Shannon (2008). The contribution of HBCUs to the preparation of African American women for STEM careers: A case study. *Review of Higher Education, 50*(1), 1–23.

Read, F. M. (1961). *The story of Spelman College*. Princeton, NJ: Princeton University Press.

Spelman College (2009). *Spelman College Strategic Plan Report*. Atlanta, GA: Matthews Consulting Group.

——— (2012). *History and traditions reference guide*. Atlanta, GA: Office of Alumnae Affairs.

Tierney, W. G. (1992). An anthropological analysis of student participation in college. *Journal of Higher Education, 63*(6), 603–618.

Tinto, Vincent. (1993). *Leaving college: Rethinking the causes and cures of student attrition*. Chicago, IL and London: The University of Chicago Press.

Watson, Y. L. & Gregory, S. T. (2005). *Daring to educate: The legacy of the early Spelman College presidents*. Sterling, VA: Stylus Publishing, LLC.

Yin, R. K. (1989). Case study research: Design and methods (4th ed.). Newbury Park, CA: Sage Publications.

Zumeta, W., Breneman, D. W., Callan, P. M., & Finney, J. E. (2012). Financing American higher education in the era of globalization. Cambridge, MA: Harvard Education Press.

CHAPTER THREE

The Crisis: Decreasing Male Enrollment at HBCUs

MATTHEW NELSON AND
PHILLIP SCOTTON

> There is a decline in the number of men going to college, period. When America has a cold, Black America has pneumonia.
>
> Walter Kimbrough, Dillard University

If you were to sit in on a lecture at an average American college, you would likely observe a well-trained professor who is well versed in their respective area of study imparting their expertise to eager pupils. You would notice that the students come from varying cultural backgrounds. You might even notice that certain ages are more prominent in the classroom. One key element of said classroom that you may or may not notice, but would almost certainly be present, is that women in the lecture hall would outnumber men.

The inequities present on American college campuses continue to reflect the myriad moral flaws and inequalities in our larger American society. Most startling of the inequities in higher education is the disproportionate number of Black males currently enrolling in college. In 2010, Black men accounted for nearly 8% of the population of 18- to 24-year-olds but represented less than 4% of undergraduate enrollment at our nation's flagship universities (Harper, 2012; Lundy-Wagner & Gasman, 2011; Toldson, 2011). These dismal enrollment statistics are the product of many years of racial inequity not only in our colleges but also systemic factors built into our society.

These dismal enrollment statistics in the greater landscape of American higher education may not surprise many, given the negative way that Black males are often portrayed in academic literature (Davis, 1994; DiPrete & Buchmann, 2006; Toldson, 2011; West, 2008). However, it is shocking (at least to the authors of this chapter) that Historically White Institutions (HWIs) are not the only culprits.

Since 1987, Black women have represented the majority at four-year public and private HBCUs. Overall, Black women represent 14.8% of the undergraduate population, and more specifically they are representative of more than 60% of the population at HBCUs (Lundy-Wagner & Gasman, 2011; Provasnik et al., 2004). In fact, the enrollment gap between Black men and their female counterparts has grown nearly every year for the past three decades as more females rush the college gates and Black male enrollment remains stagnant (Cross & Slater, 2000). This disparity cannot be taken lightly, particularly when the enrollment trend is more closely examined. In 1900, Black men represented 72% of enrollment at HBCUs, a number that has dwindled to only 39% in 2012 (Johnson, 1939; NCES, 2011). To better illustrate just how problematic this dwindling percentage of Black males enrolling at HBCUs is, we use the historical losses mentioned above to create a direct projection of future enrollment. Based on a loss of 33% in a little over a century, if this trend was to persist, Black males would constitute only 9% of students at HBCUs at the end of the twenty-first century!

While most scholars might scoff at a projection of this magnitude, we imagine scholars in the early 1900s would have had a similar reaction to the idea that Black male enrollment would shrink 33% at HBCUs during the twentieth century. We do have faith that the enrollment gap at HBCUs will be curbed eventually, but many questions must be asked in the meantime: What kind of work must be done to reach equity goals? How long will it take to achieve gender parity at HBCUs? And most importantly, what impact does this growing gender gap have on our institutions, the Black community, and society at large?

Purpose of Study

As revealed, the importance of understanding the gender parity at HBCUs has been overlooked and understudied. Some researchers (Allen et al., 2007; Gasman, 2007; Palmer & Gasman, 2008; Harper et al., 2004; Lundy-Wagner & Gasman, 2011) have focused on race and gender at HBCUs individually, but most have not looked at the historical dynamic of Black males and their enrollment in these institutions of higher education. In this chapter, we use existing literature to shed light on male enrollment with particular attention to the shrinking population at HBCUs, where Black males once were well represented. Second, we focus on dialogue between the presidents of HBCUs and the issue of male enrollment nationally and on their respective campuses, to identify trends and strategies that are relevant to institutions that either have a low disproportionate rate of males enrolling or a balance in gender enrollment on their campus.

Since the mid-nineteenth to the present twenty-first century, Black males have been ignored regarding analysis of degree completion and especially enrollment (Lundy-Wagner & Gasman, 2011). The lack of research done on Black male enrollment, leads to the belief that the overall depreciation in Black male enrollment and attainment has not been labeled as an important issue. This chapter attempts to clarify and validate that some HBCUs have started to holistically impact the growing gender gap and also note the unfortunate circumstances that Black males are facing today.

Context

When Alexander Twilight graduated from Middlebury College in 1823, he pioneered an era where Blacks would be educated in American colleges (Middlebury &Wiley, 1917). While his accomplishment marked important progress in the fight for racial equality, slavery was still legal for another 40 years. Before the Civil War, there were approximately 40 Blacks with degrees in the United States, with only three of them being women (Cross & Slater, 2000). This demonstrates that Black men (at least at one point) were considerably more likely to attend college than their female counterparts. Following the signing of the Emancipation Proclamation, several schools were opened to educate the newly freed slaves. These schools created a huge demand for teachers, an occupation that was almost exclusively held by women during the antebellum period. This increasing demand for Black teachers meant the beginning of a shift in the occupational focus at many HBCUs from theological studies, a field dominated by men, to teacher training (Lundy-Wagner & Gasman, 2011).

Further, noticeable inequities, remnants of slavery (e.g., Jim Crow), persisted for another century and continue to shape the America we see today. As capitalism often seems like a race, it cannot be overlooked that Black men began receiving a college education almost two centuries after their White counterparts (Thelin, 2011). It is no surprise, then, that Blacks have not attained equity in representation on most postsecondary campuses. What is surprising, is Black males' progress in attaining equitable representation not only continually trailed Whites, but also that they have fallen behind Black women, who were not conferred degrees until 1862 (Logan, 1969).

Adding to delayed access to higher education for Blacks are such factors as drastically increasing incarceration rates of Black males in the last 30 years, which are compounding the issue and continually exacerbate inequity in all institution types; HBCUs are no exemption. Incarceration rates in the United States were stable between 1925 and 1975, where roughly 100 of every 100,000 of the standing population were incarcerated (Pettit & Western, 2004). This number saw enormous growth after 1976, to the point where in 2001, the number had grown fivefold (DiPrete & Buchmann, 2006). As this number grew for the general population, it failed to grow proportionately for the respective races, with Black men comprising the vast majority of the new prisoners. In fact, by 2002, 12% of Black males in their twenties were incarcerated, meaning 12,000 young Black men per 100,000 are behind bars (compared to a national average of 472) (Pettit & Western, 2004). Many sociologists attribute this mass incarceration, particularly as it pertains to the longer sentences received by Black males, to police and court perceptions of Blacks as threatening or troublesome (Davis, 1994; Slater, 1994). Although it is a simple thought, it must be said: a Black man in prison is a Black man not in college. The authors of this chapter assert that many Black men who are serving time behind bars could (and likely should) be a large portion of Black males that are missing on HBCU campuses. This is one of many examples of forces working to sustain the inequities in Black male enrollment.

While getting more Black Americans to college has been touted as a priority in the past, and increases in Black enrollment have been publicized as successes by governments and institutions alike, a closer look at the data is necessary. Black males require specific focus because of the lack of progress historically. In 1976, Black men only made up 4.3% of students enrolled in college, a percentage that did not increase *at all* over the following 25 years (Harper, 2006)! This means all percentage increases in Black enrollment are reflective of women. The promise of educational and gender equity could not be fulfilled just by policies alone; thus, continuing a distinct enrollment pattern by Blacks that has continued for decades and still is an issue today (Allen, 1992; Carter, 2007).

Despite Black men having a 40-year head start from when they were first allowed to enroll in college, when gender-specific data on Blacks were first collected in 1953, the Black women already outnumbered men by approximately 18% (Lundy-Wagner & Gasman, 2011). More worrisome, Harper (2006) found the gap has grown significantly, citing that "across all racial/ethnic groups, gender gaps in enrollment are widest among Black students" (p. 2).

Focus on increasing Black male enrollment at our universities is necessary because US employment inequities indicate that Black males need college degrees the most. Among the total Black populace, only 42% of high school graduates who *opted* to not enroll in college were employed in October of the year they graduated compared to 69% for their White counterparts (West, 2008). The average unemployment rate for Blacks in 2011 was nearly 16%, twice the percentage of unemployed Whites (U.S. Department of Labor, 2012). The Department of Labor (2012) also notes that Black unemployment rates saw the largest increase during the recession, partially attributable to workers with less education being more negatively affected during recessions. Making the causal connection between education and employment in America is paramount if we are to fully understand the wide range of parties affected by low Black male enrollment.

Case Study

To better understand the current state of the gender enrollment gap at HBCUs, what causes and exacerbates it, its implications, and possible prevention methods, we take a deep dive into the presidents' offices at Saint Augustine's University and Dillard University. We explored the two universities by conducting detailed interviews with Dianne Suber and Walter Kimbrough, respectively. We have chosen to analyze these two universities for this chapter due to their many similarities in founding, institutional type, and general makeup, yet vast differences in the gender makeup of their enrollment.

Saint Augustine's University

Saint Augustine's University (SAU), which was founded by prominent Episcopal clergymen in 1867, first started as a normal school. Like many

HBCUs, SAU was founded with the purpose of educating freed slaves during the Reconstruction era in the South. As a normal school, SAU offered technical and trade-related programs while adopting a liberal arts curriculum a few years later. Although SAU started out as a normal school, the church understood the value of having a mission that catered to the Black male and the professional demands of the time. Located in Raleigh, North Carolina, it served as a primal hub for the local Black neighborhoods that still surround it today

SAU has survived through many name changes and became Saint Augustine's University in August of 2012, a change that attests to the evolution it has continued since inception. With the numerous changes throughout time, SAU prides itself on its nonnormative gender parity: its student body is approximately 1,600 undergraduate students, with 51% being male and 49% being female (St. Augustine University Institutional Research Office, 2013). In this study, Saint Augustine's University was selected primarily because of its gender parity, which is rare and significant not only in the realm of HBCUs, but also in the greater arena of higher education.

Dillard University

Similar to Saint Augustine's University, the foundation of Dillard University expanded from the religious extraction of the United Church of Christ and the United Methodist Church. These two religious affiliations laid the results from the merger between Straight College and Union Normal School (eventually becoming New Orleans University) dating back to 1869 in Louisiana. Dillard's creation was in response to the need to educate the freed slaves of the South, specifically New Orleans, which at the time held the largest population of Black Americans (Bernard & Clytus, 2000).

After the merger, the Board of Trustees saw it fit to form a private institution that would adhere to Christian principles and values. Also, they felt that the institution should implement coeducation and an interracial learning environment, but only to continue its mission by serving predominately Black American students. Through the proposed ideals, Dillard University would also take part in offering a traditional liberal arts curriculum, similar to Saint Augustine's revisions to its mission during its founding years (Bernard & Clytus, 2000; History, n.d.). Dillard University continues to be a historically Black university enrolling approximately 1,300 students with 28% and 72% being male and female, respectively.

In selecting these schools, we hope that the proximities in founding date (within two years), being privately funded, similar total undergraduate enrollment, and both being religiously affiliated liberal arts colleges will allow them to be more reasonably compared than would institutions of different size, type, and founding date. We also chose these universities because of the large variance in their gender makeup within the student bodies. We assert that Dillard's and Saint Augustine's similarities in many aspects will allow for better understanding of the issues, influences, and implications that institutions face when creating gender parity (or lack thereof) in their enrollment.

Methodology

To further examine the current state of Black male enrollment on HBCU campuses and the impact that it could possibly generate, we piloted a set of interviews to assess the observations of current HBCU leadership and the importance of having Black males represented on HBCU campuses. This consisted of choosing the president at each institution who has an expert understanding of enrollment and the institution's mission. We specifically chose to interview one male and one female president, in case of unforeseen bias in the unparalleled gender issue. In society we have come to know that women have to embrace the male norm in order to secure career advancements or assert power in times of need (Eddy & Cox, 2008). Being aware of the gendered perpetuation of leadership, we understand that this can cause a misleading affect within the interpretations. Interviewing the president from Saint Augustine's University and Dillard University, both being privately funded, provided an equal link between gender parity on each campus. Saint Augustine's University and Dillard University's full-time enrollment is approximately 1,600 and 1,300, respectively. Although, the schools' full-time enrollments are similar, their gender enrollments are vastly different. With a closely similar full-time enrollment equivalency, Dillard sounds a significant alarm for having only 28% of males represented on their campus and Saint Augustine providing a small majority at 51% male representation on its campus.

With a lack of research guiding this study, a qualitative methodology was used to guide the conversation with professionals on their individual campuses. We find it important to measure our outcomes through qualitative actions for the reason that the figures and history of Black male enrollment at HBCUs are known, but the knowledge of the leadership at institutions has not yet been sought after. Many scholars (Cuyjet, 2006; Harper, 2006; Lundy-Wagner & Gasman, 2011; Slater, 1994) have stated that the male population as a whole has tremendously declined on college campuses across the United States but none have delved into the racial population that is seen mainly at HBCUs and what this oversight could potentially mean for the shrinking population of Black males in higher education in the near future. Although, our findings may not be generalized to each and every HBCU, we do feel that many will overlap and also be able to notice the trends that Saint Augustine's University and Dillard University has in common and most importantly the differences and understanding the leadership has on the ever-changing campus environment.

Findings

To understand the ongoing phenomena on HBCU campuses, we used a set of interview questions to gain adequate knowledge of what the leadership on two similar HBCU campuses has identified with respect to Black male enrollment and the implications that may/have arisen. Through these accounts, the responses offer personal and professional observations of the campus environment, community, and society. Also, we have delineated three main thematic areas that each institution found to be a part of Black male enrollment: applicant pool, recruitment, and the general consensus of the gender enrollment gap on HBCU campuses. The interviewees have agreed that the responses are their own personal thoughts and that no HBCU campus is the same.

Dianne Suber of Saint Augustine's University has served as the president for over 13 years. Through these years, she contributes the beginning growth of Saint Augustine's male population to the revitalization of the football team among other things. She notes that being from the southeastern part of the nation has always allowed her to enjoy the sport of football and she jumped at the opportunity of being able to bring the program back to St. Augustine's University upon her arrival.

Walter Kimbrough of Dillard University has only served as the current president since July of 2012, after concluding his tenure of eight years as president of Philander Smith College. He attributes the overwhelming majority-female campus to the successful nursing program that Dillard University has built over the years but also notes that their statistics fall in line with the national average, rather than the

HBCUs, Black American gender average in postsecondary institutions (W. Kimbrough, personal communication, April 17, 2013; D. Suber, personal communication, April 22, 2013).

Recruitment

Although Dillard University is consistent with its enrollment numbers year to year, President Kimbrough credits the challenge of achieving gender parity in part to high schools graduating more women; they represent two out of every three Black high school students. Ultimately, this leaves only 33% of high school graduates who are Black males and results in an even smaller percentage when each college and university is pushed to recruit these students. This leads us to believe that recruitment is a top priority for institutions with a seemingly ever-shrinking Black male population.

SAU and President Suber view recruitment more from a local perspective rather than from a national perspective. Even though the football program was revitalized more than 10 years ago, Suber offers two theories to explain the continued male enrollment at her institution. As mentioned previously, the football program at SAU was one contributor for the initial spike in Black male enrollment but realizing that the first cohort of the football program has long since graduated provides for a more holistic perception, with Suber asserting that there may be other reasons for this phenomena. The first theory, Suber notes, is "the institution has a female head that began her work in early education" (D. Suber, personal communication, April 22, 2013). She suggests that her background comes from a nurturing student development perspective, which has also trickled down to the staff and faculty on the campus. At the end of the day, the nurturing environment allows for males who come from female-dominated homes to feel like they are in a safe place/environment (i.e., right at home).

Her second theory illustrates the recruitment that has come from the athletic department on campus. This type of recruitment is not to be credited to all admitted Black males being football players but to raise awareness that many of the students that are recruited to play football tend to bring friends from their high school along with them. Football was not placed in the strategic plan of balancing the gender enrollment but to cultivate a campus environment that is welcoming to SAU's students. Being that Kimbrough took office almost a year ago, a lot of the recruiting efforts have been overshadowed at Dillard University by the continued fight to regain campus strength following Hurricane Katrina. He noted that they still have two buildings that will not be up and running for a number of months. Once completed and the newly hired staff has had a chance to sit down, Kimbrough declares that one of their top priorities will be the current Black male enrollment and graduation rates, their causes, and getting to the bottom of the issues. He is passionate about this issue, and in the past has worked at Philander Smith College, where he increased the Black male graduation rate from 11% to 33% within six years. He spoke with enthusiasm, adding, "Increasing enrollment and attainment can be done!" (W. Kimbrough, personal communication, April 17, 2013).

Applicant Pool

One major factor that both Presidents Suber and President Kimbrough attribute to the growing gender gap at HBCUs is the general makeup of the applicant pools at their respective institutions. To better illustrate this, we must take a close look at who is applying to these institutions as well as their acceptance and enrollment rates to better understand the nature of the issue and how it might be curbed. Dillard University received 7,533 applications for undergraduate admissions for the fall of 2012, of which only 2,421 were males (NCES, 2013). These applicant numbers align directly with Kimbrough's earlier observation that institutions are competing for a high school graduating pool where two out of every three graduates are women. According to Kimbrough, Dillard generally admits around 28% of the applicants and enrolled 16% of total applicants (W. Kimbrough, personal communication, April 17, 2013; NCES, 2013). This percentage has only a 3% difference between males and females, which varies slightly year by year (NCES, 2013).

When the last admissions season ended, Dillard enrolled 95 males and 252 females, or 27% males and 73% females. These numbers have only a 1% variance from the gender makeup of the university at large: 28% males and 72% females (NCES, 2013). Based on these admission and enrollment numbers, it becomes very clear that given the applicant pool, admission and enrollment that is gender neutral is a direct contributor to the growing gender gap at Dillard and other institutions with similar applicant demographics and admissions practices. While the applicant pool and admissions narrative at Dillard University is telling of the circumstances many universities face today, it is important to understand that not all HBCUs see the same types of gender discrepancy in applicants.

SAU has achieved gender equity in enrollment, and offers some insight as to how some institutions work with very different circumstances and therefore achieve different results. SAU received 3,502 applications for undergraduate admissions in 2012, 1,550 of which were males (about 44%) (NCES, 2013). While we know from Suber's statements that SAU's recruitment strategies play a large role in the number of male applicants they receive, what happens next is particularly interesting. In 2012, SAU admitted 43% of their male applicants and 51% of their female applicants (NCES,2013). This means that nearly three of every five students SAU admits are female. The game changer however is the fact that St. Augustine enrolled 34% of those males who are admitted while only enrolling 19% of the admitted females (NCES, 2013). This means that of the admitted students, more Black male students are choosing to enroll at St. Augustine's University than their female counterparts. This set their incoming first year students in 2012 with a gender makeup of 55% males and 45% females. The male leaning gap that SAU creates with its admissions is increasingly important to gender equity over the career of the students because females are nearly 20% more likely to persist and graduate in six years (NCES, 2103). The end result is an overall undergraduate gender makeup that is an example of what can be achieved when favorable circumstances, sound strategy, and strong, thoughtful leadership come together.

More research is necessary to determine exactly why Black males tend to choose to attend some HBCUs (like St. Augustine's) more than others. Suber posits that creating an environment that provides more structure is particularly important when trying to attract Black males since so many of the male students SAU serves come from homes where structure is minimal (D. Suber, personal communication, April 22, 2013). More detail around what President Suber is referencing when she mentions structure is covered in our recommendations. The authors of this chapter offer this analysis not as a critique to gender neutral admissions, but simply to point out that given the circumstances of the growing gender gap in the applicant pool, treating genders equally contributes to the enrollment gap and shrinking male population on HBCU campuses.

Views on Black Male Enrollment

Suber and Kimbrough both agree that gender parity is an issue of high importance that has not received the necessary attention on a national level. While Kimbrough states that awareness is a key factor and advocacy groups have not made a strong push for this disparity to be reconciled, Suber believes that the problem at hand resides with the present day economic and political policies governing K-12 and higher education. Both presidents acknowledge that the trend will and can persist if no innovative programs, intentional strategies, or increased structure is implemented to foster Black male success and increase the national enrollment rate coming from a secondary education. "Black male enrollment is at risk and Black males are the most vulnerable after graduation. The Black male shrinkage is of volatile importance at the present moment and not being proactive about the issue allows for an uneducated population to be a population at risk" (D. Suber, personal communication, April 22, 2013).

Recommendations

Closing the gender gap in enrollment at HBCUs will require thoughtful and creative solutions and many resources, both economic and otherwise. In this section, we will make recommendations as to how positive progress can be made in the short term and will recommend strategies to create gender equity on a larger scale.

One path to greater enrollment equity for Black males in HBCUs is an educational focus on what works and the abandonment of what does not. While this seems obvious, the deficit-orientation many researchers and institutions use says otherwise. By focusing only on Black males who are perceived as unprepared, we are ignoring the wealth of insight held by those who excel in high school and go on to college. Leadership and scholars at HBCUs must amplify the successes of Black males on their campuses rather than the failures.

Anti-Deficit Black Male Research

Harper (2012) developed an anti-deficit achievement framework as part of his Black Male Achievement Study and a similar study on Black and Latino males in select New York public high schools that he used to explore what factors contribute to Black males' success in college. The assumption being that if we as educators can find out what works, we can use our resources more intelligently and produce high-achieving students, inevitably sending more minority males to college, an increasing number of whom will attend HBCUs. These types of initiatives must continue to be encouraged and funded by federal, state, and local governments as well as foundations and institutions. It will be important for HBCUs to play a role in this research and acknowledge and learn from their current superstars' successes.

Community College Partnerships

Another strategy to promote gender equity at HBCUs is for individual institutions to forge relationships with community colleges in their respective locales. When implemented correctly, these relationships and the programs they produce can funnel specific types of students directly into an institution. A good example of this is Cheyney University, which offers dual admission to students at the Community College of Philadelphia (CCP). This type of partnership promotes student-friendly, seamless transitions to the transfer institution by guaranteeing admission and acceptance of credits at Cheyney. Students commit to these programs before entering or early in their community college careers. Oftentimes, similar programs offer financial incentives that are allotted to students from certain cultural or socioeconomic backgrounds. By proposing to students the possibility of remaining home, a student is provided relief from some of the financial burdens normally attached to higher education. Since we know that Black students are much more likely to come from low socioeconomic backgrounds and have significantly lesser social capital than their White counterparts (Perna, 2000), the combination of financial incentives, relief from financial burden of having to move away, and the ease of transfer could be the perfect storm to increase Black male enrollment. Furthermore, the students will have already proven themselves academically at a collegiate level, increasing their chances of persevering to graduation.

Creating Ideal Environments

"If you put students in a situation where they have the potential to succeed and give them more structure and potential to do so you are going to see more Black Americans as a whole, step up" (D. Suber, personal communication, April 22, 2013). Suber ties this type of environment to her outstanding male enrollment percentages at SAU. She believes in providing students with more structure to allow them to grow as a person on her campus. This structure may not have been given or received during the student's secondary education, so it is imperative that higher education professionals keep this in mind when advancing their students and institutions. Kimbrough credits more of a programming approach on how to help Black males succeed after enrolling into a postsecondary institution. Many institutions today have taken on this approach as well. While both presidents have a different way of increasing enrollment and attaining and retaining their students, institutions must determine what best serves students in their campus environment and for their culture.

Focus and Emphasis on Male-Dominant Fields of Study

President Kimbrough prides himself on using data to inform and direct many of his leadership decisions. While he admits that adding sports teams (specifically football) may attract more males, Kimbrough also notes that this "fix" may not be a good fit in all institutions. He notes specifically that this tactic may come with some baggage including, but not limited to, the redistribution of scholarships. Kimbrough spoke about the ways that Dillard University's emphasis on nursing has undoubtedly contributed to the vast majority of women on his campus. As he attempts to alleviate the gender gap at Dillard, President Kimbrough, although early in his tenure, looked to the same idea that perpetuates the gender gap and how it can be used to alleviate it. One idea President Kimbrough is considering is the introduction of new majors that traditionally attract males. During our conversation, he spoke specifically of the possibility of introducing Sports Management as a new field of study at Dillard University (W. Kimbrough, personal communication, April 17, 2013). Since we know that sports management programs are generally dominated by males (Fullagar & Toohey, 2008), taking this type of action, when employed with intentionality and thoughtfulness, is a huge step toward attracting males and closing the gender gap.

Additionally, an increased focus on STEM majors would also increase the likelihood of male enrollment, given that the fact that men currently represent 80% of BA, MA, and PhD degrees awarded in engineering (Cohen & Deterding, 2009; Freeman, 2004; National Science Foundation, 2004). Kimbrough is undoubtedly on to something by thinking about introducing and placing emphasis on majors that typically attract men. As institutions address an issue as complex as this, it is always important to acknowledge that HBCUs and their respective students are not monolithic, which means what works on one campus or for one student may not be best for another. That said, the authors of this chapter completely endorse these presidents' recommendations and charge other HBCUs to think critically about how employing similarly innovative and intentional tactics might help close the gender gaps on their campuses.

Conclusion

There are disputes on the many disparities that continue to go unseen, which overall play a major part in closing the race and gender gaps. If our governments, colleges, and community educators work together, change can be created in the lives of not only Black males but also in our greater society. The enrollment and success of Black men in our institutions strengthens our nation and helps create more diverse and intellectually stimulating learning environments. Education is the means by which we create change and the path is drawn by scholarly research. If we invest appropriately and thoughtfully in proven initiatives that promote Black male enrollment, we can prove in the decades to come that we have learned from our shortcomings and deliver on the promises of equality our nation was founded upon. Our HBCUs and our Black males need and deserve one another, and it will be up to us as educators to find ways to make the match and effectively circumvent the crisis with which the data tells us we are currently on a collision course.

References

Allen, W. R. (1992). The color of success: African-American college student outcomes at predominantly White and historically Black public colleges and universities. *Harvard Educational Review, 62*(1), 26–45.

Allen, W. & Jewell, J. (2002). A backward glance forward: Past, present and future perspectives on historically black colleges and universities. *The Review of Higher Education, 25*(3), 241–261.

Allen, W., Jewell, J., Griffin, K., & Wolf, D. (2007). Historically black colleges and universities: Honoring the past, engaging the present, touching the future. *Journal of Negro Education, 76*(3), 263–280. Retrieved from http://www.jstor.org/stable/40034570.

Bernard, L. & Clytus, R. (2000). *Within these walls: A short history of Dillard University.* Office of the President, Dillard University.

Carter, R. T. (2007). Racism and Psychological and Emotional Injury Recognizing and Assessing Race-Based Traumatic Stress. *The Counseling Psychologist, 35*(1), 13–105.

Cohen, C. C. D. & Deterding, N. (2009). Widening the net: National estimates of gender disparities in engineering. *Journal of Engineering Education, 98*(3), 211–226.
Cross, T., & Slater, R. B. (2000). The alarming decline in the academic performance of African-American men. *Journal of Blacks in Higher Education, 27,* 82–87.
Cummins, M. W. & Griffin, R. A. (2012). Critical race theory and critical communication pedagogy: Articulating pedagogy as an act of love from black male perspectives. *Journal of Performance Studies, 8*(5), 85–106. Retrieved from http://www.liminalities.net/8-5/love.pdf.
Cuyjet, M. J. (2006). *African American men in college.* San Francisco, CA: Jossey-Bass.
Davis, J. (1994). College in black and white: Campus environment and academic achievement of African American males. *Journal of Negro Education, 63*(4), 620–633. Retrieved from http://www.jstor.org/stable/2967299.
DiPrete, T. A. & Buchmann, C. (2006). Gender-specific trends in the value of education and the emerging gender gap in college completion. *Demography, 43*(1), 1–24.
Eddy, P. L. & Cox, E. M. (2008). *Gendered leadership: An organizational perspective.* New Directions for Community Colleges. Hoboken, NJ: Wiley Periodicals.
Freeman, C. E. 2004. *Trends in educational equity of girls & women: 2004.* Washington, DC: National Center for Education Statistics, U.S. Department of Education.
Fullagar, S. & Toohey, K. (2008). Introduction to gender and sport management special issue: Challenges and changes. *Sport Management Review, 12*(4), 199–201.
Gasman, M. (2007). Swept under the rug? A historiography of gender and black colleges. *American Educational Research Journal, 44*(4), 760–805.
Gasman, M., Baez, B., Drezner, N., Sedgwick, K., & Tudico, C. (2007). Historically black colleges and universities: Recent trends. *University of Pennsylvania Scholarly Commons, 93*(1), 69–78.
Harper, S. (2004). The measure of a man: Conceptualizations of masculinity among high-achieving African American male college students. *Berkeley Journal of Sociology, 48*(1), 89–107. Retrieved from http://www.jstor.org/stable/41035594.
——— (2006). *Black male students at public universities in the U.S.: Status, trends and implications for policy and practice.* Washington, DC: Joint Center for Political and Economic Studies.
Harper, S. R. (2012). *Black male student success in higher education: A report from the National Black Male College Achievement Study.* Philadelphia: University of Pennsylvania, Center for the Study of Race and Equity in Education.
Harper, S., Karini, R., Bridges, B., & Hayek, J. (2004). Gender differences in student engagement among African American undergraduates at historically black colleges and universities. *Journal of College Student Development, 45*(3), 271–284.
History [n.d.]. Retrieved from http://www.st-aug.edu/history-374.html.
Johnson, C. J. (1938). *The Negro college graduate.* Chapel Hill, NC: University of North Carolina Press.
Kim, M. & Conrad, C. (2006). The impact of Historically Black Colleges and Universities on the academic success of African American students. *Research in Higher Education, 47*(4), 399–427. Retrieved from http://www.jstor.org/stable/40197410.

Lundy-Wagner, V. & Gasman, M. (2011). When gender issues are not just about women: Reconsidering male students at historically black colleges and universities. *Teachers College Record, 113*(5), 934–968.
Libertella, A. F., Sora, S. A., & Natale, S. M. (2007). Affirmative action policy and changing views. *Journal of Business Ethics, 74*(1), 65–71.
Logan, R. W. (1969). *Howard University: The first hundred years, 1867–1967.* New York, NY: New York University Press.
McKinnon, J. (2003). *The Black population in the United States: March 2002.* U.S. Census Bureau, Current Population Reports, Series P20-541. Washington, DC.
Middlebury College & Wiley, E. J. (1917). *Catalogue of officers and students of Middlebury College in Middlebury, Vermont: And of others who have received degrees, 1800–1915.* Middlebury, VT: The College.
National Center for Education Statistics (2011). Institute of Education Sciences, U.S. Department of Education. Integrated Postsecondary Education Data System (IPEDS), Fall, HBCU Enrollment Rates component.
National Center for Education Statistics (2013). Institute of Education Sciences, U.S. Department of Education. Integrated Postsecondary Education System (IPEDS). *Dillard University.* Retrieved from http://nces.ed.gov/globallocator/col_info_popup.asp?ID=158802.
National Science Foundation, Division of Science Resources Statistics (2004). *Women, minorities, and persons with disabilities in science and engineering: 2004.* Arlington, VA: National Science Foundation.
Palmer, R. T. & Gasman, M. (2008). "It takes a village to raise a child": The role of social capital in promoting academic success for African American men at a black college. *Journal of College Student Development, 49*(1), 52–70.
Perna, L. W. (2000). Differences in the decision to attend college among African Americans, Hispanics, and Whites. *Journal of Higher Education, 71,* 117–141.
Pettit, B. & Western, B. (2004). Mass imprisonment and the life course: Race and class inequality in US incarceration. *American Sociological Review, 69*(2), 151–169.
Provasnik, S. & Shafer, L. L. (2004). Historically Black Colleges and Universities, 1976 to 2001. EDTAB. NCES 2004-062. National Center for Educational Statistics.
Slater, R. B. (1994). The growing gender gap in Black higher education. *Journal of Blacks in Higher Education,* (3), 52–59.
Thelin, J. R. (2011). *A history of American higher education.* Baltimore, MD: Johns Hopkins University Press.
Toldson, I. A. (2011). Breaking barriers 2: Plotting the path away from juvenile detention and toward academic success for school-age African American males. Washington, DC: Congressional Black Caucus Foundation.
U.S. Department of Labor, Bureau of Labor Statistics. (2012, February 29). The African American labor force in the recovery. Retrieved from http://www.dol.gov/_sec/media/reports/BlackLaborForce/BlackLaborForce.pdf.
West, C. (2008). Foreword. In E. Anderson (ed.), *Against the wall: Poor, young, Black, and male.* Philadelphia, PA: University of Pennsylvania Press.

CHAPTER FOUR

Three Layers of Underrepresentation: Academic Pipeline Issues for African Americans

UFUOMA ABIOLA

The underrepresentation of African American doctoral students, African American faculty, and African American college and university presidents in the United States are major issues in American higher education. The significance of these topics stems from the fact that the rate of African Americans who are doctoral students, faculty members, and presidents within the academy has remained relatively unchanged in the United States. Without Historically Black Colleges and Universities (HBCUs) in existence, there would be even fewer African Americans occupying these important seats. HBCUs play a critical role in the production of African Americans who earn doctoral degrees and eventually become faculty members (Perna, 2001). HBCUs are largely responsible for the employment of African American faculty members, as they employ over half (58.2%) of the African American faculty in the United States (Smith, Tovar, & García, 2012). African Americans also comprise the majority (95%) of the HBCU presidency (American Council on Education, 2012). Predominantly White Institutions (PWIs) can learn much from HBCUs about enhancing their environments to ensure the success of African American students, faculty, and presidents.

Due to access and equity issues in US higher education, there are few African Americans who are admitted to and persist through doctoral programs greatly limiting the applicant pool for a faculty position and yielding a shortage of African American faculty (Anderson et al., 1993). As a result, African American presidents continue to be underrepresented relative to the higher education workforce because the traditional route to the presidency of the academy entails having first been a tenured faculty (American Council on Education, 2012; Birnbaum & Umbach, 2001). With the changing demography and economy in the United States, diversity among the students, faculty, and presidents of American higher education institutions is necessary.

First Layer: The Underrepresentation of African American Doctoral Students in Academia

The first PhD earned by an African American at a US institution of higher learning was in 1876 by Edward Bouchet (Thurgood et al., 2006). He received his doctoral degree in physics from Yale University. While this was a major academic accomplishment by a person of color in the United States during that era, in present-day America, African Americans are still greatly underrepresented with regard to doctoral degree earnings. For example, in the most recent *Minorities in Higher Education* report (2011), African Americans earned only 6.2% of the doctoral degrees awarded in the United States in 2008, while Whites made up 59.9% of doctoral degree earnings (Kim, 2011). These statistics are rather alarming considering the fact that ten years prior, in 1998, merely 5.9% of African Americans earned doctoral degrees in the U.S., and Whites made up 67.9% of doctorates awarded (Kim, 2011). With only a 0.3% increase in African American doctoral students from 1998 to 2008, this low percentage exemplifies the vast racial disparity in doctoral degree earnings between African Americans and Whites, and is a highly problematic issue in US higher education.

Additionally, in a survey of the nation's earned doctorates, completed by the National Science Foundation in 2000, African Americans represented 6% and Whites represented 82% of the 27,888 PhD's conferred that year (Jackson, 2002). The majority of African Americans earned their PhD in education and worked primarily within the K-12 system as opposed to higher education (Jackson, 2002). In 2000, only 86 African Americans across the nation earned doctorates in the physical sciences and within this figure only 14 doctorate degrees earned were in math, which is an essential field of study in higher education that significantly lacks African American scholars nationally (Jackson, 2002).

The origins of the underrepresentation of African American doctoral students in the academy can be attributed to equity issues and the lack of access to these institutions of higher learning (Harper et al., 2009; Perna et al., 2006). The fight for educational equity and equal access to the academy has been an ongoing battle for African Americans. Regarding a historical account of the success of African Americans and the academy, access to higher education began in the 1820s. In 1823, Alexander Lucius Twilight became the first African American to have earned a bachelor's degree from an American institution: he earned his degree from Middlebury College (Bennett, 2007). The first Historically Black Institution (HBI) of higher education in the United States was Cheyney University, created in 1837 for freed slaves and their children (Funke, 1920). Then, Lincoln University and Wilberforce University followed, and the establishment of HBCUs began, which was a significant access movement for African Americans (Funke, 1920). African American women were later allowed access to US postsecondary institutions, and in 1862, Mary Jane Patterson, the first African American female college graduate, earned her degree from Oberlin College (Lawson & Merrill, 1983).

Even with the aforementioned strides, African Americans were still very far behind in terms of educational attainment. For example, out of the four million freed slaves, only twenty-eight earned bachelor's degrees from US institutions after the Civil War (Bowles & DeCosta, 1971; Roebuck & Murty, 1993). With the passing of the second Morrill Act of 1890 that required educational funds to be dispersed annually on a "just and equitable" basis to African Americans, 17 HBCUs were created (Bowles & DeCosta, 1971; Thelin, 2004). However there was controversy surrounding this act, as it legalized the segregation of Black and White institutions; and the Black institutions were less academically rigorous, and trained students on technical and vocational skills. The passing of *Plessy v. Ferguson*, in 1896, which declared schools to be "separate but equal," further intensified that racial disparity among African Americans and Whites in the academy (Anderson, 1988). Moving into the 1900s there was limited progress, as in the late 1940s, 90% of all African Americans who earned degrees were educated at HBCUs (Davis, 1998). Less than 1% of entering first year students at PWIs was African American. In 1954, the landmark *Brown v. Board of Education* court case mandated the cessation of racial segregation in education; however, it can be argued that there has been limited progress since the passing of *Brown*, as there are still very few African American doctoral students in the United States (Brown, 2001; Kim, 2011).

The unequal and discriminatory policies and practices in academe make it particularly challenging for African Americans to enroll, thrive, and persist through their course of study, especially at the doctoral level. The paucity of African Americans in doctoral programs at US institutions can be attributed to numerous factors, including their underrepresentation at PWIs and the usage of racially biased standardized testing for college admission (Harper et al., 2009; Perna & Thomas, 2009).

> Over a century of gainful policy efforts have been undermined by the following:...consistent attempts to dismantle affirmative action; increased statewide admissions standards for public postsecondary education, without corresponding advances in public K-12 schools; reports of racism and negative African American student experiences at PWIs; low African American male student persistence and degree attainment rates; forced desegregation of HBCUs; inequitable funding for HBCUs; and the decline of need-based federal financial aid. (Harper et al., 2009, pp. 397–398)

Thus, educational opportunities and advancements for African Americans in the United States are greatly narrowed due to the "pervasive attitudes of racism, as well as differential access and power" (Allen et al., 2000, p. 113).

Though nationally African American doctoral students are underrepresented in academia, HBCUs serve a critical role in educating African American students. For example, 30 of the top 50 undergraduate producers of African American female doctoral degree recipients in science and engineering between 1980 and 1990 were HBCUs (Solorzano, 1995). 23 Of the top 50 undergraduate institutions among African American male doctoral degree recipients in science and engineering 23 were HBCUs (Solorzano, 1995). In the early 1990s, HBCUs were providing education for approximately 40% of African American college graduates (Jackson, 2002). Seventy-five percent of all African American PhDs, 85% of African American doctors, 80% of African American federal judges, 50% of African American engineers, and 46% of African American business professionals completed their undergraduate education at HBCUs (Jackson, 2002). In addition, HBCU graduate professional schools have educated and groomed 40% of African American physicians, 40% of African American dentists, 50% of African American pharmacists, and 75% of African American veterinarians across the nation (Jackson, 2002). HBCUs produce the vast majority of African American students who receive degrees in science, engineering, technology, or mathematics—these institutions comprised 17 of the top 21 undergraduate producers of African American science PhDs (U.S. Commission on Civil Rights, 2010). Even with fewer resources than PWIs, HBCUs have managed to successfully serve African American students.

Second Layer: The Underrepresentation of African American College and University Faculty

In terms of the underrepresentation of African American faculty in the academy, during the 1960s and 1970s, there were affirmative action plans established at many US institutions of higher learning; however, the percentage of African American faculty has hardly changed since then (Anderson et al., 1993). Affirmative action stemmed from the social justice mission of the Kennedy and Johnson administrations. It is a set of public policies and initiatives created to help eradicate the discrimination based on race, color, religion, sex, or national origin (Niemann & Maruyama, 2005; Zamani-Gallaher, 2007). Even with affirmative action, there has been minor progress in 20 years in many of the most prestigious institutions of higher education in the United States with regard to the hiring of African American faculty.

The origins of the underrepresentation of African American faculty in the academy dates back to 1849, when Charles Lewis Reason became the first African American university professor at a PWI in the United States, teaching at New York Central College, McGrawville (Allen, 1971). In 1941, there were only two African American tenured faculty members at PWIs in the United States (Anderson et al., 1993). By 1961, when President Kennedy signed Executive Order 110925, which mandated affirmative action practices in education and other fields, there were still very few African American faculty members at PWIs. Most of the African American scholars in the United States taught at HBCUs. Interestingly, the faculty at HBCUs is approximately 26.8% White, as HBCUs have always had a more racially integrated faculty than at PWIs (Smith et al., 2012). In 1965, when President Johnson signed Executive Order 11246, which was an affirmative action initiative, African American faculty at PWIs grew from close to 0% to over 2% by the 1970s (Anderson et al., 1993). However, there was a 12-year period of limited progress in the hiring of African American faculty when President Reagan threatened to overturn President Johnson's executive order and affirmative action policy. As a result, during that time period, affirmative action practices were not enforced (Anderson et al., 1993).

There was a slight increase in African American faculty in the late 1970s, as African Americans made up 4.3% of all full-time faculty at US higher education institutions in 1979 (Anderson et al., 1993). By 1985, the percentage of US African American faculty decreased to 4.1% and then slightly increased to 4.5% in 1989. This drop in the hiring of more African American faculty was a result of the US government not enforcing affirmative action initiatives (Anderson et al., 1993). More recently, in 2007, the average of African American faculty in the United States only grew to 5.2% and then 5.5% in 2009—providing evidence for the limited progress and paucity of African American faculty (Smith et al., 2012). In addition, the applicant pool for African Americans to teach at the collegiate level is further narrowed as a vast proportion of African Americans with PhDs teach within the K-12 system (Jackson, 2002).

Without HBCUs in existence there would be even fewer African American faculty members. African Americans are largely employed at HBCUs and the majority of African American faculty at HBCUs earned their undergraduate degrees at HBCUs (Jackson, 2002; Smith et al., 2012). In particular, HBCUs largely produce African American faculty in the fields of education, science, mathematics, and engineering (Perna, 2001). Nineteen percent of African American full-time faculty with baccalaureate degrees from HBCUs, versus 11% from non-HBCUs and 46% with doctoral degrees from HBCUs versus 20% of African Americans from non-HBCUs are employed in the science, engineering, and mathematics fields (Perna, 2001). Fifty-five percent of full-time African American faculty with baccalaureate degrees from HBCUs are employed at HBCUs versus 24% of other African American full-time faculty with baccalaureate degrees (Perna, 2001). Seventy percent of African American full-time faculty with doctorates from HBCUs are employed at HBCUs versus 41% of other African American full-time faculty with doctorates (Perna, 2001). This preference of African Americans seeking employment at HBCUs can be attributed to them wanting to support larger numbers of students of color and work with more professors of color, which would decrease potential feelings of isolation most often experienced at PWIs (Perna, 2001; Tack & Patitu, 1992).

Third Layer: The Underrepresentation of African American Presidents in Higher Education

There is a shortage of African American college and university presidents in the United States. According to the American Council on Education (ACE) 2012 report, African Americans make up 5.9% of the presidents at American higher education institutions, in comparison to Whites who make up 87.2% of the presidents in the academy. Over the course of two decades, the number of African American college and university presidents has remained relatively unchanged. In 1986, the total percentage of African American presidents in higher education was 5.0%, whereas whites made up 91.9% of college and university presidents. In 1990, there were 5.5% African American and 90.4% White college and university presidents in the United States; in 1995, 5.9% and 89.3%; in 1998, 6.3% and 88.7%; in 2001, 6.3% and 87.2%; and in 2006, 5.9% and 86.4%, respectively (American Council on Education, 2012). The ACE (2012) report provides evidence of the huge disparity in the amount of African American college and university presidents, in comparison to White presidents in the academy.

Because the *American College President Study* is "the only longitudinal, comprehensive source of demographic data on college and university presidents from all sectors of American higher education," it will be further discussed (American Council on Education, 2012, p. ix). "The report includes information on presidents of public and private institutions" of higher education (American Council on Education, 2012, p. ix). According to the aforementioned study, African Americans and most presidents of color were most represented at public bachelor's, public master's, and minority-serving institutions, where they held over 20% of the presidency at each institution type (American Council on Education, 2012). Presidents of color were least represented at private master's and doctorate-granting institutions, where they led only 6% and 5% of those institutions, respectively (American Council on Education, 2012). Presidents of color were more likely to lead public institutions (17%) than private institutions (8%)(American Council on Education, 2012). This data shows that African Americans are extremely limited in the type of postsecondary institution in which they can lead.

The paths of African Americans and Whites to becoming a president at a higher education institution often differ. Whites are more likely to be promoted to the presidency from their current institution than African Americans (American Council on Education, 2012). African Americans are more likely to take a less traditional route to presidency, such as a chief student affairs professional or chief diversity officer prior to their appointment as president. Research has shown that this alternate route is not highly regarded, and those who choose this route are often viewed as underqualified for the role of president; therefore, African Americans in pursuit of the presidency position are at a huge disadvantage (American Council on Education, 2012; Birnbaum & Umbach, 2001; Holmes, 2004).

According to Birnbaum and Umbach (2001), there are four main career paths of American college and university presidents. However, due to pipeline issues African Americans are underrepresented in the most respected and most popular career path to the presidency. For example, there is the *Traditional* category, with two career paths as the "Scholar" and "Steward" (Birnbaum & Umbach, 2001). The scholar-presidents are the most desired by institutions, as these individuals were tenured professors who then had administrative positions of increasing responsibility; all of which should prepare them for the presidency (Birnbaum & Umbach, 2001). The steward-presidents have never taught, but these individuals became president after maintaining successful administrative positions in the academy (Birnbaum & Umbach, 2001).

There is also the *Nontraditional* category, with two career paths as the "Spanner" and "Stranger," in which the presidents' career has fluctuated between higher education and other fields, or the president has not had professional experience in higher education, respectively (Birnbaum & Umbach, 2001). Birnbaum and Umbach (2001) show that almost 89% of all college and university presidents followed one of the two Traditional paths, Scholar (66.3%) or Steward (22.4%). There was a minute percentage of presidents in the academy who followed the Nontraditional paths of the Spanner (7.4%) or Stranger (3.9%), which are the least desired by institutions (Birnbaum & Umbach, 2001).

As the aforementioned study has revealed, the traditional route of the scholar and professorate reigns supreme, in terms of the candidacy for president in the academy (Birnbaum & Umbach, 2001). However, because African Americans are underrepresented as full-time tenured faculty, they typically do not fit the mold of the traditional candidate for president; therefore, they are viewed as less qualified and automatically disadvantaged in pursuing the position of president (Holmes, 2004).

Earning a PhD or EdD is the norm among the traditional and nontraditional career paths (Birnbaum & Umbach, 2001). The Scholars, who are the ideal presidency candidates, are more likely to have the PhD degree. Stewards are more likely to have the EdD degree. Spanners tend to have the PhD or other professional degrees. The Strangers had professional degrees, and one-third did not have doctoral degrees (Birnbaum & Umbach, 2001).

The scholar-president is ideal. Particularly at doctoral institutions, the Scholar is the career path most preferred for the position of president (Birnbaum & Umbach, 2001). Stewards are less likely to lead doctoral institutions, but are represented in all other institution types. Spanners are more likely to lead baccalaureate institutions, and Strangers are more likely to lead specialized institutions (Birnbaum & Umbach, 2001).

Additionally, with the PhD degree there is more flexibility; as over 70% of college and university presidents have earned the PhD (Birnbaum & Umbach, 2001). With the EdD there are some limitations, particularly at doctoral institutions, where there are only 6.5% of presidents with the EdD degree. Most presidents with this degree lead associate degree granting institutions (Birnbaum & Umbach, 2001). The president's field of study also shapes the type of institution to which they are assigned (Birnbaum & Umbach, 2001). Education was the most common academic field in which African American and White presidents earned their highest degree; however, there were more African American college and university presidents with an education degree (41%) than White presidents (38%)(American Council on Education, 2012). Presidents with education degrees made up 72% of the presidency positions at associate degree granting institutions, but only made up 15.6% of doctoral institutions. Presidents of doctoral degree granting institutions were more likely to have degrees in the sciences or humanities (50%) (Birnbaum & Umbach, 2001). The aforementioned data regarding college and university presidents' education is also a contributing factor to the shortage of African American presidents in particular types of institutions, such as doctoral granting elite private institutions, as African Americans are more likely to earn degrees in education (Birnbaum & Umbach, 2001). Therefore, to maximize one's potential to reach the position of president at prestigious research institutions, earning a PhD in the sciences or humanities is ideal.

African Americans and most presidents of color are most represented at public bachelor's, public master's, and minority-serving institutions. In 2011, 27.9% of presidents at minority-serving institutions (MSIs) were African Americans versus 3.9% of African American presidents at non-MSIs (American Council on Education, 2012). More specifically, 95% of HBCU presidents were African American (American Council on Education, 2012). Though there is a national shortage of African American college and university presidents in the United States, without HBCUs there would be far less African American presidents in academe.

Pipeline Issues and the Intersection of African American Students, Faculty, and Presidents

African Americans are underrepresented in higher education due to pipeline issues in the academy that negatively shape their progress and upward mobility of African Americans. As a result of access and equity issues in higher education, there are few African Americans who are admitted to and persist through doctoral programs, which greatly limits the applicant pool for a faculty position and yields a shortage of African American faculty. Thus, African American presidents continue to be underrepresented relative to the higher education workforce.

If African Americans can thrive and persist through college, and later enroll and advance through graduate school, this would widen the applicant pool from which to choose faculty (Anderson et al., 1993). Undergraduate programs are increasingly becoming more diverse, however that is not well represented at the graduate and doctoral levels (Anderson et al., 1993). There must be more efforts made to increase the diversity of doctoral programs; as African Americans earned only 6.2% of the doctoral degrees awarded in the United States in 2008 (Kim, 2011). Earning the doctoral degree is imperative for African Americans to qualify for a tenured faculty position, which is the most respected path to the presidency (Anderson et al., 1993; Bridges, 1996).

Decades after the equal employment opportunity legislation, African Americans still encompass a small percentage of the faculties of American higher education institutions. Although affirmative action plans were established at many US colleges and universities during the 1960s and 1970s, the percentage of African American faculty has barely changed in recent years (Anderson et al., 1993). "Over 28 percent of all African American PhDs are employed in fields outside the disciplines in which they received their doctorates" (Anderson et al., 1993, p. 26). This finding is an effect of African Americans not being offered full-time professoriate positions in their elected fields. Since over half of all African American faculty members teach at HBCUs, the likelihood of a student being taught by an African American professor at a PWI is about 50:1 (Anderson et al., 1993; Smith et al., 2012).

It is imperative that higher education institutions employ affirmative action practices, in order to help eliminate discrimination and to facilitate in diversifying their student, faculty, and president population. Affirmative action is a highly debatable issue with many proponents and opponents (Niemann & Maruyama, 2005). Supporters of affirmative action believe that it is a necessary policy to enhance the diversity on college and university campuses. Opponents of affirmative action believe that this policy gives people of color an unfair advantage and preferential treatment. Research has shown that most of the individuals against affirmative action are White; and this view against affirmative action is due to their limited awareness of institutional racism (Oh et al., 2010).

Although affirmative action is a provocative issue, it is my belief that affirmative action is a positive policy that opened the doors that would have otherwise been shut for people of color. It is not preferential treatment because affirmative action was developed as a result of the discriminatory acts performed by Whites on people of color. People of color are already at a disadvantage in comparison to Whites, with

Whites having more privilege; affirmative action policies were put in place to ensure that Blacks and other people of color were afforded the same opportunities as Whites (Niemann & Maruyama, 2005; Zamani-Gallaher, 2007). Affirmative action is in effect to level the playing field for all Americans, but it still has a negative connotation in our society, which needs to be altered.

Another contributing factor to the shortage of African American college and university students, faculty, and presidents is their encounters with blatant racism and discrimination, on the rise to the top (Anderson et al., 1993). Margolis and Romero (1998) found that there was a *hidden curriculum* in doctoral programs, which are informal or implicit demands by faculty that makes it particularly difficult for women and students of color to survive and succeed. This hidden curriculum does not promote intellectual development, but reproduces stratified and unequal social relations. When one is the token person of color at their institution, one may feel uneasy and sometimes isolated from their White counterparts because of the stereotypes surrounding their race. These students believe the collegiate environment to be far too competitive versus collaborative, which often yields unfortunate results and limits the educational opportunities of African Americans in the United States (Margolis & Romero, 1998).

Further, "African American faculty members face barriers due to the historical, cultural, and social factors that frequently have shaped their relations with Whites generally" (Allen et al., 2000, p. 113). As far as tenure and promotion are concerned as a faculty member, there is still some discrimination encountered by young African American professors who focus their research on issues related to ethnicity or race, which are topics that are often looked down upon by faculty review committees (Anderson et al., 1993). Additionally, African Americans are often called upon to participate in various university committees and task forces. They are also frequently depended on to serve as mentors to African American students (Allen et al., 2000; Anderson et al., 1993). These additional responsibilities can make it particularly challenging for African American professors to find time for their own scholarly interests that they must accomplish, in order to earn tenure and promotion (Allen et al., 2000; Anderson et al., 1993).

Not only is there discrimination in the hiring practices of qualified African Americans at the faculty level, but it exists also on the presidency level. These discrimination practices are hard to prove, as institutions use subtle criteria to disqualify African American applicants (Anderson et al., 1993). Even if African Americans are hired, there are still bouts with racism that they may endure. This may cause them to leave junior faculty positions, senior faculty positions, or senior administrative positions, which would most likely negate a career as a college or university president (Anderson et al., 1993; Rolle, 2000).

Strategies PWIs Can Learn from HBCUs to Enhance African American Success in the Academy

Although HBCUs constitute a smaller amount of postsecondary education institutions nationally, have fewer resources, and serve a higher number of disadvantaged students than PWIs, HBCUs have performed exceptionally well throughout their existence (Jackson, 2002). The strengths of HBCUs include the following: they are leaders in student engagement; they are community-based institutions that uphold and foster civic engagement and service learning; they spearhead the educational attainment for low-income, first-generation, and disabled students; they are models of success in the national effort to improve the quality of science, technology, engineering, and mathematics (STEM) education and research in the United States (U.S. Commission on Civil Rights, 2010).

Anderson et al. (1993) discuss how the first step in targeting the academic pipeline issue for African Americans should be at the high school level where the graduation rates of African American young men is far lower than that of Whites and African American females. HBCUs are targeting African American youth and this gender disparity with pre-college programs to decrease the high school dropout rate and increase the rate of African American males to postsecondary education at an HBCU (Gasman et al., forthcoming). If at this early stage of development it can be instilled in the African American youth that they can aspire to achieve any goal imaginable, and they are actively being supported, this would increase their commitment to achieving academically and decrease self-limitation and dropout rates (Anderson et al., 1993). By expanding the number of African Americans who persist through high school it increases the number of those who can go on to undergraduate and then graduate/professional studies, thereby widening the applicant pool of African American candidates for faculty positions.

When enrolled as an undergraduate, if current PWI faculty offered research experiences and mentored African American students interested in college teaching, there could be an increase in the number of African Americans pursuing academic careers (Anderson et al., 1993). PWIs can learn from HBCUs, as "according to 2004 and 2005 NSSE [National

Study for Student Engagement] data from 37 HBCUs, African American students report more contact with faculty than African American students at non-HBCUs" (U.S. Commission on Civil Rights, 2010, p. 8). Research has shown that African American students at HBCUs are more likely to be involved in faculty research projects than are African American students at PWIs; and 17 of the top 21 undergraduate producers of African American science PhD's were HBCUs (U.S. Commission on Civil Rights, 2010). Faculty and higher education leaders who sit on doctoral admission committees at PWIs need to make more efforts to increase the diversity of their respective doctoral program. Developing effective minority recruitment strategies is a start in the right direction in order to diversify graduate programs at PWIs (Jackson, 2004).

Additionally and most importantly, students need to persist through their respective program in order to earn the doctoral degree. Even though HBCUs only comprise approximately 11% of the African Americans who go to college, far more eventually graduate (Davis et al., 2004; Gasman et al., 2013; U.S. Commission on Civil Rights, 2010). PWIs, on the other hand, enroll 89% of African Americans, yet far fewer eventually graduate. While the academic credentials and socioeconomic status for African Americans who attend PWIs are generally much higher, and the resources for students at HBCUs are much tighter, students at HBCUs generally go on to graduate and to become professionals at much greater rates (Davis et al., 2004; U.S. Commission on Civil Rights, 2010). "The top 20 institutions in sending African Americans to graduate school were HBCUs" (U.S. Commission on Civil Rights, 2010, p. 34). At PWIs, 70% of African Americans drop out of baccalaureate education, in comparison to 20% of those at HBCUs (Davis et al., 2004). "According to survey data collected by the National Study for Student Engagement (NSSE), students at historically black colleges and universities ('HBCUs') report higher levels of engagement on some survey dimensions than do their counterparts at non-HBCUs" (U.S. Commission on Civil Rights, 2010, p. 8). Thus, HBCUs have a higher African American student retention rate due to the supportive and nurturing environment in which they provide for their students (U.S. Commission on Civil Rights, 2010).

Unlike HBCUs, PWIs can be a less welcoming environment for student of color learning—particularly when course offerings are predominantly White or Eurocentric, students who are culturally different may feel "othered," unappreciated, or may begin to place less value on their own culture (Davis et al., 2004). PWIs need to establish the same type of proactive campus climate as HBCUs, and can benefit from using Tinto's (1993) Model of Institutional Departure, which serves as a foundation for understanding student retention at higher education institutions. The model states that students need integration into formal and informal academic and social systems (Tinto, 1993). Thus, if students are acclimated and integrated into the academic life of the institution, their persistence improves. Additionally, engaging with faculty and staff is vital, and participating in extracurricular activities and social interactions with one's peer group aids in student retention (Tinto, 1993). Although this model is not specific to solely African American students, its basic tenets can be beneficial to retaining these students at PWIs. Tinto's (1993) model can be employed by educators at PWIs to develop programming and initiatives to increase the success of African American students in the academy. Specifically, in terms of improving pipeline issues to the professoriate and ultimately the presidency, by developing intentional and effective programming, this would aid in African American students persisting through their respective program in order to earn the doctoral degree, which is an essential credential for the senior most position in the academy.

"Research shows that the most persistent, statistically significant predictor of enrollment and graduation of African American graduate and professional students is the presence of African American faculty members" (Allen et al., 2000, p. 113). There needs to be more hiring of African American faculty at PWIs, as exists at HBCUs. Currently, 58.2% of African American faculty members teach at HBCUs (Smith et al., 2012). Higher education institutions, such as HBCUs, that are successful in recruiting and retaining African American faculty members are more successful in recruiting, enrolling, and graduating African American students than those with little to no African American faculty members (Allen et al., 2000). The dilemma lies in the fact that there are extremely limited amounts of African American faculty members in the United States overall, mainly due to pipeline issues. Without the presence of African American faculty, the likelihood of African American doctoral students completing their respective programs at the same rate as White students is significantly reduced; thus, it is essential that educators who sit on faculty search committees at PWIs employ more African American faculty members (Allen et al., 2000). To reduce discriminatory hiring practices on search committees, policymakers need to mandate that there be a diverse group of individuals, in terms of gender, race, and ethnicity, who comprise the search/hiring committees at PWIs. In order to help eradicate discrimination and to facilitate in diversifying the student, faculty, and senior leadership population, higher education leaders should employ and enforce affirmative action practices at their respective PWI, and policymakers should mandate and monitor this practice. HBCUs have African American faculty members who are dedicated to teaching (U.S. Commission on Civil Rights, 2010). Like HBCUs, PWIs must enhance their campus climate to ensure the success of African American doctoral students, faculty, and presidents.

Recommendations to African American Presidents

Research has found that the tasks of successful and efficient leaders of higher education institutions include "envisioning goals, motivating, affirming values, managing, and unity"—African American presidents must incorporate these styles of leadership along with promoting their institutions and competing for students and funding (Nichols, 2004, p. 228). Bridges (1996) and Rolle et al. (2000) discuss key factors that contribute to the success of African American higher education administrators. For African Americans who aspire to become a senior-level administrator such as a president, it is important for those individuals to recognize the importance of educational preparation. Communication skills, stellar performance in writing, speaking, goal setting, and developing and strengthening one's self-confidence are imperative for success (Bridges, 1996; Rolle et al., 2000). Effective communication skills are especially vital in interactions with others from different races, cultures, and backgrounds. Also, African Americans should have mentors. By having a supportive network of professionals, this will increase success.

Without the aforementioned strategies, African Americans can fall victim to remaining stagnant in a position. Feelings of inadequacy, lack of self-confidence, and lack of self-assurance are negative attributes that will hinder one's performance (Rolle et al., 2000). It is essential that African Americans maintain a healthy sense of self. Rolle et al. (2000) discusses the hypervigilance that often occurs by African Americans when they are put into positions of leadership at PWIs. The author explains that African Americans feel that they must always be cautious and aware of their surroundings, especially in hostile environments where institutional racism is present (Rolle et al., 2000). One way to combat this is to understand the politics of one's postsecondary institution. Knowing how to effectively navigate the system will yield success (Rolle et al., 2000).

Conclusion

With the rapidly changing economy, demography, and politics in the United States, there needs to be diversity at American institutions of higher education. PWIs can learn much from HBCUs about enhancing their environments to ensure the success of African American doctoral students, faculty, and presidents. The traditional route to the college presidency entails having been a tenured faculty first (American Council on Education, 2012; Birnbaum & Umbach, 2001). However, "African American faculty members are less often tenured, earn less, work at less prestigious institutions, have lower academic rank, and have less academic stature compared to their White peers" (Allen et al., 2000, p. 125). Thus, there are pipeline issues in higher education that limit the progress of African Americans. Because there are less African Americans in doctoral programs, there are fewer African American faculty, and therefore scarcer African American college and university presidents; thus, an unfortunate vicious cycle of inequality in academe and society persists (Holmes, 2004). Without HBCUs in existence there would be even fewer African Americans holding these seats. HBCUs create a supportive social and academic environment with encouragement given to students to explore a wide range of career possibilities, and serve as a pipeline to graduate school, a pipeline to the professoriate, and a pipeline to the presidency in higher education for African Americans.

References

Allen, J. E. (1971). *Black history: Past and present.* Jericho, NY: Exposition Press.
Allen, W. R., Epps, E. G., Guillory, E. A., Suh, S. A., & Bonous-Hammarth, M. (2000). The black academic: Faculty status among African Americans in U.S. higher education. *Journal of Negro Education, 69*(1/2), 112–127.
American Council on Education (2012). *The American college president: 2012 edition.* Washington, DC: American Council on Education.
Anderson, J. D. (1988). *The education of blacks in the south, 1860–1935.* Chapel Hill, NC: University of North Carolina Press.
Anderson, M., Astin, A. W., Bell, D. A., Cole, J. B., Etzioni, A., Gellhorn, W., Griffiths, P. A., Hacker, A., Hesburgh, T. M., Massey, W. E., & Wilson, R. (1993). Why the shortage of black professors? *Journal of Blacks in Higher Education, 1,* 25–34.
Bennett, L. (2007). *Before the Mayflower: A history of black America* (8th ed.). Chicago, IL: Johnson Publishing Company.
Birnbaum, R. & Umbach, P. D. (2001). Scholar, steward, spanner, stranger: The four career paths of college presidents. *The Review of Higher Education, 24*(3), 203–217.

Bowles, F. & DeCosta, F. A. (1971). *Between two worlds: A profile of Negro education*. New York, NY: McGraw-Hill.
Bridges, C. R. (1996). The characteristics of career achievement perceived by African American college administrators. *Journal of Black Studies, 26*(6), 748–767.
Brown II, M. C. (2001). Collegiate desegregation and the public Black college: A new policy mandate. *Journal of Higher Education, 72,* 46–62.
Davis, J. E. (1998). Cultural capital and the role of historically black colleges and universities in educational reproduction. In K. Freeman (Ed.), *African American culture and heritage in higher education research and practice* (pp. 143–153). Westport, CT: Praeger.
Davis, M., Dias-Bowie, Y., Greenberg, K., Klukken, G., Pollio, H. R., Thomas, S. P., & Thompson, C. L. (2004). A fly in the buttermilk: Descriptions of university life by successful black undergraduate students at a predominantly white southeastern university. *Journal of Higher Education, 75(*4), 420–445.
Funke, Loretta (1920). The negro in education. *Journal of Negro History, 5*(1), 1–21.
Gasman, M., Abiola, U., & Freeman, A. (forthcoming). Gender disparities at historically black colleges and universities.
Gasman, M., Nguyen, T., Castro Samayoa, A., Commodore, F., Abiola, U., Hyde-Carter, Y., & Carter, C. (2013). *The changing face of historically black colleges and universities*. Philadelphia, PA: University of Pennsylvania, Center for Minority Serving Institutions.
Harper, S. R., Patton, L. D., & Wooden, O. S. (2009). Access and equity for African American students in higher education: A critical race historical analysis of policy efforts. *Journal of Higher Education, 80*(4), 389–414.
Holmes, S. L. (2004). An overview of African American college presidents: A game of two steps forward, one step backward, and standing still. *Journal of Negro Education, 73*(1), 21–39.
Jackson, D. H. (2002). Attracting and retaining African American faculty at HBCUs. *Education, 123*(1), 181–184.
Jackson, J. F. L. (2004). Engaging, retaining, and advancing African Americans in executive-level positions: A descriptive and trend analysis of academic administrators in higher and postsecondary education. *Journal of Negro Education, 73*(1), 4–20.
Kim, Y. M. (2011). Minorities in higher education: 24th status report. Retrieved from http://diversity.ucsc.edu/resources/images/ace_report.pdf.
Lawson, E. N. & Merrill, M. (1983). The antebellum" Talented Thousandth": Black college students at Oberlin before the civil war. *Journal of Negro Education, 52*(2), 142–155.
Margolis, E. & Romero, M. (1998). The department is very male, very white, very old, and very conservative: The functioning of the hidden curriculum in graduate sociology departments. *Harvard Educational Review, 68*(1), 1–32.
Nichols, J. C. (2004). Unique characteristics, leadership styles, and management of historically black colleges and universities. *Innovative Higher Education, 28*(3), 219–229.

Niemann, Y. F. & Maruyama, G. (2005). Inequities in higher education: Issues and promising practices in a world ambivalent about affirmative action. *Journal of Social Issues, 61*(3), 407–426.

Oh, E., Choi, C., Neville, H. A., Anderson, C. J., & Brown, J. L. (2010). Beliefs about affirmative action: A test of the group self-interest and racism beliefs models. *Journal of Diversity in Higher Education, 3*(3), 163–176.

Perna, L. W. (2001). The contribution of historically black colleges and universities to the preparation of African Americans for faculty careers. *Research in Higher Education, 42*(3), 267–294.

Perna, L. W., Milem, J., Gerald, D., Baum, E., Rowan, H., & Hutchens, N. (2006). The status of equity for Black undergraduates in public higher education in the south: Still separate and unequal. *Research in Higher Education, 47*(2), 197–228.

Perna, L. W. & Thomas, S. L. (2009). Barriers to college opportunity: The unintended consequences of state-mandated testing. *Educational Policy, 23*(3), 451–479.

Roebuck, J. B. & Murty, K. S. (1993). *Historically Black colleges and universities: Their place in American higher education.* Westport, CT: Praeger.

Rolle, K. A., Davies, T. G., & Banning, J. H. (2000). African American administrators' experiences in predominantly white colleges and universities. *Community College Journal of Research and Practice, 24,* 79–94.

Smith, D. G., Tovar, E., & García, H. A. (2012). Where are they? A multilens examination of the distribution of full-time faculty by institutional type, race/ethnicity, gender, and citizenship. *New Directions for Institutional Research, 2012*(155), 5–26.

Solorzano, D. G. (1995). The doctorate production and baccalaureate origins of African Americans in the sciences and engineering. *Journal of Negro Education, 64*(1), 15–32.

Tack, M. W. & Patitu, C. L. (1992). *Faculty job satisfaction: Women and minorities in peril* (ASHE-ERIC Higher Education Report No. 4). Washington, DC: George Washington University.

Thelin, J. R. (2004). *A history of American higher education.* Baltimore, MD: Johns Hopkins University Press.

Thurgood, L., Golladay, M. J., & Hill, S. T. (2006). U.S. doctorates in the 20th century. Retrieved from http://faculty.washington.edu/timbillo/Important_Documents/NSF%20doctoral%20degree%20trends.pdf.

Tinto, V. (1993). *Leaving college: Rethinking the causes and cures of student attrition.* Chicago, IL: University of Chicago Press.

U.S. Commission on Civil Rights. (2010). *The educational effectiveness of Historically Black Colleges and Universities.* Washington, DC: Author.

Zamani-Gallaher, E. M. (2007). The confluence of race, gender, and class among community college students: Assessing attitudes toward affirmative action in college admissions. *Equity & Excellence in Education, 40,* 241–251.

CHAPTER FIVE

White Faces in Black Places: HBCUs and the White Faculty Experience

ATIYA STROTHERS

Many institutions of higher education have focused on increasing the diversity of their student populations. However, many times the faculty population does not represent the diverse student body (Bower, 2002; Jayakumar et al., 2009). With an ever-increasing focus on racial diversity, the face of faculty in higher education needs to be addressed. Most tenured faculty at Historically White Institutions (HWIs) continue to be White males and these populations are not fully integrated (Gasman, 2009). It is important for students to have faculty that can relate to them culturally and serve as role models for the students (Gater, 2005). A diverse faculty also provides different and innovative perspectives for research and methodologies. Additionally, having a variety of experiences from a diverse faculty can engage students of all populations (Gater, 2005) and use a wide range of pedagogical methods (Fries-Britt et al., 2011).

Considering societal data of minority faculty, it is rather disproportionate. In fall 2009, only 7% of college and university faculty were Black, 6% were Asian/Pacific Islander, 4% were Hispanic, and 1% were American Indian/Alaska Native. On the other hand, approximately 79% of all faculties were White with 42C% being White males and 37% being White females (NCES, 2009). Conklin and Robbins-McNeish (2006) state, "Out of the 282,429 tenured professors teaching in American institutions in 2003, 6.1 percent are Asian, 4.5 percent are Black and

2.9 percent are Hispanic. Just under 85 percent of tenured professors are white" (p. 27). With such low percentages, the benefit of having a diverse faculty as mentioned above is not being made evident in higher education. However, what do the numbers depict when we take into consideration Historically Black Colleges and Universities (HBCUs)?

HBCUs are leading the way when it comes to faculty diversity. Unlike their counterparts at HWIs, HBCUs have never had restrictions of entry based on race. Though not often recognized, HBCUs are statistically ahead in providing a racially diverse faculty for their students. According to the US Department of Education in 1996, Whites made up 29% of the faculty population at HBCUs, African Americans accounted for 58% of full-time faculty and other minorities, and foreigners accounted for 13% (Johnson & Harvey, 2002). In fall 2001, African Americans comprised 60.4% of the faculty population at HBCUs, 26.2% were White, and 13.4% were labeled as other (NCES, 2004). On the other hand, African Americans accounted for only 7% of the total college and university faculty in 2009. Hispanics accounted for 4%, 6%were Asian/Pacific Islander, and Whites made up 79% of the population (NCES, 2011). While the numbers at HBCUs do not depict a drastic difference over time, they do show a drastic difference in representation across HBCUs and HWIs.

With the demonstrated success of faculty diversity compared to HWIs, it might be assumed that a plethora of research exists evaluating faculty at HBCUs. That is not the case. While research does exist, some specific areas are either outdated or nonexistent (Foster et al., 1999; Smith, 2006). In light of the percentage of non-Black faculty at HBCUs, I am curious about their experiences as faculty at HBCUs. In this chapter, I shed light on this area of research that is sometimes overlooked. I will focus on White faculty, considering they are a perceived minority population within the context of most HBCUs.

I've Always Been Here: A Historical Perspective

The presence of White scholars and administrators at HBCUs is not a new phenomenon. The history of these institutions demonstrates the involvement of Whites back to the founding of many HBCUs. Gasman et al. (2010) note that many of our Black institutions were established by Black and White missionary organizations. Aiming to Christianize the former slaves (Gasman et al., 2010), these missionary organizations were influential in producing educational opportunities for Black students (Smith, 2006). The involvement of Northern missionaries was critical because it was often the only type of education Blacks were able to gain access to (Brazzell, 1992).

Whites were also instrumental in the history of Black colleges due to their financial capabilities. Considering the debate between industrial and liberal arts education for Blacks, some liberal arts colleges experienced difficulties in sustaining themselves (Smith, 2006). White industrial philanthropists were concerned that students under the Hampton and Tuskegee model would want to pursue a liberal arts education (Smith, 2006; Urban & Wagoner, 2004), going against their philosophy of Blacks being skilled workers and not intellectual leaders. However, not all philanthropists held the same perspective as those supporting industrial education. Missionaries made liberal education their focus as opposed to industrial training (Anderson, 1988). "Without education, they concluded, blacks would rapidly degenerate and become a national menace to American civilization" (p. 241). Thus, Whites were significant in the funding aspect of many HBCUs and also assumed leadership positions in the early phases of these institutions (Smith, 2006).

Black colleges have always had a diverse faculty population in both public and private institutions (Gasman, 2009). After 1895, Black professors began replacing the Whites. By the 1930s and 40s, HBCUs employed predominantly Black faculty (Smith, 2006). Additionally, a growing population was that of Jewish scholars in the faculty position. Jews fled to the United States to avoid oppressive regimes but were then ostracized from the White community (Foster, 2001; Smith, 2006). By the 1940s Jews had a presence on Black campuses and were accepted (Foster 2001; Smith, 2006).

A pivotal moment in education was seen in 1954 with the ruling of *Brown v. Board of Education*. This case sparked a lot of political interest, involvement, and shifts in education. Some White faculty members were drawn to Black colleges because of their interest and investment in the Civil Rights Movement (Foster et al., 1999). White faculty may have also chosen HBCUs for various other reasons and maintained different roles within the institution.

As shown in this brief history of Black colleges, Whites have always played a part in HBCUs, along with Blacks as well. Historically, unlike their HWI counterparts, HBCUs have been welcoming to various populations. This atmosphere has led to HBCUs being more racially diverse than HWIs (Foster et al., 1999). Even still, there continues to be a lack in research surrounding faculty at HBCUs (Johnson & Harvey, 2002; Louis, 2005; Smith, 2006).

Generalize Me: White Faculty at HBCUs

The White faculty population is a worthy group to study considering their contributions and the scarcity of information regarding this population. At the same time, Black faculty at PWIs are highly researched (Louis, 2005; Foster et al., 1999) however, there is a dearth of information regarding Black faculty at HBCUs (Johnson, 2001). As the discussion of diversifying faculty in higher education continues to permeate, we must be sure to include the experiences of faculty at HBCUs.

Black administrators and faculty have been a driving force in creating educational environments for Black students (Foster, 2001) by providing models of excellence that defy what is perceived in society of Black success. These individuals stand as role models and examples of what young Black men and women can aspire to be or attain. Black students make visual and personal connections with Black administrators and faculty serving as support systems and inspiration, which is often lacking at HWIs (Foster, 2001). Most HBCU communities are seen as supportive, encouraging, inspirational, and motivational for Black students. The culture of these environments is created in part by the administrators and faculty who are employed by the institution.

The overall experience of White faculty at HBCUs cannot be compiled into a monolithic summary. There is no faculty member, HBCU, or campus environment that is exactly the same. They are all different and unique in their own right. However, research does produce some thematic concepts that are helpful in understanding their experience. Smith and Borgstedt (1985) conducted a study looking at the factors influencing the adjustment of White faculty at HBCUs. Although this study is more than 20 years old, it is highly cited and continues to be one of the few that analyzes the adjustment of this population. In this study they found that 75% of participants felt socially accepted on campus and 92% perceived themselves as committed to the goals of the university and supportive of the college community. Also, 40% indicated that friends make derogatory remarks about their employment at an HBCU. With regard to feeling trusted by Black students, only 13% perceived Black students preferring a Black faculty member. Last, 56% perceived limitations in their career advancement because of their race and 60% saw the administration as more rigid than HWIs. Foster et al. (1999) found that White faculty members have positive experiences in the classroom that could be connected to the power dynamics seen in professor versus student. The highest satisfaction was seen with White faculty and their interactions with Black students. Overall, Smith and Borgstedt (1985) imply that the White faculty experience at HBCUs seems to be more positive than that of the Black faculty experience at HWIs.

White faculty members also have a role in the creation of the environment that is seen at HBCUs. They continue to maintain a presence at Black colleges and at some colleges they are large in number. White faculty members represent nearly a majority of faculty members in some HBCUs. They comprise at least 40% or more at the following schools: Xavier University of Louisiana, Harris-Stowe State College, Lincoln University in Missouri, Delaware State University, Tennessee State University, and Shaw University (Foster, 2001). At Bluefield State College and West Virginia State University, we see an extreme exception where White students and White faculty are now the majority population at these HBCUs. Specifically, White faculty represented 92% at Bluefield State College and 80% at West Virginia State University (Foster, 2001).

Excluding the exceptions seen at Bluefield State and West Virginia State, White faculty members have to adjust to teaching in settings where they must become the minority. For some who have never addressed or recognized their "Whiteness," this may be a daunting and sometimes impossible task. Smith (2006) draws parallels between new faculty experience and the experiences of their White HBCU faculty counterparts (Smith, 2006). Connections are made in that these faculty members have to learn the culture of the institution, understand the politics of the institution, and so on. However, the difference (a very significant difference) is that it involves the racial component.

Oh Snap, I'm White!: Temporary Minority

For the first time in my life I really felt white. I had always thought of myself generically as just a person. Now I was conscious of myself specifically as a white person. Of course, I was simply experiencing an awareness that many of my students have had to deal with their whole lives, of being being in others' eyes specifically persons of a certain race.

Karl Henzy, White Professor at Morgan State University
(Foster et al., 1999, p. 17)

This is just one example of thoughts had by a White faculty member becoming a minority within the context of this professional space.

When in the environment of a Black college, these faculty members face the likelihood of experiencing a role reversal opposite to that of their privilege in being a part of the dominant group. Considering this privilege and the norms connected to the dominant group, they possess limited understanding as to the values and norms when existing as a member of the racial minority population (Smith, 2006).

To further understand this dynamic, it is helpful to discuss how Whites develop their identity as a majority and a minority. Helms (1995) outlined a model in which there are six statuses that Whites go through to develop their identity: *contact, disintegration, reintegration, pseudo-independence, immersion/emersion, and autonomy.*

The *contact* status is a place where the person is satisfied with the racial status quo and is oblivious to racism as well as their participation in it. They have minimal experiences with Black people and may consider themselves to be color-blind. People in this status may not recognize their dominance or their own prejudices within.

The *disintegration* status is evident by unresolved racial dilemmas that cause disorientation or anxiety. People in this status become conflicted between humanism and loyalty to their own group. Examples of this may include believing one is not racist but not wanting their son or daughter to marry a minority, or witnessing oppression yet not acknowledging it.

In the *reintegration* status, idealization of one's socioracial group occurs. This could be considered regression as it facilitates a strong belief in the superiority of the White race. In this status, persons are intolerant of minority groups and blame them for their own problems.

The fourth status developed by Helms (1995) is *pseudo-independence.* People in this status begin to reshape their reality and re-conceptualize their commitment to their own racial group as well as their tolerance level of others. They try to understand differences in others and interact with minority members that have some shared commonalities. Moving into this status often occurs after a meaningful event.

The *immersion/emersion* status includes a redefinition of Whiteness and a personal search/understanding of racism. Reaching this status involves questioning the benefits received from White privilege and confronting their own biases. The difference in this status is increased experiential and affective understanding.

The last status in this model is *autonomy.* Persons in this status have a commitment to socioracial groupings that are positive and informed. They are aware of their Whiteness, accept individual role and actions in the perpetuation of racism, and relinquish fear or intimidation surrounding race. Their ability to abandon their White privilege leads to this level of autonomy.

It is important to highlight that this model was updated to using the word "status" as opposed to "stage." This was done to demonstrate the complex management of racial material and behavioral manifestations seen in statuses, as opposed to the linear categories perceived by stages. Identity development for Whites as the majority is important because they have the potential to perpetuate racism if they remain in one of the first three statuses discussed. Helms (1995) highlights that the developmental issue here for Whites is often giving up their entitlement to White privilege. As with any human being, it may be a challenge to relinquish your own individual privilege for the sake of humanity, as seen in the disintegration status. Persons not fully developed in their White identity may experience challenges in socialization and interactions with their minority counterparts. White faculty members at Black colleges who take heed of their development and mature into the autonomy status also need to understand their identity as a minority within the institution.

When Whites become part of the minority, as is the potential on Black campuses, there are different stages they must go through in reconstructing their identity (Smith, 2006). The stages of microcultural identity development (Jablin, 1982) are of particular interest as they force the intersection of the majority and minority perspective in one's experience. This four-stage model consists of: *unexamined identity, conformity, resistance and separatism, and integration.*

In the first stage, *unexamined identity,* the individual has very little information regarding their membership in the minority population. In the next stage, the person begins to recognize minority labeling as insensitive and connects negative values to their cultural background. This is the *conformity stage.* The third stage is *resistance and separatism.* At this stage the individual is able to resist blaming the minority for their situation and begins to make the separation as to the contributions of their own dominant group to racial problems. In the final stage, *integration,* the person has a strong sense of their identity and can contribute positively within the new minority group he/she is a part of.

This model is very helpful in understanding the process White faculty may go through in their development of a minority identity. With both models presented here (Helms, 1995; Jablin, 1982), the reader is able to gain insightful understanding as to what White faculty may go through in this challenge between majority/minority. Those that are able to progress through the final stages of the majority model, as well as the minority model, have a better chance at full integration within the institution (Smith, 2006). Discussing these models is beneficial not only for White faculty but also for the entire HBCU community.

Wearer of Many Hats: Roles of White Faculty

> Trustees may serve terms, students cycle in and out, but once tenured, faculty are there to stay.
>
> Park & Denson, 2009, p. 416

Faculty members, particularly tenured ones, play a very important role within the institution. They are in many ways, one of the few entities that may never leave the university. Faculty fulfill the role of developing curriculums, producing research to advance their work and the institution's, and they also have the power to determine many standards on their campus (Park & Denson, 2009). Some of the traditions, customs, and unspoken culture at universities are still in place due to the longevity seen in the presence of tenured faculty, active alumni, and so on. That being said, faculty members wear many hats at the institution and fulfill many roles. In addition to the roles they fill as a faculty member, two pieces of scholarship have been developed to outline the roles they fill as a White faculty member at a predominantly Black institution.

Thompson (1973) categorizes White faculty into four types: *missionary zealot, dedicated professional, young idealistic scholar,* and *academic reject.* The *missionary zealot* (including guilt-ridden zealot) is considered an advocate for the Black community. White faculty members in this category join the Black community's journey toward equality. These persons are often overly enthusiastic about assisting on campus and taking on additional tasks. The *dedicated professional* is deeply committed to the HBCU. They are passionate about the mission of HBCUs and the vision of the institution. The dedicated professional values their position and attempts to do all that is possible to uplift the institution in a professional manner. *Young idealistic scholars* are usually young professors with a different perspective on diversity. Because of their youth and generational differences, there is an obvious difference as to how they view minority-serving institutions. They may possess a perceived understanding of diversity at the surface level, but may not have dealt with their own identity development as a minority. Last, the *academic reject* categorizes the White professor who cannot secure a job at a HWI and thus obtains a position at a HBCU. Persons in this category may be considered less competent in their area of expertise and chooses to "settle" for a position at a Black institution.

Following Thompson (1973), Winifred Warnat (1976) of Howard University developed four roles for White faculty: *moron, martyr, messiah,* and *marginal man.* The *moron* has limited academic ability or no access to HWIs. They may be considered incompetent in their discipline and choose to remain at the HBCU in fear of rejection or having to face the reality of their limited ability. Faculty in this category can blame their own lack of proficiency on the environment at the Black college. This category aligns with Thompson's (1973) notion of academic reject. The *martyr* is similar to that of a missionary. They have a level of guilt within themselves and use this position as a relief for that guilt. This person willingly takes on boring tedious work without complaint and has no aspiration to achieve a higher status. Black colleagues pity White faculty in this role. The *messiah* provides direction that has been lacking in HBCUs. They "bring in the sheep." White faculty in this category consider the Black institutions as needing their help to continue functioning. Not surprisingly, this group is mistrusted and fosters feelings of alienation and hostility. The *marginal man* lives in two worlds and struggles to find his/her place in each. They are sensitive to the culture that surrounds them and struggle to maintain a balance between their dual identity: as representing white social structure and as member of Black college faculty. This particular group is similar to Carter's (2003) notion of being a cultural straddler. Straddlers are able to understand the values and norms of the dominant and nondominant cultures. They embrace the skills needed to actively participate in each of the differing environments.

These roles presented by Thompson and Warnat are not inclusive categorical groupings for all White faculty members. Furthermore, persons of color may fit into some of these categories as well (Warnat, 1976). Considering the era of development for both of these groupings, one would suspect some change to occur. However, these roles that White faculty can fill continue to be highly cited and referenced in literature.

The importance of faculty to the make-up of the institution has been previously discussed. Considering the similarities seen across these groupings, White faculty and the community should be cognizant of these roles and the impact they can have on the learning environment. Additionally, as we continue to explore the experiences of White faculty at HBCUs, these roles predict an impact on that experience and the interactions of their colleagues and students. Faculty members who have good intentions but criticize their own status and value to the institution may have good relationships with students but may never realize the power in their status (Warnat, 1976). This approach has the potential to lessen the power of their contributions and advancement to and within the university. Faculty who are perceived as saviors (lack of respect for history, customs, traditions of institution) may encounter the most negative feelings from colleagues and students, whereas the martyr achieves the greatest condolence from Black faculty (Warnat, 1976). It should be reiterated that the experiences of White faculty at HBCUs vary widely (Foster, 2001) but these theoretical concepts provide some of the themes related to their experience.

I Choose "U": Why White Faculty Join HBCUs

As we take into account the historical presence of Whites at HBCUs, their overall experience, their identity development, and the roles they fit into, this question comes to mind: Why be a part of the Black college experience? When one considers the gap in wages as a faculty member at HWIs versus HBCUs, the pay rate is clear. Faculty members at research-intensive universities are paid more, and, generally, faculty at HBCUs are paid less than their counterparts at HWIs (Renzulli et al., 2006). According to a recent report, *The Changing Face of Historically Black Colleges and Universities*, full professors at HBCUs make just slightly more than half of what their colleagues make at the national level. To provide specific numbers, the salary at the national level for full professors is $113,176, whereas the salary at private HBCUs is $58,456 and $78,653 at public HBCUs (Gasman et al., 2013). The question remains: Why choose an HBCU?

A body of research addresses this particular question and a few speculations have been noted. Historically, the presence of Whites on campus has not always had the best interest of Black education in mind. As mentioned previously, some Whites were active in the education of Blacks in order to control their education and maintain racial superiority within society. At the same time, there are assumptions by White dominant culture (and some in Black communities) that the Whites who join HBCUs are those who are unable to obtain faculty positions at HWIs due to their low level of competence in academic disciplines (Warnat, 1976). Furthermore, there is a stigma associated with working at HBCUs (Foster, 2001). This can be noted for both Whites and

Blacks. However, we must also consider that White faculty join HBCUs simply because it is the best decision and their personal choice.

Now, the argument can be made that White faculty are attracted to HBCUs because of the opportunities for academic employment. Tenure-track positions are increasingly shrinking and opportunities are becoming scarce in higher education (Foster, 2001). Young White faculty may also choose HBCUs in an effort to bring and learn new ideas and understandings about diversity (Foster, 2001). Also of importance are the recent debates and potential mandates for the desegregation of some HBCUs. Going forward, this discussion of diversity will shape the make-up and face of Black institutions.

Implications and Recommendations

I started this study with the hope of shedding light on the Black faculty experience at HBCUs and drawing parallels to their experience at HWIs. However, to my dismay, there was very minimal research considering the structural and environmental influences on the Black faculty experience at HBCUs. I then chose a different approach by considering the literature available and focusing on the White faculty population at HBCUs. I bring this into discussion to demonstrate the lack of scholarly research on our Black colleges overall. Much of the research on faculty at HBCUs is either outdated or minimal, as partially seen here in our discussion of White faculty and their experience at HBCUs.

This study has sought to shed light on a population that is not often discussed. White faculty has always had a presence on Black campuses and although their experiences vary, I have emphasized the existing research showing commonalities in their experience and applied theoretical concepts as well. Identity development for any person is of importance as we learn and grow individually. This development is particularly important for White faculty at Black colleges. Colleges should be involved and aware of the identity formation process that their faculty go through. As mentioned earlier, the roles presented by Thompson and Warnat can have a tremendous impact not only on the institutions but also on the students. Taking preventive measures to incorporate these concepts into professional development can lead to a deeper understanding among colleagues from diverse communities and cultures and potentially strengthen collaboration.

As mentioned earlier, the topic of diversifying HBCUs is an ongoing debate within higher education. More specifically, the topic of diversifying faculty has been a continuous topic and call for action as well. To my astonishment, HBCUs have been absent from this conversation. It has been proven here that Black colleges have always had an open door to various populations and the numbers suggest that HBCUs are in fact leading the way in faculty diversity compared to HWIs. At HBCUs, the percentage of tenured faculty for Blacks is 57% and 27% for Whites. On the contrary, the percentage of tenured Black faculty at the national level is only 4% and 84% for Whites (Gasman et al., 2013). These figures show a huge disproportion regarding faculty diversity. If you consider the positive feelings of socialization of White faculty at HBCUs, it is opposite of that for Black faculty at HWIs. Black faculty members at HWIs often have feelings of isolation, racism, and experience an uncomfortable campus climate (Fries-Britt et al., 2011). One would think that this would place Black colleges as an example for others to learn from; however, that has not happened. Given the data shown in the experiences of White faculty at HBCUs, these institutions should be leaders in faculty diversity and socialization.

HBCU faculty and students have a diverse profile, yet the question continues: "Why choose an HBCU?" As discussed in this section, there is research addressing why faculty members choose HBCUs but there is a lack of research on Black faculty at HBCUs. Furthermore, when faculty or students choose to teach or attend an HWI, are they burdened with the stigmatized question of "why"? It seems as though our scholarly priorities are out of order and the pattern of institutional racism permeates our research. If our educational systems continue to stress the importance of diversity and equity, we need to take an introspective account of our own inclusivity. More research on HBCUs and MSIs is required overall and these institutions need to be included in the many conversations surrounding diversity. HBCUs have always welcomed White faces in their Black spaces, leading the way for access and opportunity; it's time we take heed to the lessons learned.

References

Anderson, J. D. (1988). *The education of Blacks in the south, 1860–1935*. Chapel Hill, NC: The University of North Carolina Press.

Bower, B. L. (2002). Campus life for faculty of color: Still strangers after all these years? *New Directions for Community Colleges*, (118), 79–87.

Brazzell, J. C. (1992). Bricks without straw: Missionary-sponsored Black higher education in the post-emancipation era. *Journal of Higher Education*, 63(1), 26–49.

Carter, Prudence (2003). "Black" Cultural Capital, Status Positioning, and Schooling Conflicts for Low-Income African American Youth." *Social Problems, 50*, 136–155.
Conklin, W. & Robbins-McNeish, N. (2006). *Four barriers to faculty diversity. Diversity Factor, 14* (4).
Foster, L. (2001). *The not-so-invisible professors: White faculty at the black college.* Sage Publications.
Foster, L., Guyden, J., & Miller, A. (1999). *Affirmed action: Essays on the academic and social lives of white faculty members at historically black colleges and universities.* Lanham, MD: Rowman & Littlefield Publishers.
Fries-Britt, S. (2011). Underrepresentation in the academy and the institutional climate for faculty diversity. *Journal of the Professoriate, 5*(1), 1.
Gasman, M. (2009). Diversity at historically black colleges and universities. Message posted on http://diverseeducation.wordpress.com/2009/06/05/diversity-at-historically-black-colleges-and-universities/.
Gasman, M., Lundy-Wagner, V., Ransom, T., & Bowman III, N. (2010). *Unearthing promise and potential: Our nation's historically black colleges and universities* (ASHE Higher Education Report No. 5). Hoboken, NJ: Wiley Periodicals.
Gasman, M., Nguyen, T., Castro Samayoa, A., Commodore, F., Abiola. U., Hyde-Carter, Y., & Carter, C. (2013). *The changing face of historically black colleges and universities.* Philadelphia, PA: University of Pennsylvania, Center for Minority Serving Institutions.
Gater, L. (2005). Diverse faculty reflects diverse world. *University Business, 8*(3), 22–23.
Helms, J. E. (1995). An update of Helms's White and people of color racial identity models. In J. G. Ponterotto, J. M. Casas, L. A. Suzuki, & C. M. Alexander (Eds.), *Handbook of multicultural counseling* (pp. 181–191). Thousand Oaks, CA: Sage.
Jablin, F. M. (1982). Organizational communication: An assimilation perspective. In M. Roloff & C. Berger (Eds.), *Social cognition and communication* (pp. 255–286). Beverly Hills, CA: Sage.
Jayakumar, U. M., Howard, T. C., Allen, W. R., & Han, J. C. (2009). Racial privilege in the professoriate: An exploration of campus climate, retention, and satisfaction. *Journal of Higher Education, 80*(5), 538–563.
Johnson, B. (2001). Faculty socialization: Lessons learned from urban black colleges. *Urban Education, 36*(5), 630.
Johnson, B. J. & Harvey, W. (2002). The socialization of Black college faculty: Implications for policy and practice. *Review of Higher Education, 25*(3), 297–314.
Laird, T. N. (2012). Study finds HBCU faculty are more supportive of students than faculty at other schools. *Journal of Blacks in Higher Ed*, May 6.
Louis, D. A. R. (2005). *Attributes influencing the adjustment of white faculty at selected historically black colleges and universities in Texas.* Unpublished Doctor of Philosophy thesis, Texas A&M University.
Musil, C. M. (1996). The maturing of diversity initiatives on American campuses: Multiculturalism and diversity in higher education. *American Behavioral Scientist, 40*(2), 222–233.

Park, J. J. & Denson, N. (2009). *Attitudes and advocacy: Understanding faculty views on racial/ethnic diversity*. Ohio State University Press.

Renzulli, L. A., Grant, L., & Kathuria, S. (2006). *Race, gender, and the wage gap: Comparing faculty salaries in predominately white and historically black colleges and universities*.Thousand Oaks, CA: Sage Publications.

Smith, Kimya (2006). "White Faculty at Historically Black Colleges and Universities." University of New Orleans Theses and Dissertations. Paper 1044.

Smith, S. L. & Borgstedt, K. W. (1985). Factors influencing adjustment of white faculty in predominantly black colleges. *Journal of Negro Education*, 54(2), 148–163.

Thompson, D. C. (1973). Black college faculty and students: The nature of Their interaction. In C. E. Willie & R. R. Edmonds (Eds.), *Black colleges in America* (pp. 180–194). New York, London: Teachers College Press.

Urban, W. J. & Wagoner, J. L., Jr. (2004). *The American education: A history* (3rd ed.). New York: McGraw-Hill.

U.S. Department of Education, National Center for Education Statistics (1996). *Historically Black colleges and universities, 1976–1996 (NCES 96–902)*. Washington, DC.

U.S. Department of Education, National Center for Education Statistics (1999). *Predicting the need for newly hired teachers in the United States to 2008–09*. Washington, DC.

U.S. Department of Education, National Center for Education Statistics (2011). *Digest of Education Statistics, 2010* (NCES 2011–015), Chapter 3.

Warnat, W. (1976). The role of white faculty on the black college campus. *Journal of Negro Education*, 45(3), 334.

CHAPTER SIX

HBCU Young Alumni: Paying It Forward

BRANDY JACKSON AND JACQUELINE AMPARO

Historically Black Colleges and Universities (HBCUs) are an integral part of American higher education. Since the founding of the first HBCU, Cheyney University, these institutions have provided access to postsecondary education for African Americans. Presently, over half of African American professionals are graduates of HBCUs (Knight et al., 2012). About 30% of bachelor's degrees awarded to Blacks in STEM fields are granted by HBCUs (Perna et al., 2009). HBCUs are also the largest producers of African American science PhDs (Gasman & Bowman, 2012). However, historically these institutions have had limited resources to keep their infrastructure in place—today it is no different (Holloman et al., 2003). For HBCUs to survive in the twenty-first century alumni involvement is key. Alumni are particularly important for the development and advancement of institutional resources. Yet, the research on the subject indicates that HBCU alumni are giving less or not giving at all (Cohen, 2006; Reaves, 2006; Williams, 2010).

While it is important to highlight the low rates of alumni-giving at HBCUs, it is also critically imperative to showcase stories and efforts of alumni that are giving to their alma mater. Mainstream media continues to paint a negative image of HBCUs, which does not help their plight or financial stability (Gasman & Bowman, 2010). Further, institutions use a narrow concept of alumni-giving that excludes alumni that are giving nonmonetary resources (i.e., volunteering and advocating) (Weerts & Ronca, 2007). Therefore, this chapter is an effort to provide a positive perspective on young alumni-giving at HBCUs.

We want to move beyond the conventional financial concept of giving and illustrate that when thought of broadly, giving is multifaceted. By doing so, we can initiate change in mainstream discourse on HBCU alumni-giving and chronicle efforts of young alumni that are paying it forward.

Changing the Rhetoric

According to the 2013 *Merriam-Webster's Dictionary*, giving is "to make present of." This definition can encompass many forms of giving such as clothing donations, volunteering, and monetary donations. However, giving in the higher education setting most commonly refers to monetary donations (Weerts & Ronca, 2007). Monetary donations are important for colleges and universities to be able to provide adequate facilities and services to their students but there are other ways by which alumni give that also help in resource development (Tillman, personal communication, April 2013). With a majority of the research focusing on charitable giving, little is known about nonmonetary forms of giving by alumni (Weerts & Ronca, 2007). A comprehensive view of giving that includes monetary donations, volunteerism, and advocacy will adequately demonstrate alumni-giving at postsecondary institutions (Weerts & Ronca, 2007). In an effort to provide an adequate image of alumni-giving at HBCUs, this analysis will use an inclusive framework of the concept of giving that includes both monetary and nonmonetary forms.

Negative Image of HBCUs

This chapter began because of the negative perceptions the public has of HBCUs. Many of these perceptions focus on questioning the existence of HBCUs, the quality of their education, and alumni involvement (Gasman & Bowman, 2010). Tiffany Tillman, a Prairie View A&M University alumnus and now a student at the University of Pennsylvania Graduate School of Education, told us that the common view she often hears about HBCU alumni-giving is "that they do not give." While it is true that HBCU alumni have low monetary donation giving rates (9%) compared to the national rate (20%) (Gasman & Bowman, 2010), the rates do not necessarily capture a comprehensive picture of alumni involvement. The problem is that alumni financial giving is used to measure alumni involvement. There is a lack of research on alumni that are paying it forward. Therefore, it is important to highlight the efforts of HBCU young alumni engaging and paying it forward to their alma mater as an attempt to improve the image of HBCUs. The surge in negative portrayal of HBCUs by mainstream media (Hill & Fiore, 2011) does not help in engaging alumni. Therefore, to change the conversation it is necessary to start moving beyond what is wrong with HBCUs and start recognizing their achievements.

Early Funding at HBCUs

As Black colleges formed throughout the United States, higher education served as a tool to unite African Americans as a race. Faragher and Howe (1988) note the African American perspective in the early 1800s was centered on the philosophy of racial uplift (as cited in Peeples, 2010). However pursuing this goal was difficult due to discrimination against Blacks and the lack of financial support to their colleges. Though the Morrill Act of 1890 helped establish land-grant HBCUs, many institutions still struggled to operate. Thelin (2011) states, "The seventeen black institutions were disproportionately neglected with respect to facilities, salaries, and staffing. They were ill equipped to conduct advanced, original research" (p. 136). Nevertheless, Black institutions without land grants progressed with monetary assistance from Northern and Southern White missionaries, such as the American Baptist Home Mission Society, American Missionary, and the Freedmen's Bureau. Though these institutions were dedicated to financially supporting Black institutions, they also had their own agenda—transforming former slaves into productive citizens of society. Gasman highlights that "the missionaries' stated goals in establishing these colleges were to Christianize the freedman (i.e., convert formerly enslaved people to their brand of Christianity) and to rid the country of the 'menace' of uneducated African Americans" (Gasman, 2007 p. 20).

Just as there were White missionaries dedicated to supporting Black colleges, there were Black denominations committed to establishing and founding HBCUs. With the help of the African Methodist Episcopal (AME) church, many universities were established. Some include institutions such as Allen University, Morris Brown, and Paul Quinn College; Livingstone College was developed through the efforts of the African Methodist Episcopal Zion church (Smith et al., 2002). While most of these institutions were dependent on financial donations from missionaries, they also gained support from the surrounding Black communities that they specifically served (Hunter et al., 1999). The ways in which many Black communities gave back to Black colleges were through tithing and volunteering with the church. Though these activities were successful in terms of fundraising, they were mostly done in private, "partly because the formation of voluntary associations by Blacks was forbidden and often considered subversive" (Hunter et al., 1999, p. 525). Gasman and Anderson-Thompkins indicate:

> These educational efforts for Blacks were made possible by money saved—sometimes one penny at a time—by African American communities and churches. As a result of the "obligation to give" instilled by their churches, Blacks supported their own advancement in society. (2003, p. 285)

In the 1930s, as aid from missionaries started to disappear, Northern philanthropists, such as Slader, Rosenwald, Peabody, Carnegie, Rockefeller, and the Anna T. Jeans Foundation that focused on industrial education ideology, began to give to HBCUs (Hunter et al., 1999).

Trends in HBCU Alumni-Giving

Reviewing African American giving trends, there is a lack of research indicating how Blacks give in higher education. As Cohen (2006) states in his findings, "research related to higher education is scant and almost nonexistent when investigating alumni givers as vested stakeholders" (p. 203). Further, US institutions do not make the effort to collect this important data, nor does the Council for the Support and Advancement of Education (CASE) (Gasman & Bowman, 2013). However, recently, research on Black alumni-giving has increased and is being found in dissertations rather than in scholarly writings (Wallace, 2012).

Black people typically give in small increments to mainstream organizations because there is a historic lack of trust. Conversely, when trust is established and Black people are familiar and comfortable with the organization, research has shown that their giving increases in terms of amounts (Gasman & Bowman, 2012). This may explain why alumni-giving at HBCUs is significantly low. In order to increase giving HBCU institutions must establish strong relationships with alumni. Blacks need to first feel trust in order to give in large sums to an organization.

On the other hand, HBCUs lack the infrastructure to cultivate that trust. Because most HBCUs have budgets that are undersized they have small institutional advancement offices composed of three to five staff members. As a Jackson State University professional notes, "Our greatest liability in the area of fundraising at Jackson State University is budget. We are unable to attract or recruit professional fund raisers due to a lack of funds" (Gasman & Anderson-Thompkins, 2003, p. 59). Since most HBCUs development offices are small and have limited capacity, institutional advancement officers have less access to engage with alumni and officers lack the training and knowledge to effectively fundraise. As a result having fewer funds implies that donations to the institution are unrestricted rather than restricted to specific programs (Tindell, 2007).

Another key problem that occurs at HBCUs is that most institutions do not cultivate giving with their current student body. Some institutions wait ten years to facilitate alumni-giving with new graduates because they believe that young alumni are bound by student loan debt and need time to become established as professionals (Gasman et al., 2010). Nevertheless, if institutions desire to increase their young alumni-giving they need to provide education on the importance of philanthropy during the students' undergraduate experience.

A recent study of 200 institutions revealed that getting young alumni to become active donors is a challenge for development offices (Ezarik, 2010). Research has also shown that there are only a few Historically White Institutions (HWIs) that have high young alumni involvement (Wampler, 2013), indicating that low young alumni-giving rates is an issue at both HBCUs and HWIs. Though institutions all over the nation are using student outreach programs to connect with young alumni, many institutions fail to unite the experience with the student's new identity as an alumnus (Wampler, 2013). Therefore, HBCUs need to develop opportunities for students and young alumni to give what they can (i.e., donations, volunteering, and mentorship), which will result in larger donations in the future.

Why Are Young Alumni Important?

Institutions thrive on having a strong alumni base. With alumni donations, institutions have the ability to sustain the university and carry on the rich history and traditions to the next generation. However, in order to achieve this goal, HBCUs must instill in students the importance of young alumni-giving once students arrive on campus (Drezner, 2008). Research indicates that colleges and universities are more likely to have strong annual giving programs and high alumni-giving rates when their strategies from fundraising are clear and encourage alumni-giving among their current student body (Ayers & Ayers, 2002). Regardless of race, alumni-giving is largely based on the student's undergraduate experience (Gasman, 2001; Holloman et al., 2003).

Tara Hill (personal communication, March 2013), a 2009 alumnus from Morgan State University, explains her reason for giving and how the faculty and staff made a difference in her decision to give back:

> Ms. Tanya Rush was my main reason I gave back to my alma mater. She put everything into perspective for me very early. My first year I was fortunate to make the Dean's list and was put into honors housing. However because I paid for everything out of pocket I did not have enough money to pay for books. Because Ms. Rush heard about my situation, she gave me a grant to pay for my book expenses. When she sat me down she said, "I'm going to give you this but you have to pay it forward. I'm not asking you to pay me now, nor am I asking you to pay in a year. But when you graduate it is your responsibility, it is your duty to pay it forward."

The nurturing and commitment showed by the institution motivated Tara to pay it forward. Similarly, there are two other institutions that are making student philanthropy a priority on their campus—Spelman College, a four-year liberal arts women's college, and Claflin University, a United Methodist liberal arts institution.

Spelman College, located in Atlanta, Georgia, is in the midst of a $150 million campaign, which was launched in 2009 and is to be completed in 2015. Under the leadership of President Beverly Daniel Tatum, the college has already passed the $100 million mark. With their committed alumnae and dedicated faculty and staff, the college is confident they will raise the additional $50 million. As the college reaches out to alumni to support the institution, they are also educating their students on the importance of giving to Spelman as a student. Spelman seeks to impart to its students the importance of giving from the very beginning. Spelman's annual giving officer, Jennifer Moore (personal communication, March 2013), also a 2005 graduate of Spelman, notes how the college is instituting an "all student approach to giving" for the 2012–2013 fiscal year:

For our senior legacy program we encourage all graduating seniors to give $20.13 to the Spelman fund. In exchange we give each student a commemorative Spelman Blue tassel to be worn as part of the Founders Day Convocation regalia and on Class Day. Not only are we encouraging seniors to give back, but this year we have also provided a suggestive giving amount for underclassman. To recognize our students' philanthropic efforts, all students who gave this year will be highlighted in the Spelman honor roll.

Because giving has become a part of the culture of Spelman, in 2011 the college was the first HBCU to establish an Association of Fundraising Professional Collegiate Chapter. Through this organization students are able to give to specific campus priorities, such as the Spelman Fund, scholarships, or the college campaign. By participating in this organization students learn the fundamentals of fundraising and how to appropriately use and apply ethical principles.

In April 2012, Claflin University, located in Orangeburg, South Carolina, had a huge success in their student philanthropy campaign. The students raised $150,000 to contribute to the institution's $96.4 million capital campaign. President Henry N. Tisdale states "the student body of Claflin University is to be commended for taking ownership and exhibiting leadership during this historic campaign." Marcus Fogle (personal communication, March 2013), a 2009 graduate of Claflin and manager of the annual fund, states how the university cultivates student philanthropy on the campus:

> Our goal is educate students about the importance of alumni giving from the time they are a freshmen [until] they become young alums of the university. Because we educate students on the impact they are making, we don't have a problem of getting 100% of our seniors to contribute to the annual fund. To educate our students on how they can be fundraisers of the university, each year the university hosts in April a student philanthropy day. On this day students are able to purchase buttons that say, I support my Claflin education.

Claflin has made student alumni-giving a key priority of the university's vision and strategic plan. As a result, the student body has truly worked tirelessly this past year to make giving a part of the culture at Claflin (Fogle, personal communication, March 2013).

Young Alumni Paying It Forward

Every day young alumni from HBCUs are making a great difference within their own communities and in the HBCUs they represent. However, the public rarely hears about the positive work they are doing. To change the current rhetoric on and image of HBCUs, it is important to highlight alumni efforts as they work to sustain HBCUs through volunteerism, fundraising, and advocacy. In this chapter we will discuss three organizations in which alumni are actively engaged to strengthen their alma maters as well as HBCUs as a whole. These organizations include: Fisk University Young Alumni Association (YAA), The H.O.P.E. (Helping Others Pursue Education) Scholarship Initiative, and HBCUStory.

Fisk Young Alumni Association

Fisk University's Young Alumni Association (YAA) is a great example of an organization that promotes young alumni engagement. The organization was originally created during the fifth year reunion of the Class of 2000 with the goal of implementing an annual fundraiser (Demetrius Short, personal communication, April 2013). The Fisk YAA later evolved into a young alumni association that would inform and educate young Fisk alums about university events and news (*Fisk Young Alumni Association*, 2010, website). As many young alumni find it difficult to relate to older alumni, Gasman and Bowman note that the creation of young alumni associations is instrumental to institutions. These organizations create a bond between younger graduates but also aid in bridging the generational gap that exists between current students and older alums (Gasman & Bowman, 2011). Demetrius Short, a '99 Fisk graduate and Chairman of the Fisk YAA, speaks on how it manages to cultivate a bond between the institution and younger alumni:

> FYAA was created by a group of young alumni who saw the importance of connecting and creating a culture of social responsibility of Fisk University from a younger alumni perspective. As we have the General Alumni Association of Fisk University, Inc. (GAAFU), we thought it would be best to create FYAA in conjunction to the university. In creating this young alumni component to Fisk, we initially thought that we were establishing

something new; however unbeknown to us our eyes were opened to how young alumni associations were thriving throughout the country. (Demetrius Short, personal communication, April 2013)

During the research process of establishing Fisk YAA, the team realized how late they were in tapping into creating a young alumni division for the university (Short, personal communication, April 2013). However, seeing other alumni organizations such as "Howard University, the Morehouse, the Spelman, the Harvard, the Yale, and Vanderbilt" (Short, personal communication, April 2013) gave the team motivation and assurance that the Fisk YAA was essential in connecting Fisk to its alumni. Short (personal communication, April 2013) states that FYAA should not be seen as a separate entity of Fisk University but as an integral division of the GAAFU, one that is disseminating the goals of Fisk to a younger audience.

Understanding that young alumni today tend to give to smaller local social causes where they feel they can make more of a difference (Wampler, 2013), FYAA developed the Fisk 50/50 Protégé Program (Short, personal communication, April 2013). The program creates mentorship relationships by matching a current Fisk student with a Fisk alumnus (Short, personal communication, April 2013). Through this program, young alumni engage current students and encourage them to give back by tutoring inner city Nashville high school students.

This creates a culture where Fisk alumni within FYAA give back by mentoring current Fisk students, and current Fisk students are making an immediate impact by giving back to underprivileged inner city students. As a result a life cycle of success is created. "The kids that we mentor here in Nashville, their opportunity of success is graduating from junior high school. However, putting a Fisk University student in their face empowers them to achieve to be more" (Short, personal communication, April 2013).

The H.O.P.E. Scholarship Initiative

The H.O.P.E.—Helping Others Pursue Education—Scholarship Initiative is a 501c3 nonprofit organization started by Howard University alums Jeffery Chance '09 and Michelle Janaye '07. The organization was designed to empower financially challenged students attending HBCUs. Since its inception in 2010, the H.O.P.E. Scholarship team has successfully given out three $1,000 scholarships to needy and deserving HBCU college students (Chance, personal communication, April 2013). Jeffrey notes:

> The H.O.P.E. Scholarship Initiative was created so at least one continuing student does not have to stress about finding funding for college and have to make the decision to drop out of school. Additionally, H.O.P.E. was created to preserve HBCUs; we never want to hear someone say, 'Right here once stood a historically black college and university.' The work that we do reminds me that young people can have an impact on society now. It reminds me that young people can transform communities now. (Personal communication, April 2013)

The executive team of H.O.P.E. consists of five individuals who are all graduates of HBCUs (H.O.P.E., 2010). Each member knows firsthand the challenges of paying for tuition, looking for scholarships and working part-time jobs, all the while maintaining an impressive GPA (Chance, personal communication, April 2013). H.O.P.E. maintains a blog that has attracted more than 11,000 visitors in the past two years and features guest bloggers (Paul Quinn College) President Michael Sorrell, (Dillard University) President Walter Kimbrough, (University of Pennsylvania) Professor of Education Marybeth Gasman, and Grammy award-winning, Chicago-based rapper Che "Rhyme Fest" Smith. Furthermore, according to Michelle Janaye, one of H.O.P.E.'s founders:

> We invest in HBCUs students in ways that allow them to graduate. We encourage HBCU students/alumni/ to reinvest in their institutions. On our website, there is a page where you can find a long list of HBCUs to donate to. We've done the research for you. More importantly, the board of this organization is comprised of all HBCU graduates who lead impressive careers in their varying fields and represent the best of what their HBCU education has to offer, in terms of producing fruitful, community-empowering students.

The ultimate message the H.O.P.E. scholarship wants HBCU young alumni to comprehend is the value of an education. "Everyone, regardless of their socioeconomic income, deserves access to great teachers, a stimulating curriculum and a supportive learning environment. By educating a young person is to empower a family, uplift a community, sustain a people and improve a generation" (Michelle Janaye, personal communication, April 2013). As H.O.P.E. looks to the future, the goal is to inspire more people to follow their dreams, assist more students financially through scholarship, and empower more of the next generation of young philanthropists. Chance concludes, "If this means more intuitive blog posts, stronger branding, better events, and larger H.O.P.E. tours–let's do it" (personal communication, April 2013).

HBCUStory

HBCUStory is an emerging initiative to unify HBCU alumni for the continued support of these institutions. Motivated by her undergraduate experience at Fisk University, Crystal A. deGregory, a professor at Tennessee State University, founded HBCUStory with her personal funds in 2012 (personal communication, April 2013). For deGregory, Fisk was "the place that allowed me to find my voice, it allowed me to really grow as a person, it is the place that nurtured me and loved me but also challenged me and encouraged me." Therefore, as a young alumnus, deGregory was motivated to give back to Fisk. In her words:

> I think shortly after I graduated I began giving in a monthly automatic withdrawal from my account. There were times where it was a real sacrifice for me. I didn't have money and I would have to borrow money so that my account wouldn't go into overdraft. Since that time I also believe you can give more than money, you can give other than money. Some give their time and their energy.

Crystal deGregory was committed to Fisk because it not only fostered her educational and leadership development but it also provided her with the tools that enabled her to complete her master's and doctoral degrees in history from Vanderbilt University (personal communication, April 2013). While deGregory continues to give financially to Fisk, she was also prompted to create a platform that would unite alumni from all 105 HBCUs:

> I decided to do HBCU story because I thought about a woman historian who had dubbed herself the *herstorian*. And I thought well if she is the *herstorian*, I am the *HBCUStorian* because I tell the HBCU story. And I used the singular version because we collectively write one story. (Personal communication, April 2013)

On April 27, 2013, months of work culminated in the first HBCUStory symposium held in Nashville, Tennessee, where a hundred of HBCU alumni came together to share their stories and encourage others to actively participate in supporting the advancement of these institutions. This event is part of the initiative "to do a better job of saying to the world who we are, what it is we've done, what it is we are doing and going to do moving forward" (Crystal deGregory, personal communication, April 2013). For deGregory, HBCUStory is a way for alumni to counteract the negative portrayal of HBCU in mainstream media— "we tell positive stories about the HBCU experience."

Conclusion

Alumni-giving is critical for the future of HBCUs. However, the focus has been largely on the low rates of financial giving by young alumni, often ignoring the nonmonetary efforts by this population. Though HBCU young alumni are often constrained monetarily, they are giving back through projects such as FYAA, H.O.P.E Scholarship, and HBCUStory. It is through these initiatives that HBCU young alumni are becoming more involved in their alma maters. Therefore, it is important to recognize these actions as legitimate forms of giving.

Broadening the definition of giving will paint a more positive image of HBCUs and their alumni involvement. Most young alumni may not have the financial means to become major donors but they are willing to give their time and energy to advance their institution. Therefore, it is imperative that HBCUs start highlighting these efforts by young alumni in order to combat mainstream criticism. Unfortunately, the public lacks understanding of the history and purpose of HBCUs, and unjustly compares them to established HWIs that have traditionally enjoyed more resources (Gasman & Bowman, 2011). We believe that if we start changing the way we speak about alumni-giving at HBCUs and highlight positive examples of young alumni who are actively involved, we can successfully encourage current students and other alumni to pay it forward.

Recommendations

It is imperative that young alumni at HBCUs are cultivated early and given the opportunity to give in monetary and nonmonetary ways. Gasman and Bowman have produced *A Guide to Fundraising at*

Historically Black Colleges and Universities (2012) in which they have taken into consideration the limited resources HBCUs have and tailored the recommendations for increasing alumni donations accordingly. While the recommendations below are in line with some of the ones posed by Gasman and Bowman they are designed to increase young alumni giving through nonmonetary means. We see these recommendations as alumni-engagement strategies that can lead to more monetary donations.

Education
- To start the tradition of giving among young alumni, and educate students on the importance of giving during the new student orientation.
- Explain to young alumni what the institution's annual fund is and how their donation makes a difference.
- Start a campus philanthropy program to cultivate student-giving.

Multimedia
- Use social media sites to engage current students and young alumni.
- Highlight stories of students and alumni.
- Demonstrate through technology the accomplishments of HBCUs.

Volunteer Opportunities
- Have young alumni represent the institution at college fairs and other recruiting events.
- Develop mentor programs with current and young alumni.
- Engage young alumni, asking them to call prospective students to share their experiences and encourage them to attend the institution.

Stewardship
- Establish a procedure to recognize alumni that are giving of their time.
- Young alumni may prefer recognition electronically rather than traditional mailings.
- Social-media sites can be used to provide public recognition of young alumni that are giving donations, volunteering, and advocating for their institution.

The recommendations provided will of course vary from campus to campus. We strongly suggest that each campus use the methods and practices that work best for them. However, as suggested, early education on giving to the institution must be cultivated when students are freshmen. Though every alumni may not have the means to give financially, it is important that institutions make sure that alumni are included and are able to give back through volunteering. They should share with alumni the ways in which they can aid in sustaining their alma mater, through recruiting students, being elected to their alumni board, or participating in mentoring or tutoring students. The only way HBCUs will progress and survive through generations is through the help and leadership of alumni. It is our responsibility to continue to "Pay it forward."

References

Ayers & Ayers (2002). *Alumni giving in the new millennium: A guide to securing support.* Washington, DC: Ayers & Associates.

Baade, R. A. & Sundberg, J. O. (1996). What determines alumni generosity? *Economics of Education Review, 15*(1), 75–81.

Cohen, R. T. (2006). Black college alumni giving: A study of the perceptions, attitudes, and giving behaviors of alumni donors at selected historically black colleges and universities. *International Journal of Educational Advancement, 6*(3), 200–220.

Drezner, N. (2008). Cultivating a culture of giving: An exploration of institutional strategies to enhance African American young alumni giving. Unpublished doctoral dissertation. University of Pennsylvania, Philadelphia, PA.

Ezarik, M. (2010). Cultivating a culture of giving back—starting freshman year. *University Business, 13*(3), 15–15.

Faragher, J. M. & Howe, F. (Eds.) (1988). *Women in higher education.* New York: W.W. Norton.

Fisk University Young Alumni Association (2010). *About: Fisk Young Alumni Association*—Moving Forward by Giving Back. Retrieved May 2, 2013 from http://fiskyoungalumni.com/site/.

Fiore, D. J. & Hill, W. W. (2011). *Creating personal success on the Historically Black College and University campus.* Retrieved on May 2, 2013 from www.cengagebrain.com.

Gasman, M. (2001). An untapped resource: Bringing African-Americans into the college and university giving process. *The CASE International Journal of Educational Advancement, 2*(3), 280–292.

——— (2007). *Envisioning Black college: A history of the United Negro Fund.* Baltimore, MD: The Johns Hopkins University Press.

Gasman, M. & Anderson-Thompkins, S. (2003). *Fund-raising from Black college alumni: Successful strategies for supporting alma mater.* Washington, DC: Council for the Advancement and Support of Education.

Gasman, M. & Bowman III, N. (2011). How to paint a better portrait of HBUCs. *American Association of University of Professors, Academe, 97*(3), 24.

——— (2012). *A guide to fundraising at Historically Black Colleges and Universities: An all campus approach.* New York: Routledge.

——— (2013). *Engaging diverse college alumni: The essential guide to fundraising.* New York: Routledge.

Gasman, M., Lundy-Wagner, V., Ransom, T., and Bowman III, N. (2010). *Unearthing promise and potential: Our nation's Historically Black Colleges and Universities.* San Francisco, CA: Jossey-Bass.

Holloman, D. B., Gasman, M., & Anderson-Thompkins, S. (2003). Motivations for philanthropic giving in the African American church: Implications for Black college fundraising. *Journal of Research on Christian Education, 12*(2), 137–169.

Hunter, C. S., Jones, E. B., & Boger, C. (1999). A study of the relationship between alumni giving and selected characteristics of alumni donors of Livingstone College, NC. *Journal of Black Studies, 29*(4), 523–539.

Knight, L., Davenport, E., Green-Powell, P., and Hilton, A. A. (2012). The role of historically Black colleges or universities. *International of Journal Education, 4*(2), 223–235

Peeples, Y. T. (2010). Philanthropy and the curriculum: The role of philanthropy in the development of curriculum at Spelman College. *International Journal of Educational Advancement, 10,* 245–260.

Perna, L. W., Lundy Perna, L. W., Lundy-Wagner, V., Drezner, N., Gasman, M., Yoon, S., Bose, E., & Gary, S. (2009). The contribution of HBCUs to the preparation of African American women for STEM careers: A case study. *Review of Higher Education, 50*(1), 1–23.

Reaves, N. (2006). *African American alumni perceptions regarding giving to Historically Black Colleges and Universities.* Unpublished doctoral dissertation. North Carolina State University, Raleigh, NC.

Smith, W. A., Altbach, P. G., & Lomotey, K. (2002). *The racial crisis in American higher education: Continuing challenges for the twenty-first century.* New York: SUNY Press.

Thelin, J. R. (2011). *A history of American higher education.* Baltimore, MD: Johns Hopkins University Press.

Tindall, N. T. J. (2007). Fund-raising models at public historically Black colleges and universities. *Public Relations Review, 33*(92), 201–205.

Wallace, C. (2012) African-American Alumni Perceptions and Motivations toward Philanthropic giving (A case study of an African-American alumni council at a midwestern university). Dissertation.

Wampler, F. H. (2013). Bridges to a lifelong connection: A study of Ivy Plus young alumni programs designed to transition recent graduates into engaged alumni. Dissertation.

Weerts, D. J. & Ronca, J. M. (2007). Profiles of supportive alumni: Donors, volunteers, and those who "do it all." *International Journal of Educational Advancement, 7*(1), 20–34.

Williams, M. G. (2010). Increasing philanthropic support through entrepreneurial activities at Historically Black Colleges and Universities. *International Journal of Educational Advancement, 10*(3), 216–229.

PART II
People and Programs

CHAPTER SEVEN

Expanding the HBCU Legacy: Enrolling and Supporting the Rising Latino Population

PAOLA ESMIEU AND ANDREW MARTINEZ

By 2050, it is estimated that non-Hispanic Whites will make up less than half the population of the United States (U.S. Census Bureau, 2007). Already, California, Hawaii, New Mexico, Texas, and the District of Columbia have a majority population of historically underrepresented groups. Other states, such as Arizona, Georgia, Maryland, Mississippi, and New York, will be among the next to shift to having a majority of historically underrepresented groups among its population (U.S. Census Bureau, 2007). This shift in demographics is also affecting the number of historically underrepresented groups enrolling in higher education institutions. Latinos[1] are the largest and fastest growing minority group in the nation; however, they have the lowest educational attainment among any other ethnic group (Liu, 2011). Rising Latino enrollment presents a unique opportunity for Historically Black Colleges and Universities (HBCUs) to attract these students to their institutions. HBCUs have a legacy of providing a unique and culturally relevant education to Black students across the United States, and we believe that they can adapt to expand this legacy to other marginalized groups. Through evaluating literature on how HBCUs excel in graduating such a high percentage of Black students compared to Historically White Institutions (HWIs), literature on how current HBCUs are adapting to the rising Latino enrollment, an exploration of the Latino and Black student experiences, and best practices in serving

Latino students within higher education, we will develop key recommendations to help HBCUs adapt and take advantage of the rising Latino enrollment.

Latino Enrollment

According to the Pew Hispanic Center, the number of 18- to 24-year-olds attending college in the United States was at its highest in 2010 with 12.2 million students. Of those 12.2 million students, college-age Latinos accounted for 1.8 million (15%). Data collected from the 2010 U.S. Census Bureau reveals that the percentage of Hispanic young adults enrolling in college is growing faster than any other ethnic group while the percentage of White students enrolling is leveling off. However, it is important to note that Latinos are not the largest minority group on four-year college campuses (Fry, 2011).

According to 2010 U.S. Census data, nine states, many concentrated in the South, witnessed growth of the Latino population by 50% or more. There are several contributing factors to this phenomenon, including the rise in immigration into the United States, increasing birth rates amongst Latinos, and the increasing K-12 educational attainment of Latinos. As more Latinos graduate from K-12 schools, enrollment is bound to increase. The U.S. Census Bureau predicts that by 2020, about one in four college-age adults will be Latino. It is important for the nation to plan for the shifting demographics of college students to ensure that students are able to gain entrance and graduate from a higher education institution.

The Latino College Experience

Latino students' college experience is one marked by stress, pressure, and tribulations, which come in various formations. Despite the increasing number of Latino students and the advances institutions have made in their attempt to better serve this growing population, Latino students face several issues as they attempt to navigate their way through HWIs. Though there is variance in what issues are prominent for an individual student and the degree to which it affects them, these issues have a significant influence on the collegiate experience of Latino students, regardless of the institution type. Latino student issues can be categorized as follows: cultural and familial issues, institution-based issues, and issues of racism.

Cultural and Familial Issues

Traditionally, Latino students have generally been raised with extremely close family ties. As reported by Fiske (1988), one of the greatest strengths of Latino culture is the close family relationships it fosters, which have a profound influence on the experience of Latino college students. These ties transcend the American perception of a nuclear family unit to include grandparents, aunts and uncles, and cousins. Latino college students must often cope with the anxiety of breaking close family ties as they leave home to find their way in institutions built around an alien culture (Fiske, 1988). The collectivistic ideology Latinos have of putting the family before the individual can serve as a cultural norm that may create internal conflict and affect a student's experience and engagement (Dayton et al., 2004; Mmeje et al., 2009). Leaving home and breaking close family ties can also result in feelings of guilt, wherein Latino students feel as though they have abandoned their family. In addition to these feelings of anxiety and guilt, Latino students have to learn to live without the constant presence of their family, which can lead to issues of loneliness and homesickness.

When Latino college students decide to go away for college, they must not only contend with the issues mentioned above, but they must also deal with stress brought on by their families, who may not understand the campus lifestyle and may not want their children to adopt too many American norms (Torres, 2003). In traditional Latino homes, children, especially females, are expected to live at home until they marry (Torres, 2003). This becomes challenging when Latino students want to go away to college and live on/near the campus. For some Latino students the desire to please their parents is connected to their acknowledgment of how much their parents have sacrificed to send them to college (Torres, 2003). This can lead to compromises, whereby the student agrees to attend a college closer to home so that they can commute—affecting their on-campus experience and ability to become heavily invested and involved with the campus community. In addition, when Latino college students live at home, they are expected to meet strict familial obligations such as helping out around the house, taking care of siblings or grandparents, or contributing financially to the household (Mmeje et al., 2009; Saunders & Serna, 2004; Torres, 2003). These expectations create additional pressures for Latino students, who must balance their collegiate experience, academics, and meeting familial obligations (Torres, 2003).

Often, Latino college students have the additional responsibility of serving as role models for younger family members. Older siblings, particularly those who are first in their family to attend college, are looked upon as someone who has "made it." They are expected to set a good example and to make the family proud. The collectivistic nature of Latino culture nurtures a tight-knit familial unit. In this regard, any gains made by a Latino college student are often viewed as gains for the entire family. The responsibility that Latino students have to be role models is felt not just from the familial unit but also from the Latino community at large. One student explains: "Everyone from my community is watching me. If I do well, people will encourage their children to do well in school and go to college" (Fiske, 1988, p. 32).

Latino college students are constantly juggling between two cultures and are pressured into retaining their culture while at the same time maintaining a status quo in mainstream culture (Fiske, 1988; Torres, 2003). Traditional cultural values can sometimes clash with attributes and behaviors that are valued in mainstream culture as identifiers of academic success. For example, looking someone in the eye could be a sign of disrespect, even if that person is standing in front of you in a classroom (Fiske, 1988). Often times, a Latino student must adopt and identify with dominant values in order to thrive within higher education (Herring, 1998). Acculturating and "losing one's culture" can lead to Latino students being branded as "sellouts" or "coconuts" (Fiske, 1988; Herring, 1998), which can contribute to a student's feeling of isolation. Latino students are constantly battling the opposing tensions caused by wanting to maintain their Latino culture in environments that warrant them to acculturate if they are to succeed. This is a difficult balance to maintain.

Latino parents are generally supportive of their children being in college. However, they have very limited understanding of what the college experience is like. A study by Fred Ramirez (2003) concluded that Latino parents desired to be part of their children's education, "but forces within their school prevented them from doing so." These parents, particularly those of first-generation college students, are unable to assist their children with their academic careers due to their lack of knowledge and experience with higher education (Clark & Dorris, 2007). Thus, Latino students often find themselves navigating the institution with inadequate parental support and assistance (Mmeje et al., 2009). Having to navigate systems of financial aid, housing, and making academic decisions becomes burdensome, especially at large and impersonal campuses, and can negatively impact Latino students' college experience.

Institution-Based Issues

Most students would agree that navigating any institution of higher education can be an overwhelming, intimidating, and tedious process. When Latino college students are charged with managing this process on their own, with minimal parental support, the institution itself becomes a challenge that directly affects the experience of students. Especially at large HWIs where Latino students and other historically underrepresented students are the significant minority, students can feel isolated and unsupported by the institution. Feelings of isolation and lack of support can make a Latino student feel disconnected from the institution resulting in lower levels of integration and higher levels of alienation on these campuses (Jones et al., 2002).

Another factor contributing to Latino students' feeling of loneliness at HWIs is being academically underprepared. It is possible that some Latino students feel as though they are not prepared for the university environment and expectations. A student can feel underprepared in regard to social behaviors, academic expectations, or any other institutional norms. Latino students are often thrust into institutions that were not created around the unique needs of Latino and other historically underrepresented students in mind. In addition, many Latinos often come from weaker high schools (Fiske, 1988). In general, Latinos are academically underprepared when compared to their White counterparts and have access to fewer academic resources (Perna, 2002), making the realm of academia a foreign place where failure is a definite and looming fear. The combination of being underprepared to manage all the various aspects of the college experience can result in Latino students feeling jaded and beset by personal sentiments of loneliness, inadequacy, and incompetence.

In addition to feeling underprepared and having access to fewer resources, Latino students tend to struggle at HWIs, and often feel that being an ethnic minority on these campuses can create a "frustrating and lonely experience" (Quaye et al., 2009). In these institutions, the curriculum itself has been created to serve the interests of the majority and the faculty teaching the material is usually White. As stated by Fiske (1988), "since curricula rarely reflect [Latino] interests, even the classroom can contribute to a sense of alienation" (p. 30). Many Latino students will often progress through their education without ever sufficiently learning about America's history of racial oppression (Quaye et al., 2009). The history and perspectives of Latinos are completely left out of the curriculum and renders Latino peoples as "immigrants" and "foreigners" with no claim to the Americas (Ladson-Billings, 2009; Villenas & Deyhle, 1999). Assigned literature and classroom discussions often fail to discuss issues pertaining to the cultures of Latino students (Banks, 1996, 2001). In addition to the alienation students feel because of the classroom curriculum, the lack of Latino faculty can affect the Latino student experience. As stated by Fiske (1988), "[Latino] students say that they feel the absence of "role models" once they get to predominately Anglo colleges and universities" (p. 32). This is not surprising given the fact that Latino faculty represents only 4 percent of all faculty members nationwide (Digest of Education Statistics, 2010). Data reveal the difficulties that Latino students face when they wish to find ethnic minority faculty members that understand their struggles and that can serve as mentors and advisors (Quaye et al., 2009). The lack of Latino representation within the academic institutional context can lead to uncomfortable and exclusive learning environments and can affect the racial tension students perceive, which inevitably affects their academic success and overall college experience (Quaye et al., 2009).

Issues of Racism

Attending colleges and universities that are predominately White exposes Latino students to issues rooted in racist ideologies and ignorance. Upon stepping foot on these HWI campuses, many Latino students feel the pressure to continually justify their presence, are constantly having their academic capabilities questioned, and must contend with being labeled "affirmative action" admits (Chang, 1999; Fiske, 1988; Quaye et al., 2009). A number of Latino students feel as though they carry a stigma and have endured aggressions from White students as described in the following experience: "We carry a stigma in a sense... when I first came here as a freshman, a White undergraduate said to me, 'You're here, and my friend, who is better qualified, is not'" (Fiske, 1988, p. 31). Some Latino students feel like they always have to perform at high levels to prove they are competent, can keep up, and can cope with the rigorous academics. One student highlights this experience: "I feel as a Chicana that I always have to perform. I have to know my material, then deliver it in a forceful, articulate manner. Otherwise, you're stereotyped as not being able to cope"(Fiske, 1988, p. 31). Latino students feeling like they constantly have to prove their presence and intellectual abilities can lead to a profound sense of loneliness (Quaye et al., 2009). Even high-achieving students must cope with self-doubt and feeling like they have to justify their belonging in higher education (Fries-Britt & Turner, 2002). In addition, negative stereotypes and deficit-minded approaches to understanding Latino student achievement pose additional barriers and could lead to lowered teacher expectations which negatively impacts classroom performance (Villenas & Deyhle, 1999; Quaye et al., 2009). The Latino student experience is often marked by discrimination and racism that has been perpetuated in society. For Latino students, racism is evidenced in their grouping as a monolithic "Hispanic Other" (Hidalgo, 1998) and in their construction in the public sphere as being undeserving (Villenas & Deyhle, 1999). Despite their strong achievement characteristics upon entry, many Latino undergraduates complain of pervasive discrimination, both subtle and overt, at HWIs (Fiske, 1988). Furthermore, Latino students are constantly stereotyped and are victims of insensitive comments and jokes regarding these perceived stereotypes. As stated in a Latino student's interview, "people will joke around—at least, I hope they're joking—and say, 'Oh he's Mexican, hide your wallet'... they're insulting you in a public setting without knowing who you are, what you've done, and what you've accomplished" (Fiske, 1988, p. 31). Another student, quoted in Fiske's article, recalls a time when students decided to host a Mexican themed party. The Latino student explained that he was offended by the nature of this party, and because he vocalized his feelings on the matter other students would be cautious around him (Fiske, 1988). These types of scenarios can become social stressors for Latino students; the pressure of standing up against racist and discriminatory activities at the risk of becoming a form of "social parasite" that other students are "cautious" of can negatively impact Latino students' experiences at HWIs.

Along with stereotypes that arise from racist and discriminatory perceptions, Latino students also have to deal with tokenism and serving as "native informants" at HWIs. Author bell hooks (1994) explains that a "native informant" is often a student of color who is objectified by other students and/or the instructor and is forced to serve as a lone spokesperson for their race, placing an unfair responsibility on that student. Many students feel as though they are constantly put in a position where they have to represent their entire racial/ethnic group and are always cognizant of their behaviors so as to not perpetuate negative stereotypes (Quaye et al., 2009). Latino students express that often they feel like others expect them to know "all about their culture," are viewed as "experts in their culture," and are called upon to discuss "what Latinos think... or to simply provide the minority perspective"

(Jones et al., 2002, p. 31). These experiences put additional pressure on Latino students; not only must they contend with familial pressures of being exemplarily role models for their younger family members, but they are also expected to be representatives and ambassadors for a wide range of Latino cultures.

Latino college students face a multitude of issues at HWIs that make it challenging for these students to succeed at the institution. However, we want to make it clear that despite all of these issues tainting the Latino student experience, these students are resilient. Latino students explained that they just have to "roll with the punches" in order to remain visible at HWIs until the next generation of students arrives (Jones et al., 2002, p. 30). A college education is worth making the effort and overcoming the struggles that Latino students face (Fisk, 1988). For Latino students, being resilient and pushing themselves to meet the expectations of their family members, peers, and the institution, means being able to achieve what other Latinos have not had the opportunity to achieve (Fisk, 1988).

We have chosen to describe the Latino student experience in such detail because it is important to understand the Latino student experience when thinking about expanding the legacy of HBCUs to include Latino students. We also wanted to highlight some of the issues they face at HWIs; issues that many Black students and students of other historically underrepresented groups must also cope with at HWIs. Highlighting the experiences of Latino students allows us to demonstrate how their experience directly parallels the experience of Black students at HWIs.

Existing literature suggests that Latino students and Black students at HWIs face similar challenges and hurdles (Nelson Laird et al., 2007). Much like Latino students, Black students at HWIs often doubt their own intellectual ability, must deal with the racial and discriminatory climate, and in general are academically underprepared when compared to their White counterparts at HWIs (Fordham & Ogbu, 1986; Perna, 2002; Solórzano et al., 2000). The problems faced by both Latino and Black students at HWIs are issues that HBCUs have historically combated on their campuses by creating campus environments tailored for Black students. For over 150 years, HBCUs have been a safe haven for Black students; a place where they do not have to feel the constant pressure, isolation, and doubt that they would feel at HWIs.

The parallels between Latino and Black students extend past their collegiate student experience. Historically, Latino and Black communities have many of the same needs regarding education, socioeconomics, and upward mobility. As explained by Larry Earvin, Huston-Tillotson University's president, HBCUs are well-positioned to appeal to Latino students and their families given that their socioeconomic profiles are similar to the families Black schools have traditionally served (Roach, 2005). Furthermore, Earvin explains that the needs of Latino communities are very similar to the needs of Black communities (Roach, 2005). These similarities among Latino and Black communities demonstrate that HBCUs' legacy could be expanded to include an increased Latino student population while at the same time staying true to their historical mission of educating Black students and socially disadvantaged populations.

The HBCU Legacy

Higher education in America has had a pattern of limited access, particularly for people of underrepresented backgrounds. HBCUs are institutions of higher education founded with the purpose to educate the descendants of former slaves and African Americans (Gasman et al., 2010). The nation has 105 HBCUs mostly located in Southern states (Gasman et al., 2010). Unlike HWIs, HBCUs have a mission to contribute to the overall racial uplift of their Black students. According to Brown, Donahoo, and Bertrand (2001), HBCUs "have always been expected to meet the same curriculum standards as other institutions while also providing African Americans with a cultural-specific pedagogy...since their inception, these institutions have continued to successfully promote an educational agenda that is both academically superior and culturally relevant" (pp. 559–560).

Although HBCUs have conferred the most degrees on Blacks in the United States, they have consistently faced challenges in garnering the support many other HWIs have achieved. According to Anderson (1988), prior to 1950, traditionally Black institutions educated more than 75% of African American college students. After laws were established to put an end to separate public institutions for Black and White students during the 1954 *Brown v. Board of Education* case, enrollment at HBCUs dropped significantly as HWIs now had to accept previously banned Black students into their schools. Although by 2005 HBCU enrollment dropped by 20% since the late 1950s, the retention rates among Black students at HBCUs were still much better than at HWIs (Dwyer, 2006). In fact, students at HBCUs reported better outcomes in their learning and self-confidence when compared to their peers at HWIs (Allen, 1992.) In a study focusing on the effect of multiculturalism on diversity outcomes among students enrolled in HBCUs, Brighid Dwyer (2006) argues that students within HBCUs have better relationships with the faculty and staff and overall have a better experience because they do not face the racial hostility that can occur at HWIs. While the *Brown v. Board of Education* case created greater access for Black students and other marginalized groups to enroll in higher education institutions, it also challenged HBCUs to recruit and admit non-Black students, even though HBCUs had always admitted students regardless of race, unlike their HWI counterparts. Dwyer argues that as a result of the desegregation of schools after 1954, HBCUs are becoming some of the most racially diverse institutions for higher education.

The HBCU environment has the positive legacy of being a place well suited for promoting the academic, social, and cultural success of Black students (Nelson Laird et al., 2007). Compared to HWIs, students attending HBCUs report better outcomes in student learning and self-confidence. These students form stronger relationships with faculty and staff at HBCUs and experience a less racially hostile campus (Dwyer, 2006). Research suggests that Black students' experiences at HBCUs are more educationally beneficial than those for Black students at HWIs (Nelson Laird et al., 2007). The existence of student activities catering to Black students' interests and needs at HBCUs helps create social support networks that facilitate student success (Davis, 1991; Nelson Laird et al., 2007). In a study conducted by Nelson Laird, Bridges, Morelon-Quainoo, Williams, and Holmes (2007), Black students at HBCUs reported higher levels of active and collaborative learning, student–faculty interaction, and gains in overall development. These students, compared to their counterparts at HWIs, were more frequently discussing grades, readings, and career plans with faculty as well as engaging with faculty more often inside and outside the classroom (Nelson Laird et al., 2007). HBCUs have been a major asset for Black students seeking a college education for over a century (Anderson, 1988) and provide the opportunity to do the same for Latino students. By and large, many HBCU officials contend that enrolling first-generation college-going Latino students represents part of their traditional mission of educating the socially disadvantaged (Roach, 2005). Thus, the unique HBCU environment that has been created to help Black students succeed can be expanded to serve the needs of Latino students in a manner that is beneficial to both the institution and Latino students.

Benefits of Increased Latino Enrollment

The growing Latino population and Latino college-bound students is a window of opportunity for HBCUs. Strategically recruiting and increasing the enrollment of Latino students at HBCUs is necessary if they are to thrive within our changing society. Enrolling more Latino students will not only increase the number of students matriculating at HBCUs, but these students could help alleviate some of the fiscal burdens these tuition driven institutions face. Increased Latino student enrollment at HBCUs will help sustain the institutions and at the same time improve Latino–Black relations on the campuses and in the local communities. Ray Winbush, director of the Institute for Urban Research at Morgan State University, states that the long-term benefits of Latinos educated at HBCUs will serve to promote a positive relationship that will strengthen ties between the communities by allowing Latinos and Blacks to get to know one another better (Roach, 2005). This social impact aligns directly with many HBCU mission statements of developing student leaders into agents of change in their communities.

The benefits of enrolling Latino students at HBCUs will be felt by the institutions and by the students themselves. Much like Black students, Latino students will benefit from the nurturing HBCU environment that caters to the needs of socially disadvantaged students by teaching courses and hosting activities that appeal to the interests of their student body. HBCUs are among the most racially diverse campuses with their students, administration, and faculty (Roach, 2004). This racial diversity contributes to minimal issues of racism and discrimination, which will allow Latino students to study in an institutional environment free from problems that taint their student experience at HWIs. In research conducted at a Texas HBCU,[2] Taryn Ozuna (2012) found that Latino participants described precollege interactions with institutional agents (Texas HBCU students, professors, and staff) as being supportive and encouraging. These interactions were impactful and informed the participants' college-going aspirations, which ultimately led to their decision to pursue their degree at Texas HBCU (Ozuna, 2012). This example demonstrates the impact that HBCU agents can have on Latino students—an impact that can transcend the recruitment realm and carry over into the classroom all the way through graduation. Latino students could greatly benefit from the HCBU culture of forming close-knit relationships between students and institutional agents. These relationships facilitate networking and mentorship for

Black students and could do the same for Latino students. The culture that promotes relationship formation at HBCUs between students and institutional agents is beneficial in and of itself; however, even if the institutional agents are not necessarily Latino, it is assumed that they will have the knowledge and ability to work with Latino students since they have the experience of working with students who have similar experiences.

When thinking about increasing Latino enrollment at HBCUs, we want to draw special attention to the Afro-Latino population. Afro-Latinos are a unique subset of the Latino and Black racial and ethnic minority groups that have adopted the customs and culture of Latinos, but exhibit physical characteristics that are typically associated with African ancestry (Ramos et al., 2003). Currently, the bulk of Latino student recruitment focuses on Southern and Midwestern campuses—areas that are heavily populated by Latinos from Mexico and Central America (Roach, 2005). However, HBCUs are well positioned to attract students from the Afro-Latino subset and should consider expanding their recruitment to northeastern United States, where there are large populations of Afro-Latinos (Roach, 2005). Strategically recruiting in these areas for Afro-Latinos will benefit both the institution and the students. Afro-Latino students could experience the benefits of being at an institution that caters to the unique needs of their intersecting ethnic and racial identities. In addition, because of the unique ethnic-racial combination of Afro-Latinos, it is possible to demonstrate that HBCUs can balance being mission-centric while at the same time increasing their Latino student enrollment.

Rising Latino Enrollment/Current HBCU Initiatives

HBCUs, especially the public institutions, offer a college education to their students at a significantly lower price than their White counterparts. Furthermore, as HBCUs begin to diversify their campuses, more financial opportunities will become available for Latino students to enroll. For HBCUs that are located in regions where the Latino college-aged population is growing rapidly, such as Texas, the likelihood of becoming a Hispanic-Serving Institution (HSI) will give the institution eligibility for more government funding. HSIs are defined in federal law as accredited and degree-granting public or private non-profit institutions of higher education, with 25% or more total undergraduate Hispanic full-time equivalent student enrollment (Laden,

2001). HSIs enroll more than 1.4 million Hispanic students and educate about 50% of all Hispanic students (Laden, 2001). Unlike HBCUs, HSI designation is based solely on their enrollment numbers, not their institutional mission, allowing these institutions to develop as demographic trends evolve. In 2008, Texas HBCU enrollment was 21% Hispanic (Crusere et al., 2014). St. Phillip's College is currently the only HBCU that is federally designated as both an HBCU and HSI. However, several HBCUs in the south are dedicated to increasing their Latino enrollment and are on their way to be emerging HSIs, which qualifies the institution for Title V funding. Some of the institutions that are intentionally recruiting and supporting their Latino students are Fayetteville State University, Huston-Tillotson University, Prairie View A&M University, Texas Southern University, and Virginia State University (Hernandez, 2010; Roach, 2004; 2005). These institutions are witnessing increasing Latino enrollment and are using this to their advantage to attract more students and to retain them by providing more services.

In North Carolina, Arkansas, and Georgia, the Latino population has increased by 300–400% since the early 1990s (U.S. Census Bureau, 2000). Although there has been much effort to promote Latino enrollment in higher education, this task is challenging as the overall public high school dropout rates for Latinos remain high (Roach, 2004). However, in North Carolina, there have been efforts to increase and support Latino college enrollment in several organizations, including HBCUs such as Fayetteville State University (FSU), which had the highest share of Latino enrollment (4%) among public institutions of the state in 2004 (Roach, 2004).

Robert Kanory, associate vice president for academic affairs in the University of North Carolina (UNC), argues that it is "imperative that all the schools become proficient in developing multi-cultural environments because demographic projections show that Latinos will surpass Blacks in the state's college-age population around 2019 and that student growth will continue to surge among Latinos while the growth numbers of Black and White students will level off after 2014" (Roach, 2004). Thus, HBCUs will have less Black students to compete for and even lower enrollment if they do not become more racially diverse. Currently, FSU has a student population that is 25% non-Black, and are continuing efforts to increase diversity in their campuses by offering literature about the school in Spanish as well as hiring admissions counselors specifically focused on community outreach and Latino students (Roach, 2004).

FSU is not the only HBCU working toward increasing Latino college enrollment. In 2010, Virginia State University (VSU) held the 2010 Hispanic Youth Symposium (HYS), which is a live-in learning experience for Latino high school students to expose and motivate them to pursue higher education. Hispanic high school students spend four days on campus attending career workshops and networking with college students, staff, and faculty to learn about college life and stay informed about scholarship opportunities. VSU was the first HBCU to host this event and offered its facilities for free, allowing the program to double the number of participants for the year (Hernandez, 2010). According to Mirta Martin, VSU's business school dean, "The values of African-Americans and Latinos are the same...if we want to double our student population, it has to be through the fastest growing group in the state" (Hernandez, 2010).

Texas HBCU, St. Phillip's College, plays an interesting role being both an HBCU and HSI. In order to combat funding and enrollment challenges, St. Phillip's College has evolved into a public community college with Hispanics making up the largest ethnic group on campus (Pluviose, 2007). Although the institution has faced challenges serving as both an HBCU and HSI, the demographics of the state as well as the increase in their enrollment overall has allowed the institution to thrive.

Huston-Tillotson University is federally recognized as an emerging HSI institution. As an institution with 15–24% fulltime Latino student enrollment, it qualifies for Title V funding and is likely to become an HSI institution (Laden, 2001). According to Ronald Roach (2005), Huston-Tillotson's leadership believes that "HBCUs are well-positioned to appeal to Hispanic students and their families given that their socioeconomic profiles are similar to the families Black schools have traditionally served." The rise in Latino enrollment in Hudson-Tillotson has allowed the school to grow and has garnered support from alumni, students, faculty, and administrators who embrace the institution's growing ties to the Hispanic community (Roach, 2005).

Challenges

HBCUs often receive criticism for perpetuating segregation despite their long tradition of providing access to higher education. According to Brown et al. (2001), HBCUs are "mistakenly perceived as homogeneous entities that only serve Black students" (p. 567). While HBCUs were created primarily for the education of African Americans, these institutions did not prohibit admission for other groups. HBCUs continue to be ignored when discussing diversity within higher education institutions although they are prime examples with racially diverse student bodies, staff, and faculty.

Since HBCUs play such a significant and historic role in the lives of African Americans, some HBCU advocates worry that the increase in diversity developing in HBCUs may result in the institutions losing sight of their mission. However, other HBCU leaders believe that the increasing diversity strengthens the institutions, allowing them to continue their legacy of enrolling low-income and underrepresented students (Gasman, 2012). Gasman argues that HBCUs no longer have a choice on whether or not they should recruit students of all racial and ethnic backgrounds. HBCUs must come to the realization that African-Americans are choosing to attend HWIs and if they want to compete, and keep their enrollment up, they must fully embrace diversity on their campuses (Gasman, 2012).

Recommendations

If HBCUs take the opportunity to extend their legacy of providing a high quality education to Latino students, it is important for these institutions to consider their individual strengths and weaknesses in serving this population. Through our research of what HBCUs are currently doing to increase Latino student enrollment as well as our understanding of what resources best aid Latino college students, we have devised the following recommendations to help HBCUs increase their Latino student population and to best support this population at their institutions.

Hire Staff Specifically Targeting Latino Applicants

Some HBCUs, such as Fayetteville State University, are located in areas where the Latino population is skyrocketing; these institutions have already hired staff members who are dedicated to recruiting Latino students (Roach, 2005). With staff members who specialize in Latino recruitment, HBCUs are able to better connect with these students and their families. For parents that do not understand English, having staff members within the institution that they can communicate with helps alleviate any concerns that they may have about the college process and sending their child off to school. This also helps the family and the prospective student see the institution as a good fit for their particular needs because these staff members will be able to directly address any concerns and communicate the value of the institution.

Market the Institution as an HBCU that Embraces Diversity

Due to the historical legacy of HBCUs, it is possible that many Latino students do not see these institutions as accessible or as viable options. In order to adapt to demographic and enrollment trends occurring within higher education and attracting Latino students, it is important for HBCUs to demonstrate how diverse their institutions actually are. Highlighting the various diaspora, religions, ethnicities, and interests represented at HBCUs as well as utilizing their student, faculty, and staff demographics can help highlight the diversity at HBCUs. More importantly, HBCUs need to market their institution as an environment that is welcoming to Latino students and their families. HBCUs can do this by including parents in new student orientation programs and translating marketing materials into Spanish to better inform and connect with Latino families (Ozuna, 2012). Institutions that already have Latino student organizations or programs dedicated to serving Latino students should highlight this in their brochures and in other recruitment materials as well.

Create Ties with the Latino Community in the Area

As articulated previously, Latino students come from extremely tight-knit families and communities that have a great amount of influence over the pre-collegiate decisions of Latino students. For HBCUs located in areas with rapid Latino population growth, it is critical for the institutions to create ties with the Latino community. Investing in the Latino community reinforces HBCUs commitment to diversity and allows HBCUs to expand their reach by planting roots in these communities. Establishing relationships with the Latino community will create a more inclusive campus environment where students can witness the engagement their institution has in their community. HBCUs can also utilize these relationships to enhance the connection between local Latino and Black communities and create a feeling of intercultural connectedness. In doing this, HBCUs will demonstrate their commitment to supporting both Latino and Black students on their campus and in creating students who will serve as social change agents.

Use Currently Enrolled Latino Students to Assess HBCUs

The experience of Latino students currently enrolled in HBCUs should be examined. HBCUs should create focus groups of Latino students at their institution in order to help assess what the Latino student experience is like at their particular institution. This will help HBCUs assess their strengths and weakness regarding the way they recruit, matriculate, and support Latino students. Interviewing current Latino students at HBCUs could provide information regarding campus inclusivity, first-year-experiences, peer-to-peer relationships, perceived institutional support, and other information that will allow the institution to assess where they are and where they need to progress. Additionally, collecting this data may demonstrate to the Latino population at HBCUs their institution's commitment to diversifying the campus and meeting the needs of their increasingly varied student body.

Create Inclusive Student Organizations and Programs to Facilitate Intercultural Competencies within the Campus Community

There should be an institution-wide commitment to helping develop intercultural competencies within the campus and local community. HBCUs should spearhead inclusive organizations and programs and provide full support, to demonstrate to the students, staff, faculty, community, and alums how committed the institution is to supporting good relations among all of its constituents. Developing programs for increased communication between student populations will provide an outlet for students to address racial climate perceptions at HBCUs, which may arise with increased Latino students on campus. More importantly, developing these types of organizations and programs will foster collaboration among racially and ethnically diverse students, students and institutional agents, and the institution and local communities. Thus, not only will Latino students feel welcomed and supported at HBCUs, but also HBCUs will build a reputation for being culturally relevant institutions for Black students, Latino students, and other historically underrepresented groups.

Implications for Further Research

Latino and Black students share similar experiences of being marginalized and excluded in the sphere of higher education. As institutions with a historic legacy of providing an education to historically underrepresented groups, enrolling and retaining Latino students provides HBCUs with an opportunity to expand their legacy. However, more research is needed to better understand how current Latino students experience HBCUs and how those experiences differ from Latinos at HWIs. While we suggest that HBCUs are institutions that will allow the growing Latino population to thrive, the literature of Latino students within HBCUs is limited. Furthermore, the limited research available about Latinos within higher education spheres does not offer a range of information according to the type of Latino. As stated before, HBCUs have a unique opportunity to attract Afro-Latinos; however, research on specific Latino groups is limited.

Conclusion

Despite the setbacks some HBCUs may face from alumni, current students, and other key stakeholders at specific institutions, enrolling more Latino students will provide more opportunities to HBCUs across the nation to sustain their enrollment. Although HBCUs continue to produce a significant amount of Black graduates, the enrollment of Black students in HBCUs have steadily decreased as other institutions are increasingly embracing racial diversity in their campuses. By focusing on increasing Latino enrollment at HBCUs, these institutions will offset the decrease in their Black student enrollment, and depending on the region of the HBCU and the demographic shifts in the nation, they may be dealing with their highest applicant pool, thus becoming more selective institutions. We believe HBCUs should continue to reach out and provide higher education opportunities to the Black population. However, due to the shifting demographics occurring in the nation and in order to thrive, HBCUs need to expand their legacy by actively recruiting and supporting Latinos.

Notes

1. The terms "Latino" and "Hispanic" are used interchangeably throughout this chapter.
2. The university studied by Ozuna was selected based on its publicly stated interest in recruiting Latino students. In the study, the institution is referred to by the pseudonym "Texas HBCU." The qualitative study included four female and four male self-identified Mexican American students at Texas HBCU.

References

Allen, W. R. (1992). The color of success: African-American college student outcomes at predominantly White and historically Black public colleges and universities. *Harvard Educational Review, 62*(1), 26–45.

Anderson, J. A. (1988). Training the apostles of liberal culture: Black higher education, 1900–1935. In James D. Anderson (Ed.), *The education of Blacks in the South, 1860–1935*. Chapel Hill, NC: University of North Carolina Press.

Banks, J. A. (1996). *Multicultural education, transformative knowledge, and action: Historical and contemporary perspectives*. New York: Teacher's College Press.

——— (2001). Multicultural education: Goals, possibilities, and challenges. In C. F. Diaz (Ed.), *Multicultural education in the 21st century* (pp. 11–22). New York: Longman.

bell hooks (1994). *Teaching to transgress: Education as the practice of freedom*. New York: Routledge.

Brown, I. I. M. C., Donahoo, S., & Bertrand, R. D. (2001). The Black college and the quest for educational opportunity. *Urban Education, 36*(5), 553–571.

Brown v. Board of Educ., 347 U.S. 483 (1954).

Chang, M. J. (1999). Does racial diversity matter?: The educational impact of a racially diverse undergraduate population. *Journal of College Student Development, 40*(4), 377–395.

Clark, A.A. & Dorris, A. (2007). Partnering with Latino parents. *The Education Digest, 72*(7), 44–50.

Crusere, M., Fernandez, C., Fletcher, C., & Rice, E. (January 2014). *State of Student Aid and Higher Education in Texas*. Retrieved from http://www.tgslc.org/research/sosa.cfm.

Davis, R. (1991). Social support networks and undergraduate students academic-success-related outcomes: A comparison of Black students on Black and White campuses. In W. R. Allen, E. G. Epps, & N. Z. Haniff (Eds.), *College in Black and White: African American students in predominately White and in historically Black public universities* (pp. 143–157). Albany, NY: State University of New York Press.

Dayton, B., Gonzalez-Vasquez, N., Martinez, C. R., & Plum, C. (2004). Hispanic-Serving Institutions through the eyes of students and administrators. In A. Ortiz (Ed.). *Addressing the unique needs of Latino American students. New directions for student services* (No. 105, pp. 29–40). San Francisco, CA: Jossey-Bass.

Dwyer, B. (2006). Framing the effect of multiculturalism on diversity outcomes among students at Historically Black Colleges and Universities. *Educational Foundations, 20*, 37–59.

Fiske, E. B. (1988). The undergraduate Hispanic experience: A case of juggling two cultures. *Change: The Magazine of Higher Learning, 20*(3), 29–33.

Fordham, S. & Ogbu, J. U. (1986). Black students' school success: Coping with the "burden of 'acting White.'" *The Urban Review, 18*(3), 176–206.

Fries-Britt, S. L. & Turner, B. (2010). Facing stereotypes: A case study of Black students on a White campus. *Journal of College Student Development, 42*(5), 420–429.

Fry, R. A. & Pew Hispanic Center. (2011). *Hispanic college enrollment spikes, narrowing gaps with other groups: 24% growth from 2009 to 2010*. Washington, DC: Pew Hispanic Center.

Gasman, M. (2012). Historically black colleges and universities must embrace diversity. *The Chronicle of Higher Education.* http://chronicle.com/blogs/conversation/2012/11/08/historically-black-collegesand-universities-must-embrace-diversity/.

Gasman, M., Lundy Wagner, V., Ransom., T., & Bowman, N. (2010). *Unearthing promise and potential: Our nation's Historically Black Colleges and Universities.* San Francisco, CA: Jossey-Bass.

Hernandez, A. (2010). Virginia HBCU hosts Latino student symposium. *Diverse Issues in Higher Education.* http://diverseeducation.com/article/13963/#.

Herring, R. (1998). *Career counseling in schools: Multicultural and developmental perspectives.* Alexandria, VA: American Counseling Association.

Hidalgo, N. M. (1998). Toward a definition of a Latino family research paradigm. *International Journal of Qualitative Studies in Education, 11*(1), 103–120.

Jones, L., Castellanos, J., & Cole, D. (2002). Examining the ethnic minority student experience at predominantly White institutions: A case study. *Journal of Hispanic Higher Education, 1*(1), 19–39.

Laden, B. V. (2001). Hispanic-serving institutions: Myths and realities. *Peabody Journal of Education, 76*(1), 73–92.

Ladson-Billings, G. (2009). Critical Race Theory in Education. *The Routledge International Handbook of Critical Education.* New York: Routledge, 110.

Liu, M. C. (July, 2011). Investing in higher education for Latinos: Trends in Latino college access and success. *National Conference of State Legislatures.*

Mmeje, K., Newman, C. B., Kramer II, D. A., & Pearson, M. A. (2009). The changing landscape of higher education: Developmental approaches to engaging emerging populations. In S. R. Harper & S. J. Quaye (Eds.), *Student engagement in higher education: Theoretical perspectives and practical approaches for diverse populations* (pp. 99–116). New York: Routledge.

Nelson Laird, T. F., Bridges, B. K., Morelon-Quainoo, C. L., Williams, J. M., & Holmes, M. S. (2007). African American and Hispanic student engagement at minority serving and predominantly White institutions. *Journal of College Student Development, 48*(1), 39–56.

Ozuna, T. (2012). Latino/a knowledge community: The first-year experiences of Mexican American students enrolled in the Texas HBCU. *NASPA Knowledge Communities,* Fall, 22–21. Retrieved from http://www.naspa.org/kc/Fall-2012-KC-Publication-FINAL.pdf.

Perna, L.W. (2002). Precollege outreach programs: Characteristics of programs serving historically underrepresented groups of students. *Journal of College Student Development, 43*(1), 64–83.

Pluviose, D. (2007). The evolution of a Texas HBCU. *Diverse: Issues in Higher Education, 24*(13), 24–25.

Quaye, S. J., Tambascia, T. P., & Talesh, R. A. (2009). Engaging racial/ethnic minority students in predominantly White classroom environments. In S. R. Harper & S. J. Quaye (Eds.) (2009). *Student engagement in higher education: Theoretical perspectives and practical approaches for diverse populations* (pp. 157–178). New York: Routledge.

Ramirez, F. A. Y. (2003). Dismay and disappointment: Parental involvement of Latino immigrant parents. *The Urban Review, 35*(2), 93–110.

Ramos, B., Jaccard, J., & Guilamo-Ramos, V. (2003). Dual ethnicity and depressive symptoms: Implications of being Black and Latino in the United States. *Hispanic Journal of Behavioral Sciences, 25*(2), 147–173.

Roach, R. (2004). Surging in the Southeast: North Carolina HBCUs expected to play significant role in facilitating college access for the increasing Latino population in the region. *Black Issues in Higher Education, 21*(16), 32.

— (2005). HBCUs reach out. *Diverse: Issues in Higher Education, 22*(16), 28–29.

Saunders, M. & Serna, I. (2004). Making college happen: The college experiences of first-generation Latino students. *Journal of Hispanic Higher Education, 3*(2) 146–163.

Solórzano, D., Ceja, M., & Yosso, T. (2000). Critical race theory, racial microaggressions, and campus racial climate: The experiences of African American college students. *Journal of Negro Education*, 60–73.

Torres, V. (2003). Mi casa is not exactly like your house. *About Campus, 8*(2), 2–7.

U.S. Census Bureau (2000). Resident population of the United States by sex, race, and Hispanic Origin: April 1 to July 1, 1999, with short-term protection to June 1, 2000. Washington, DC: U.S. Department of Commerce.

U.S. Census Bureau (2007). Minority population tops 100 million. Press release. Washington, DC: U.S. Department of Commerce.

Villenas, S. & Deyhle, D. (1999). Critical race theory and ethnographies challenging the stereotypes: Latino families, schooling, resilience and resistance. *Curriculum Inquiry, 29*(4), 413–445.

CHAPTER EIGHT

Beyond the Fifth Quarter: The Influence of HBCU Marching Bands

Yulanda Essoka

Music matters. Soulful rhythmic beats have a long, significant lineage in Black culture—both spiritually and secularly. For years, song has been used by Blacks to worship, soothe, stir, celebrate, and entertain. The aesthetics of music has inspired people to move in various fora, both holy and worldly, by swaying and handclapping in church, dancing in the club, or high-stepping on the football field. This chapter will focus on the latter—the linkage between music and dance in the form of marching bands at Historically Black Colleges and Universities (HBCUs).

Blacks and higher education have a connection that was established in 1826 with the initial awarding of baccalaureate degrees to Edward A. Jones and John Russworm (Drewry & Doermann, 2001). However, these Black men were graduates of Historically White Institutions (HWIs), Amherst College and Bowdoin College, respectively. From the granting of Jones's and Russworm's degrees until the end of the Civil War only 26 additional Blacks out of a population of 4.4 million earned baccalaureates (Drewry & Doermann, 2001). However, these sparse numbers grew substantially after the founding of HBCUs.

Black colleges have a rich legacy of providing educational opportunities to masses of Black people. Three HBCUs (Cheyney University, Lincoln University, and Wilberforce University) were created before the start of the Civil War. The remainder of the current existing 105 Black higher education institutions began operating after 1861. The majority of the resulting schools were spawned by the Freedman's Bureau, an agent of the federal government, and other religious affiliates and missionary organizations, such as the Baptists, Congregationalists, African Methodist Episcopalians, and the American Missionary Association (Gasman & Bowman, 2012). Yet, the motivation to educate Blacks was not exclusively altruistic and puritanical. Many pedagogical efforts were driven to avert the country from the alleged "menace" of uneducated Blacks (Anderson, 1988).

The second Morrill Act in 1890 generated additional HBCU growth. The act "stipulated that those states practicing segregation in their public colleges and universities would forfeit funding unless they established agricultural and mechanical institutions for the Black population" (Gasman & Bowman, 2012, p. 119). The prospect of fiscal forfeiture was an effective stimulus for states to erect Black colleges, and they did. However, the newly established Black schools had subpar facilities and course offerings in comparison to their White counterparts despite federal legislation directing just and equitable division of government funds (Gasman & Bowman, 2012). The financial deficit Black institutions were forced to endure imposed limitations on more than facilities and curricula, and additional formalized activities like bands, or the prospect thereof, were stalled. Ironically, however, once some HBCU marching bands took root at their institutions, these fledgling groups helped transform and grow schools, serving as effective recruitment, fundraising, and promotional vehicles.

Historical Background of Marching Bands

American marching bands are derivatives of their European forerunners whose genesis stemmed from militias. Historically the first colonial bands were used to give orders, surreptitiously transmit messages, and boost morale (Lewis, 2003). Although free mulattos, Blacks, and Native Americans were required to join the military, they were circumscribed in their possession of weapons due to Whites' fear of revolt. Therefore, colored military personnel were relegated to serve as drummers, fifers, and trumpeters. Many nineteenth-century Black musicians obtained their training and instruments during the War of 1812. These enlisted men served double duty by performing at civilian events like cotillions, in addition to their martial duties. Eventually, Black military marching bands were used as armed forces recruitment tools at parades and other social events. Experts estimate that by the close of the Civil War the bands' efforts resulted in over 185,000 Black men joining the army as the United States Colored Troops (Southern, 1997).

Once the Civil War concluded, many Black band members remained in the military and became a part of the first Black units in the army. Other Black men who separated from the military post–Civil War joined civilian bands and minstrel shows. Minstrels were a premier form of entertainment from 1830 to 1900. The official shows were cast at night, but during the day the minstrel performers would stage parades through town centers showcasing their talents to boost attendance (Southern, 1997). The traveling musical and comedic shows provided an avenue for Blacks to display and cultivate their instrumental and theatrical talents for compensation during a time when pathways of steady employment were limited.

Musical legends like W. C. Handy, often hailed as "Father of the Blues," cut their teeth in minstrels. Handy played the coronet in minstrel shows until 1900 when he was hired by Alabama A&M College as its musical director. During his tenure, Handy often "instructed the band to slip in ragtime pieces among more traditional fare" (Fausset, 2011). Handy's clever musical innovation infected his students, many of whom went on to become great performers and band directors. His novel approach to music also forecast how HBCU bands would distinguish themselves from HWI bands by integrating popular, modern melodies with classical selections to stir the crowd.

Brass bands' popularity also took off in tandem with minstrel shows. Many consider the period 1880–1910 to be the "golden age of the brass band in America" (Schafer, 1977). Participation of Blacks in brass bands swelled post–Civil War, due to the abundance and accessibility of highly trained musical Black former military personnel and a plenitude of cheap military musical instruments (Lewis, 2003). There were about 10,000 bands, many of them marching bands, by 1890 (Malone, 1996). The brass ensembles' missions were multifaceted. Some merely entertained, while others were used to fundraise and served as community outreach vehicles to promote various social causes. The prominence of brass bands continued, but a shift was felt with the precipitation of America's entry into World War I, which drew many Black musicians back into the military. Once again, Blacks assumed the roles of overseeing military bands as directors or drill sergeants (Malone, 1996).

The ingenuity of these band leaders continued to thrive as they displayed musical showmanship to recruit troops and differentiate themselves from their White counterparts (Badger, 1995). "While White-American soldiers of World War I ardently strove to march like well-oiled war machines, like battle-ready robots, Black bandsmen of the 369th Regiment stepped to the beat of a different drummer"

(Malone, 1990, p. 59). Black World War I drill sergeants introduced melody and foot-stomping syncopation into military cadence counting, which permanently transformed the standard European marching call that had been around for centuries (Szwed & Morton, 1988). James Reese's 369th Regiment "Harlem Hellfighters" band won critical acclaim abroad and at home for its distinctive performances. Black colleges eagerly solicited the exceptional talents of these Black military bandsmen to join and spearhead their music departments and bands, after the war ended (Lewis, 2003; Malone, 1990).

Therefore, HBCUs overflowed with a wealth of premier Black educators because many were prohibited from working elsewhere due to America's strict racist structure. According to Anderson, "Until 1941 no African American scholar, no matter how qualified, how many degrees he or she had earned, or how many excellent articles and books he or she had published, was hired in a permanent faculty position at any predominantly [W]hite university in America" (1993, pp. 153–154). This proscribed top-tier talent included those affiliated with Black college music programs. Despite Blacks' proven band expertise, they continued to be deemed inferior to Whites. HBCU leadership, however, recognized the twofold benefit of having preeminent musicians at their institutions and dually charged Black former bandsmen to educate students on campus and promote their school in surrounding communities. Like its minstrel show precursors, Black college bands recruited students and raised money, in addition to entertaining crowds.

Experts posit that the first HBCU marching band was formed around 1890 at Tuskegee Normal School (Harlan et al., 1974). A long tradition also exists at Alabama State College, Alabama A&M College, and Florida A&M College (FAMC). Given Tuskegee president Booker T. Washington's penchant for self-promotion, establishing a marching band for recruitment and fundraising would have been considered a sound investment. A marching band would have been deemed by Washington as the ideal mechanism to declare and inspire Black people's aspirations—a critical focus of his dual role as spokesman and political manipulator (Harlan, 1975; 1983). Therefore, Army Major Nathaniel Clark Smith was recruited to Tuskegee in 1907 and is presumed to be the first Black band director who had faculty status at an HBCU. Prior to this formal appointment, it was not uncommon for early college bands to be informal and led by students (Lewis, 2003).

Army Captain Frank Drye assumed band directorship from Smith in 1918. He continued to lead and innovate for 12 years and is hailed by many music scholars as being the best-known college band director in the country during his tenure (Malone, 1990). Many of Drye's students became stellar teachers in their own right and bandmasters. The excellent musicianship spawned at Tuskegee germinated throughout the network of HBCUs.

An example of this musical evolution is demonstrated by FAMC's growth. The golden period of Florida A&M College's development is directly attributable to what started at Tuskegee Normal School. When FAMC appointed J. R. E. Lee, a former Tuskegee professor, president in 1923, his plan to grow the college was modeled after Booker T. Washington's Golden Tigers blueprint. President Lee appointed a Tuskegee alumnus and former student of renowned bandmaster Drye, Arnold W. Lee (who was not related), as the first band director compensated by FAMC. Bandmaster Lee was responsible for FAMC's increasing prominence (Malone, 1990). Alumni directly attribute FAMC's current success to President Lee. "It is through the tone that he set and the things that he did that Florida A&M is what it is today," according to Julian Adderley, Sr., whose brother Nathaniel started FAMC's first 16-piece band as a student in 1910 before President Lee formalized a school marching band (Malone, 1990, p. 65).

Notably, early marching bands at HWIs and HBCUs did not typically perform at sporting events, since outdoor activities were more conducive to wind-band performances. College bands tended to augment school ceremonies and social events. According to music historian Kenneth Berger, eventually they became attached to the military or ROTC departments, or in select cases, unofficially sponsored by the athletic department (Lewis, 2003). At FAMC "the band played for the cadet, daily dress parades, for special occasions during the week, and for chapel on Sundays. Throughout the year, the band also participated in the celebrations of local towns and accompanied the baseball and football teams on trips all over the state" (Malone, 1990, p. 64). An interesting distinction of early bands' presence at sporting games in comparison to modern ensembles is that "there was no such thing as a band playing a game in those early days. Between halves they just sat down, they didn't think about having music during a game... The band was just a thing of itself" (Malone, 1990, p. 64). This is in stark contrast to today's Black college Battle of the Bands and HBCU Bowls where musicianship and band presentation overshadow athletics. In fact, at many HBCU football games foot traffic and concessions usually peak during half-time or "the fifth quarter"—after the band performs.

The Broad Influence of HBCU Marching Bands

HBCU marching bands, much like athletic programs at HWIs, can be very powerful organizations on college and university campuses. However, their significant influence extends far beyond their entertainment aspect. HBCU band programs possess multidimensional sway. They play a substantial role in Black college student recruitment and retention, fundraising, and leadership/student development.

Student Recruitment and Retention

Although typically HBCU marching bands are merely viewed as sparks that ignite football half-times, these ensembles have served as catalysts inspiring many young people to enroll in Black colleges. In some cities throughout the country, there are high schools that serve as "pipelines" for future HBCU marching band members. Southwest Dekalb High School in Georgia is such an example. It has had several of its band directors graduate from Florida A&M University (FAMU), including Don Roberts and James Seda, and many of the high school's students enroll in FAMU as well. This Atlanta-metro high school band is renowned for being showcased in the 2002 American hit movie *Drumline*, starring Nick Cannon, being featured in Rose Bowl parades, and having its own reality show (Tagami & Emerson, 2011).

For many young people, attending a HBCU and making the band represents a peak of post–high school graduation success. Of course, college graduation is the paramount accomplishment, especially since HBCUs' graduation rate for its Black students lags behind the nationwide graduation rate for Black students—37% in comparison to 41% (Gasman, 2011). Recognizing that stark disparities related to student populations served at HBCUs do exist and are linked to disproportionate high levels of poverty, poor high school quality, and below par study skills, notwithstanding, HBCU marching bands make no excuses for members failing to meet academic standards (Gasman, 2011). Therefore, students' participation in marching bands is often contingent upon them maintaining passing grades and exemplary behavior. Band scholarships also offer a recruitment and retention incentive, since the awards help students to supplement school tuition and expenses.

Fundraising

The immense popularity of HBCU marching bands yields many opportunities for schools to capitalize on raising money from performance competitions and from loyal fans and alumni interested in sustaining the honored institutions. The Honda Battle of the Bands (HBOB) is a long-standing tradition among Black colleges that was devised to recognize the skillfulness of band members and the unique academic experience provided by HBCUs. It has served as a major fundraising and promotional vehicle as audiences convene from far and wide to witness legendary HBCU band battles brimming with expert musicianship and glamorous pageantry. HBOB is currently in its eleventh year. This annual celebration awards more than $200,000 in grants to participating marching bands.

However, Honda's commitment to HBCUs encompasses more than their support of pleasurable musical performances. The company also sponsors the Honda Campus All-Star Challenge (HCASC), a program that highlights the academic talents of HBCU students. HCASC has existed almost 25 years and is the first-ever academic competition between students at Black colleges. Since its inception, over 100,000 HBCU students have participated and demonstrated their intellectual shrewdness and earned over $7 million in grants for their schools to enrich programs and students' college experience.

Although significant capital is generated by HBCU bands' participation in various bowls like HBOB, more could be done to harness the revenue generating power of these programs throughout the school year and among their alumni after graduation. Alabama A&M University devised a clever fundraising initiative known as "Adopt a Band Student Uniform." It allows marching band admirers to underwrite the cost of a band member uniform (Gasman & Bowman, 2012). Institutions should also create unique ways to petition fans and alumni *during* game time when emotions are transparent and adoration and exhilaration are at their highest. For many, like after a stirring church sermon, this is the time they are most likely to give.

Additionally, a thoughtful fundraising strategy should be implemented by college and university development officers. Gasman and Bowman (2012) discuss the "family" relationship and high level of camaraderie that exist among marching band members and their alma maters. They encourage development officers to draw upon these warm memories when soliciting alumni donations. Furthermore, due to band members' strong connection and affinity for their music programs, Black college fundraisers should create a dossier of these individuals and actively communicate with them, both before and after graduation. Tapping into band members' rich experiences could result in them remaining connected to their campus through volunteerism and financial donations.

This author was particularly moved to witness the fellowship among marching band members when in attendance at a friend's father's funeral. After 30 years, the bereaved Hampton University alumnus had his entire section show up to support him during his loss. Moreover, the alumnus has consistently donated to his alma mater after graduation, even during times of non- and underemployment. He views it as a responsibility to give back to an institution and program that gave a considerable amount to him.

Leadership/Student Development

At many colleges and universities there is a traditional hierarchy of leadership—a top-down model that showcases the president as the primary campus authority. However, some college presidents at formidable HBCU marching band campuses discover they have titular positions. The real power resides in the hands of the marching band director, much like HWIs' football coaching dynamos the late Joseph Vincent "JoePa" Paterno of Pennsylvania State University and Nicholas Lou "Nick" Saban of the University of Alabama. The cult of personality and mega revenue generating programs overshadow campus presidential leadership.

Such was the case with George Edwards, Prairie View A&M University's band director. During his 31-year tenure, "Prof Edwards'" name was not only synonymous with the campus band known as the Marching Storm, his name was also associated with the entire higher education institution.

Oftentimes, since fabled band instructors' length of employment with colleges and universities exceeds that of college presidents', which is merely seven years according to the American Council on Education, they are able to cultivate sustainable, deep-rooted relationships with the campus community and its neighbors and partners (Stuart, 2012). Prof Edwards' lofty reputation is especially notable because during his reign the band's popularity grew despite the Prairie View A&M football team's 80-game losing streak for over a decade—one of the worst college football team records of all time. Therefore, it was evident that Prairie View fans came to see the band, not the football team. Even HWIs were enamored with the Marching Storm. Under Edwards' tutelage, Prairie View became the first Black college to perform in the Rose Bowl Parade (Watson, 2010).

Serving as band director is not the only position of leadership amid a HBCU marching band. Students are also groomed to govern. Holding certain positions of authority within the marching band (like drum major or section leader) affords students leadership opportunities and sometimes confers superior or "hero" status upon them, akin to the praise and admiration typically reserved for celebrated sports jocks. However, adept band leaders do not subscribe to creating singular heroes within the marching unit, they work at developing all their band members into confident, productive young adults.

A student of Professor Edwards reflected how Edwards always stressed the need for his students to be leaders. Edwards continually told them they could do anything they put their mind to, and often saw more in his students than they saw in themselves (Watson, 2010). Many Black college students who participate in band often cite their band experience as being more meaningful to their development than anything else during their college tenure. A former band participant recalled, "I learned more from band staff about...a standard of excellence, and about the importance of completing a mission, than from any other experiences, courses, or activities that I had in college" (Malone, 1990, p. 73).

Conclusion

Despite the broad influence of HBCU marching bands on higher educational institutions, students (both secondary and postsecondary), and American culture, there is scant educational research about them. Considerably more analysis of marching bands' contributions is needed. There is much to be learned from these organizations that have little to do with the entertainment value for which they are acclaimed.

HBCU marching bands are composed of and have fostered academics. They also have a history of being a major source of financial contributions, which help to sustain struggling institutions and provide scholarships for fiscally strapped students. Many of the HBCU marching bands are led by serious scholars who are multitalented regarding book knowledge, business acumen, and community engagement. Black college bandleaders' magnetic personalities and musical savvy does not diminish their wits. These leaders and the programs they oversee, offer a valuable window into what works at HBCUs, and the findings could prove beneficial to both Black colleges and HWIs.

References

Anderson, J. D. (1988). *The education of Blacks in the South, 1865–1930.* Chapel Hill, NC: University of North Carolina Press.

Anderson, J. D. (1993). Race, meritocracy, and the American academy during the immediate post-World War II era. *History of Education Quarterly, 33*(2), 151–175.

Badger, R. (1995). *A life in ragtime: A biography of James Reese Europe.* New York: Oxford University Press.

Drewry, H. N. and Doermann, H. (2001). *Stand and prosper: Private Black colleges and their students.* Princeton, NJ: Princeton University Press.

Fausset, R. (2011, December 17). Hazing investigation is sour note for Georgia marching bands. *The Los Angeles Times.* Retrieved from http://articles.latimes.com/2011/dec/17/nation/lana-band-hazing-20111218.

Gasman, M. (2011, September 7). Being fair about graduation rates at Historically Black Colleges and Universities (HBCUs). *The Huffington Post.* Retrieved from http://www.huffingtonpost.com/marybeth-gasman/hbcus-graduationrates_b_948678.html.

Gasman, M. & Bowman, N. (2012). *A guide to fundraising at Historically Black Colleges and Universities: An all campus approach.* New York: Routledge.

Harlan, L. R. (1975). *Booker T. Washington: The making of a Black leader 1856–1901.* New York: Oxford University Press.

——— (1983). *Booker T. Washington: The wizard of Tuskegee 1901–1915.* New York: Oxford University Press.

Harlan, L. R., Kaufman, S. B., & Smock, R. W. (1974). *The Booker T. Washington papers, Vol. 3, 1889–95.* Urbana, IL: University of Illinois Press.

Lewis, W. D. (2003). Marching to the beat of a different drum: Performance traditions of Historically Black College and University marching bands. M.A. Thesis, University of North Carolina at Chapel Hill.

Malone, J. (1990). The FAMU Marching 100. *The Black perspective in music, 18*(1/2), 59–80.

——— (1996). *Steppin' on the blues: The visible rhythms of African American dance.* Champaign, IL: University of Illinois Press.

Schafer, W. J. (1977). *Brass bands and New Orleans jazz.* Baton Rouge, LA: Louisiana State University Press.

Southern, E. (1997). *The music of Black Americans: A history.* New York: W.W. Norton & Company.

Stuart, R. (2012, July 5). Analysis: The college president—higher education's toughest job. *Diverse Issues in Higher Education.* Retrieved from http://diverseeducation.com/article/17189/#.

Szwed, J. F. & Morton, M. (1988). The Afro-American transformation of European set dances and dance suites. *Dance Research Journal,* Summer.

Tagami, T. & Emerson, B. (2011, December 14). Marching band suspended in DeKalb over FAMU ties. *The Atlanta Journal Constitution.* Retrieved from http://www.ajc.com/news/news/local/marching-bands-suspended-in-dekalb-over-famu-ies/nQPW9/.

Watson, G. (2010, February 26). PVAMU band a legacy to Edwards. *ESPN.* Retrieved from http://sports.espn.go.com/ncf/news/story?id=4946680.

CHAPTER NINE

Study Abroad at HBCUs: Challenges, Trends, and Best Practices

SARAH MULLEN

In a world that is increasingly global and interconnected, study abroad programs provide the "greatest potential for experiential international education" (Brux & Fry, 2010, p. 508). International experience is considered important in today's job market. However, the population of American students going abroad has historically been quite homogenous; even today, nearly 80% of such students are White, and mostly upper middle class (Brux & Fry, 2010, pp. 511–514). Concurrently, demographics in the United States are shifting in such a way that the American undergraduate population is increasingly composed of non-White and lower-income students—groups that have historically had low participation rates in study abroad, and have been underserved by higher education more broadly.

Historically Black Colleges and Universities (HBCUs) serve a significant number of low-income students of color.[1] It is therefore important that we understand how study abroad is (or is not) approached at such institutions. This chapter will examine study abroad at HBCUs with the aim of understanding how international educational opportunities can be expanded at these institutions. First, it will briefly examine the development of study abroad within American higher education. Second, it will discuss existing barriers to study abroad for students of color. Third, it will explore challenges facing HBCUs as they seek to provide study abroad opportunities. Fourth, it will provide a brief overview of the available information on study abroad programming across the spectrum of historically Black institutions. Fifth, it will perform an in-depth examination of two HBCUs' current approaches to study abroad. Finally, it will draw a number of conclusions regarding best practices in study abroad at HBCUs, listing proposed actions that institutions can take in order to ensure that their students are globally competitive.

Study Abroad in the United States: Past and Present

Study abroad is by no means a recent phenomenon. In the United States, study abroad has historically been the purview of the White, wealthy elite. Its existence can be traced back to the colonial era, during which a small number of wealthy individuals participated in self-directed travel to Europe for their studies. While the American Revolution gave rise to significant vocal opposition to international education, "American faculty and students continued to flow to Europe throughout the nineteenth century" (de Wit, 2002, p. 21). However, this practice declined toward the end of the century as the number and quality of American institutions and programs increased, and the flow of students began to reverse.

While "academic mobility from and to the United States became a regular phenomenon" as the nineteenth century drew to a close, this occurred largely on an informal basis (p. 21). Yet the early twentieth century showed the development of a more "formal and institutional structure...when private organizations, foundations, and universities began to recognize the educational value of study abroad" (p. 21). In the aftermath of World War I, internationalism took on a new fervor; "peace and mutual understanding became a driving rationale" as study abroad organizations such as the Institute of International Education and the development of institutional programming became increasingly prevalent (p. 23). Since World War II, the federal government has become deeply involved in supporting study abroad initiatives, resulting in a focus on more non-Western locales. Such efforts were seen as an effective foreign policy tool, which combines "the prewar idealism of peace and mutual understanding and the postwar foreign policy and national security rationales" (p. 25).

The end of the Cold War resulted in a renewed interest in international education, with "reasons of defense, public diplomacy, and security...[continuing] to be the main rationales for federal support"

(p. 28). This interest can also be attributed to concerns about the impact of economic globalization and the role that internationalization plays in US ability to compete. The federal government has developed a wide range of scholarships, including those that provide funding for low-income students pursuing education abroad (Institute of International Education, 2013).

Despite policy and funding foci on non-Western locations, study abroad destinations for American students continue to be overwhelmingly concentrated in Western Europe. At the same time, "only one percent of U.S. undergraduate students participate in a study abroad program during their degree program; and the numbers are even worse for minority students" (Walker et al., 2010, p. 3). "Traditionally, black students [and other students of color] have not participated in study abroad in large numbers" (Ganz, 1991, p. 29), and this continues to be the case, despite the significant expansion of access to institutions of higher education over the past 50 years. Study abroad has remained a predominantly White phenomenon. As a report produced by the Council on International Educational Exchange in 1988 observed:

> Students who study abroad are from a narrow spectrum of the total population. They are predominantly white females from highly educated professional families, majoring in the social sciences or humanities. They are high achievers and risk-takers. Many have had earlier overseas travel or international experience. Whether by their own choice or lack of encouragement to do so, there are fewer men, members of minority groups, students from nonprofessional and less-educated families, and there are fewer students from science, education, or business majors among undergraduates who study abroad. (p. 8)

A quarter century later, this statement continues to ring true. The total number of students of color studying abroad has increased from 15.7% in 2000/2001 to 22.2% in 2010/2011 (Institute of International Education, 2012). Black students represented 3.5% of all students studying abroad in 2000/2001, a proportion that rose to 4.8% in 2010/2011 (Institute of International Education, 2012). Though an improvement, these figures illustrate that students of color are still significantly underrepresented in study abroad when compared with their representation in American institutions of higher education, and in the US population.

Barriers to Study Abroad for Students of Color

In recent years, as the globalized economy has placed an increasing premium on international experiences and intercultural competencies, underrepresented students "may find themselves at a disadvantage as they enter the workplace and continue to live and to cope in a global society" (Sebeck, 2005, p. 38). In this context, people of color in the United States have had the greatest difficulty adjusting to the realities of international competition (Akomolafe, 2000), due to their historic underrepresentation in higher education and in fields considered essential to the growing "knowledge economy." In this context, study abroad experiences can be "more than enriching...they can also produce profound and lasting changes in students' self-image, their academic and professional goals, and their attitudes about their roles in society" (Burkart et al., 2001). Yet despite the proven, transformative effects, students of color continue to be the least likely to participate in study abroad or in other international educational opportunities. Such students make up less than a quarter of the total number of American students pursuing studies abroad. Among this group, Black and African American students comprise less than 5% of the overall study abroad population, while Latino/a students are less than 7% of the total (Institute of International Education, 2012).

There are a wide variety of explanations as to why participation rates among students of color are disproportionately low. Overall, scholars suggested four major barriers to students of color, Black students specifically, that prevent them from "engaging in international educational exchange" (Cole, 1991, p. 2). These are often referred to among practitioners as the "four Fs": "Faculty and staff, finances, family and community, [and] fears [of racism abroad]" (Cole, 1991, p. 3). In recent years, this list has been refined, expanded, and prioritized; it now includes "finances; family concerns and attitudes; fear of racism and discrimination; historical patterns, expectations and attitudes; institutional factors; and a lack of relevant study abroad programs" (Brux & Fry, 2010, p. 513). Each of these barriers, with the exception of institutional factors, will be addressed below.

Traveling and living overseas is expensive. As a result, finances are often the primary concern for all students planning to study abroad. However, this factor is important for students of color, and particularly for "black students...[who] are disproportionately found among students who simply cannot attend college without substantial financial aid" (Cole, 1991, p. 3). The costs of study abroad are not confined to tuition, travel expenses, room, and board. Many students from low-income backgrounds, including those at HBCUs "work full-time...just to be able to pay their way through college" (Akomolafe, 2000, p. 105). Consequently, "financial concern extends beyond actual expenses, because the opportunity cost of foregone earnings while studying abroad can be a major constraint" (Brux & Fry, 2010, p. 513). Due in large part to the "prohibitive cost of study-abroad programs, many students from minority institutions cannot afford the luxury of studying overseas...without a full or at least partial scholarship" (Akomolafe, 2000, p. 104). Moreover, "even when students are presented with full or partial scholarships, [many] still cannot afford to take advantage of the opportunity" (p. 105)

Students of color who hope to study abroad must often do so in the face of both implicit and explicit disapproval from their families. As research has indicated, "negative parental attitudes and other family issues have been found to constrain the participation of specific multicultural groups of students in study abroad" (Brux & Fry, 2010, p. 513). This is particularly true for students at HBCUs, with one study finding that "family disapproval was a factor mentioned by 60% of African American students" (p. 513). Whether or not a student's family values or does not value international educational experiences, they are worried for their children's health and safety. In particular, they are "concerned about what racial attitudes and incidents [their children might] experience" while abroad—a worry that is often exacerbated by the fact that "African American parents are less likely to have traveled abroad than white American parents have" (Cole, 1991, p. 3). Consequently, parents and other family members are understandably apprehensive about the study abroad experience.

Parents are not the only ones who worry about racism abroad. In fact, many students of color are afraid of "encountering, miles away from home, yet another form of racism" (p. 4). This is particularly true for African American students, whose fears are often "based on experiences with racism in the United States" (Brux & Fry, 2010, p. 514). Students may first experience "a degree of anxiety regarding inter-action with other program participants or interaction with the director," in terms of being the only student of color participating in a program, or being singled out or treated differently by other program members and staff (Perdreau, 2002). Moreover, they may argue that "they know and on some level understand American racism...why venture into foreign variations on that everyday theme" (Cole, 1991, p. 4)? Interestingly, while students of color often experience both implicit and explicit discrimination abroad, it is "not unusual for returnees to state that the only racism or perceived prejudice they [encountered] abroad [was] from other Americans" (Perdreau, 2002).

With regard to "historical patterns, expectations, and attitudes," which persist among students, faculty, and institutional staff, it has already been noted that study abroad has traditionally been an activity for wealthy, White individuals. Consequently, students of color have traditionally been excluded from international educational opportunities—both in practice, and in media images portraying study abroad (Jackson, 2005, p. 16). This can result in situations where "minority students don't think of study abroad as right for them and they then filter out or ignore information" that pertains to these opportunities (Brux & Fry, 2010, p. 515). In addition, the presence or absence of faculty and staff support can have a significant influence on students' knowledge of and interest in study abroad. At predominantly White institutions, "faculty and staff tend to encourage 'the best students'...to apply for and go on study abroad programs," and many "do not see black students in those terms" (Cole, 1991, p. 3). Although this may occur much more infrequently today, such a mindset can certainly still exist among faculty and staff at all universities, including historically and predominantly Black institutions.

"Beyond academic opportunities, students who participate in quality study abroad programs...[have] educational, social, and personal learning experiences [that] can be particularly meaningful to students of African heritage" (Metzler, 2002, p. 55). Yet, most students of color face challenges in finding study abroad opportunities in locations that are personally relevant, due to the historical dominance and continuing popularity of Western study abroad destinations. These students are much more likely to be "heritage seekers" who "[select] a study abroad venue because of family background...because of some familiarity or resonance with less emphasis on the difference" (Comp, 2008, p. 30). This is particularly well illustrated by the fact that a 1996 "survey of 61 study-abroad programs in Africa revealed that...African American students made up 23 percent [of all participants], a rate of participation significantly higher than in study abroad programs worldwide (3.5 percent in 2000–2001)" (Metzler, 2002, p. 51). As many have noted, current conceptions of "internationalism" have been too geographically narrow—often referring only to the global West (Carter, 1991, p. 11). While the number of non-Western study abroad programs has increased dramatically over the past decade, study abroad programs are still largely concentrated in Western Europe. It is possible for students of color to connect with their heritage and identity while studying in traditional Western locales. However, heritage-seeking students of color tend to have fewer choices than study abroad participants of European origin. As a result, "minority students whose racial or ethnic origins are represented by geographic regions somehow omitted from the focus of international programs and courses receive the clear message that their cultural origins and identities are not important" (p. 11).

However, little has changed since many of the seminal studies on the issue were completed; study abroad participation in the United States remains overwhelmingly White. Students of color, African American students in particular, are much more likely to be first-generation college students from low-income backgrounds, for whom the cost of study abroad is an unbearable financial burden. In addition, these students may be unaware of the existence of study abroad opportunities, or may filter out information that they believe does not pertain to them. As a consequence of this wide range of highly effective barriers to study abroad, the number of students of color participating in international educational exchanges is extremely low. This dearth of opportunity in the face of often insurmountable challenges ultimately perpetuates the cycle of inequality and privilege that pervades our society, and prevents students of color from obtaining the cross-cultural competencies that will enable them to compete effectively in a global marketplace.

Institutional Challenges at HBCUs

Additional barriers to study abroad that have yet to be addressed occur at the institutional level. These include "curriculum requirements, lack of support of faculty and departments, difficulty in transferring credits, campus culture, language and other requirements, [marketing practices],...length of program and scheduling difficulties" (Brux & Fry, 2010, p. 515). Consequently, it has been argued, "institutions can undertake a major role in reducing the constraints faced by these students" (p. 516). Despite significant variation among HBCUs, these institutions tend to face similar challenges in providing their students with opportunities for study abroad. These challenges often exceed those faced by predominantly White institutions, with a particular emphasis on the following: extremely limited financial resources; an institutional commitment to serving low-income students of color, most of whom must overcome the many barriers mentioned here; and, a lack of commitment to comprehensive internationalization.

HBCUs, like all institutions of higher education, are tasked with preparing the current generation of students for an increasingly global economy. "Many HBCUs recognize the importance of study abroad programs and have begun to create their own programs and to recruit foreign scholars to their institutions" (Sebeck, 2005, p. 40). Such programs have often been in countries that are considered to be heritage sites for the student population. Indeed, "study abroad in Africa has become increasingly popular among HBCUs" (Akomolafe, 2000, p. 103)—particularly because such programs "provide the opportunity for a large heritage community to participate in study-abroad" (Metzler, 2002, p. 54). Yet despite these efforts, "African-American students who attend traditionally White institutions...tend to study abroad at a much higher rate than their peers at historically Black colleges and universities (HBCUs)" (Sebeck, 2005, p. 40).

While there are myriad reasons for the low levels of participation in study abroad at HBCUs, one must look first and foremost at the issue of cost. As many have noted, "sustainable and qualitative international education...is in large part unaffordable and thus inaccessible to most HBCUs" (Akomolafe, 2000, p. 103). Indeed, when compared with their predominantly White counterparts, HBCUs are "often working with far fewer resources to sustain a study abroad program" (Cole, 1991, p. 3). This is likely the case due to a combination of factors, including historically lower levels of government funding, smaller endowments, low alumni-giving rates, and a commitment to lower tuition rates. These circumstances are compounded at private institutions, which also do not receive consistent state funding, and are thus more tuition-driven than their public counterparts.

This lack of financial resources means that there is often a single person administering study abroad programs—many times in addition to their regular duties. "Unlike their counterparts elsewhere, study-abroad advisors in HBCUs face an extremely arduous task. Where they exist, most of the activities that deal with overseas study are undertaken on an ad hoc basis...the success or failure of the program will more likely depend on the tenacity and willingness of the study-abroad advisor to hang in" (Akomolafe, 2000, p. 104). This is further complicated by the fact that many study abroad advisors at HBCUs are faculty members who have taken on additional responsibilities. Indeed, "carrying out all the work of these programs may be viewed as a 'luxury' that folks who teach four courses a semester feel they 'cannot afford'" (Cole, 1991, p. 3).

In addition to having severely limited financial resources, most HBCUs are also committed to serving low-income and first-generation students of color—students for whom college might not otherwise be an option. In fact, the number of Pell Grant recipients who attend HBCUs is significantly higher than the national average. The nature of these students "sometimes makes it relatively more difficult to promote international education, especially where it relates to the study-abroad programs" (Akomolafe, 2000, p. 103). This is largely due to the wide range of barriers mentioned previously, which students of color—and low-income students of color in particular—must overcome in order to study abroad. Thus, for HBCUs, which "service relatively disadvantaged students who do not traditionally participate in study-abroad programs" (Metzler, 2002, p. 54), there exists an additional layer of difficulty that they must address.

Finally, among the vast majority of HBCUs, a significant and sustained commitment to comprehensive internationalization does not exist. This means that university leadership often does not actively support and prioritize international education within the curriculum, student body, faculty, and opportunities for all campus constituencies. Indeed, "most HBCUs do not have an institutionalized funding procedure for their students or faculty to study overseas" (Akomolafe, 2000, p. 103), and many are hesitant to allow students to use their financial aid for international programs. This makes it difficult for faculty and staff working to build up an institution's international offerings, despite observations that HBCUS "have real interest in working with larger universities and study-abroad consortia to offer students quality and affordable study-abroad programming" (Metzler, 2002, p. 54). At the same time, it is understandable that "internationalization is probably not one of [institutions'] top priorities" (Akomolafe, 2000, p. 103), as many struggle to stay afloat in the current financial climate.

In sum, while many HBCUs have expressed interest in increasing the international educational offerings available to their students, these institutions face multiple layers of barriers that historically and predominantly White institutions do not face. Historic governmental neglect and a dearth of external funding sources have left HBCUs with severely constrained financial resources; they can hardly afford to invest large sums in international programming. HBCUs' focus on serving low-income students of color who have individual issues that must be addressed, makes it difficult for these institutions to address other issues in a broad-based manner. These constraints, combined with a general lack of commitment from institutional leadership, stifle HBCUs' abilities to take steps toward internationalization in the same way that their predominantly White counterparts have done in recent years. Ultimately, this leaves institutions at a further disadvantage, as they search for ways to ensure their students' ability to succeed in a twenty-first-century workforce.

Overview: Current Trends in Study Abroad at HBCUs

This section will examine study abroad at HBCUs. The information was obtained through an internet-based search of the websites of each of the 105 HBCUs as well as other internet sources. I attempt only to provide a preliminary overview of study abroad at these institutions; it is by no means complete, nor is it comprehensive. However, it does represent a crucial first step in understanding the current trends and challenges that HBCUs face as they seek to increase the availability of study abroad programming.

Presence of Study Abroad Opportunities

From an extensive search of the 105 HBCU websites, a few trends are apparent—both across all institutions, and disaggregated by school type. It is clear that institutional challenges continue to reflect those discussed in the literature. Just under two-third of institutions mentioned the existence of study abroad opportunities for enrolled students on their websites. Of these, fewer than half had any sort of webpage dedicated to study abroad.

It is possible to obtain a more nuanced approach by disaggregating these institutions into public and private, two-year and four-year. Just over 10% of HBCUs are two-year institutions, of which only two are private, and the rest are public institutions granting only associate's degrees. Among these institutions, only two—Hinds Community College and Saint Philip's—indicate that they currently offer study abroad opportunities. The lack of study abroad at the two-year institutions is not surprising, given that study abroad is a rarity among community and technical colleges throughout the United States, although this has begun to change in recent years. Both institutions have dedicated webpages that discuss the programs available to students. Hinds and Saint Philip's are both public institutions; however, while Hinds programs are school-run (Hinds Community College, 2000–2012), opportunities for Saint Philip's students are available only through the wider community college system, Alamo Community Colleges (Alamo Community Colleges, 2013). An additional three institutions are private, graduate-only institutions. These three institutions—Meharry Medical College, Morehouse School of Medicine, and the Interdenominational Theological Seminary—do not seem to offer any study abroad opportunities for their students. This is also not unusual, given that study abroad at the graduate level in the United States usually occurs through foundation or national scholarships, rather than through institutional programs.

Slightly less than half of all HBCUs (49) are private, four-year institutions. Of these, only 27 (55%) mention study abroad anywhere on their websites. Just 14 (29%) provide further information on study abroad through a dedicated website addressing specific program information. One interesting case is that of Oakwood University. As a Seventh Day Adventist affiliated institution, the university is able to provide study abroad opportunities through Adventist Colleges Abroad (Oakwood University, 1996–2013), which offers programs in Europe, the Middle East, South America, and Asia. Since these programs are coordinated by an independent organization that represents a consortium of affiliated institutions, Oakwood is able to provide opportunities for students without an institutional study abroad office or adviser. More generally, the dearth of study abroad at private HBCUs can likely be explained by the fact that these institutions tend to have significantly less money than publicly funded institutions. Private HBCUs receive very little assistance from state governments, and thus tend to be very tuition driven. Consequently, they often have fewer resources to spend on study abroad programs or staff to administer them. Moreover, because of their reliance on tuition dollars, including federal loans and grants, many private institutions simply cannot afford to allow this income to be put toward study abroad programs.

Finally, about two fifths (41) of all HBCUs are public, four-year institutions. Of these institutions, 90% (37/40) mention that study abroad opportunities are available to students. Twenty-nine of these (73%) discuss these opportunities further on specific study abroad websites, with one additional institution, the University of the Virgin Islands, providing contact information on its website dedicated to domestic exchange programs (University of the Virgin Islands, 2008–2013). This widespread presence of study abroad at public institutions can likely be explained by two factors. First, the presence of consistent state funding for these institutions enables them to provide study abroad opportunities without undue burden. Moreover, public institutions are less tuition driven than private institutions, which means that they are less affected when federal and state financial aid is used for study abroad. Second, public institutions are often part of a wider state system of higher education. As a result, some are able to offer study abroad through either a statewide study abroad and exchange consortium (such as the University of North Carolina Exchange Program), or through programs offered by other institutions within the state system (as in Georgia).

Administrative Structure

In keeping with the existing literature, which notes a lack of funding and human resources as major issues that HBCUs face, relatively few institutions have fulltime employees or self-contained study abroad offices. Instead, study abroad is often located within umbrella offices, such as broader international programs offices, Centers for Academic Excellence, honors college, academic affairs or special programs offices, and specific academic departments, such as modern languages or international studies. No matter where the office is located, few institutions have faculty or staff dedicated solely to overseeing study abroad. If study abroad is housed within an international programs office, it is often the case that advising and administration fall under the responsibility of the same administrators who work with international students. If there are employees whose fulltime responsibilities focus on study abroad, they are most often lower-level administrators or coordinators. In many cases, faculty members take on study abroad advising in addition to their teaching and other professorial duties, or choose to lead their own short-term study abroad programs.

Programs

Overall, only a handful of HBCUs currently run their own study abroad programs. These tend to be short-term, faculty-led programs that are offered in the summer or during other breaks, such as that offered through Prairie View A&M University (Prairie View A&M University, 2013). The presence of these one-off, shorter-term programs can likely be explained by their relatively low cost, which would not be prohibitively expensive for either students or institutions. A few institutions also have direct exchange partnerships with foreign institutions. Such programs are often more affordable for students, as they allow students to directly pay tuition to their home institution (Ganz, 2013). By and large, however, HBCUs rely on third-party study abroad providers, whether through a system-wide consortium, another institution, or a nonprofit study abroad provider organization such as the Council on International Educational Exchange (CIEE). This is likely due to a pervasive lack of funding, which means that many institutions do not have the capacity or resources to run their own exchange or study abroad programs. By relying on third-party providers, HBCUs are able to remove a significant resource burden, as these providers are responsible for student orientation programming and dealing with any issues that arise while students are abroad.

With regard to program location, there are still far more programs available in Europe and non-heritage locations, especially if third-party provider programs are included. For public institutions, which rely on system-wide consortia or programs run through other state institutions, programs are strongly concentrated in non-heritage locales. This can likely be explained by the fact that many of the participating state institutions are historically and predominantly White. Consequently, fewer students participating in study abroad programs throughout the state are looking to study abroad in non-Western countries that might be desirable heritage destinations for HBCU students. Because the vast majority of students studying abroad in the United States are White, it stands to reason that third-party providers would cater to this population. This ultimately perpetuates the cycle whereby HBCU students and other students of color seeking to study in heritage locales are unable to find relevant programs, and thus may choose not to study abroad, while White students are almost always able to find personally relevant programs and thus continue to participate. As a caveat, it is important to note that many of the school-run, short-term study abroad programs that HBCUs operate do travel to heritage locations in Africa, the United Kingdom, and some Spanish-speaking countries are also popular destinations.

Financial Aid and Requirements

Where information was provided, institutions stressed that federal financial aid and many scholarships could be applied toward study abroad. Websites also offered links to information on school-funded and externally funded scholarships and programs that could help students pay for their programs. They encouraged students to speak with the institution's office of financial aid, in order to see what aid and scholarships could be put toward study abroad. Moreover, many institutions required explicit approval from the financial aid office, and good financial standing, in order for students to be approved to participate in study abroad programs.

The available information indicated that most HBCUs that offer study abroad opportunities also require students to be in good academic standing. The grade point average requirements ranged from 2.0–3.25; some requirements are institutionally mandated, while others are program-specific. Institutions also tend to require students to have either sophomore standing (largely for short-term or summer programs), or junior standing (for semester and year-long programs). Where study abroad programs are offered for credit, institutions also require that students have all courses preapproved by the relevant departments before departing for their studies abroad. This can be seen as an effort on the part of institutions to ensure that students are able to continue their studies and graduate on time.

Information and Communication

Overall, very few HBCUs had comprehensive study abroad websites that were easy to find, access, and navigate. In many cases, creative search techniques were required in order to find any mention of study abroad. For institutions that did have specific study abroad websites, many provided only contact information or a brief overview of available destinations. Moreover, many did not discuss program details, application processes, or other vital information that students might need in order to decide whether to explore study abroad opportunities further. For institutions that relied almost entirely on third-party providers, many only provided hyperlinks to the different study abroad providers' websites, with little to no additional information. One notable exception, however, was a handful of institutions' use of abroadoffice.net (Alabama A&M University, n.d.; Xavier University of Louisiana, n.d.), a customizable, thorough form website (Global Learning Semesters, 2006–2013). While nearly two thirds of institutions mentioned the possibility of study abroad for its students, fewer than half of all institutions had dedicated study abroad websites, and even fewer provided information in sufficient detail. This widespread lack of easily available information creates significant challenges for students, and may mean that even those interested will find it difficult to navigate the study abroad application process.

Case Studies

This section of the chapter will examine in detail the study abroad structures and practices at two HBCUs. The first is Morgan State University, a public, doctoral granting institution in Baltimore, Maryland. Morgan's study abroad program is relatively small, although it is currently expanding due to increased institutional support. The second case is Spelman College, a private four-year institution in Atlanta, Georgia. Over the past 30 or so years, the number of Spelman students studying abroad for credit has increased exponentially. For these cases, independent research has been supplemented by interviews, conducted by the author, with Dr. M'bare N'gom, senior executive director of the Center for Global Studies and Exchange at Morgan State University, and Dr. Margery Ganz, director of Study Abroad and International Exchange at Spelman College.

Morgan State University

Study abroad at Morgan State University has existed for at least 20 years. Upon his arrival at Morgan in 1993, the current senior executive director of the Center of Global Studies and Exchange began "[advising] students and also [helping] them find external resources that would help them go abroad to study" (N'gom, 2013). Around 2000, study abroad was officially brought under the umbrella of the "Center for Global Studies, which...was officially established...as an outgrowth of the East Asian Studies program" (N'gom, 2013). Today, the Center for Global Studies and Exchange is "a university-wide support unit aimed at facilitating the internationalization efforts of the university. To achieve this goal, the Center works collaboratively with academic departments to enhance student and faculty development through workshops, study abroad, internships, exchanges, and other relevant international education programs" (Morgan State University, 2013a). Currently, the Center has four fulltime staff members that oversee all aspects of international activity at the university: "a director, an assistant, a director of international services (visas, etc.), and an administrative assistant" (N'gom, 2013). In addition, the senior executive director for the Center, who is also a member of the Morgan faculty and an interim dean, allocates about 15% of his time to "coordinating and advising students who were preparing applications for study abroad [scholarships]," as well as "[sharing]...international opportunities with faculty and students" (N'gom, 2013).

Over the years, the study abroad program at Morgan has remained small, typically sending around four to five students abroad per year (N'gom, 2013). Students have the option of applying to "any of the study abroad/exchange programs offered by Morgan, [participating] in a program offered by another institution, [and creating] an independent study abroad program that must be approved by the University through the Center for Global Studies and Exchange" (Morgan State University, 2013b). Because the institution's study abroad capacity is still developing, students mainly use third-party provider programs, with the most popular longer-term study abroad destinations in Mexico, Spain, and France (N'gom, 2013). From time to time, Morgan State also offers faculty-led study abroad courses. These are not offered consistently, and are typically organized by individual faculty. For example in 2011, "one of the faculty in the department of world languages organized a faculty-led study abroad course to Oaxaca, Mexico. There were 16 students enrolled in the course" (N'gom, 2013). Finally, Morgan State has recently begun to offer students the opportunity to study in Brazil and China—two countries that are recognized as rapidly emerging players in the global economy. April 2012 saw the establishment of an exchange agreement between Morgan and Hubei University in China (Kilar, 2012). Six months later, Morgan State was selected to participate in a one-year exchange program with Brazil through the Institute for International Education's International Academic Partnership Program (*Universities News*, 2012). In addition, Morgan plays a lead role in the CAPES/HBCU-Brazil Alliance Partnership, which is "a collaborative network of historically black colleges with partnerships supporting student and faculty exchanges with universities in Brazil" (*Universities News*, 2012).

Morgan has a number of explicit requirements for students interested in studying abroad. Students must have completed two years of study on campus—largely because "Morgan cannot guarantee that a host institution will be willing to accept a sophomore" (Morgan State University, 2013b). Although grade point average requirements vary from one program to another, students must have a minimum GPA of 2.5, and must not be on academic probation (Morgan State University, 2013b). Students interested in programs where courses are taught in languages other than English must meet specific language requirements; often, "students must have at least four college semesters or the equivalent," should be "enrolled in the foreign language the semester before departing," and must "meet program-specific requirements" (Morgan State University, 2013b). Finally, students need to "submit a Disciplinary Records Release Form, which must be completed by the

Dean of students" (Morgan State University, 2013b); students with a "problematic disciplinary history" can be denied approval to participate in a study abroad program.

Among students at Morgan who choose to study abroad, most tend to come from middle-class families, and have "either had a brief stint [abroad] in high school, or heard about international education at home" (N'gom, 2013). Currently, the Center for Global Studies and Exchange utilizes a variety of outreach and recruitment tools to provide students with information on study abroad, including "brochures, open [houses], information sessions, [the study abroad] web page, in-class information, [and] e-mail" (N'gom, 2013). The Center also asks students who have returned from overseas to "serve as resource people and participate in events where [the Center] promotes study abroad" (N'gom, 2013). At the same time Morgan students face many barriers to study abroad. Two of the most prominent barriers that have been observed are "funding and [a] lack of international culture," whereby "many [students] do not consider study abroad as a transformative experience" (N'gom, 2013). While it is likely that the opinions that constitute the second major barrier are likely to change over time, particularly due to the increasing focus on international opportunities at the institution, at present, Morgan "has not been able to resolve the financial aid issue" (N'gom, 2013).

In recent years, there has been a distinct trend toward internationalization at Morgan State University. This is seen as the result of a "strong commitment, personal and institutional, to International Education on the part of President David Wilson" (N'gom, 2013), whose tenure at the university began in 2010. This commitment is apparent in the tagline for the university's strategic plan: "Growing the Future, Leading the World" (Morgan State University, 2013c). It is further illustrated by the appointment, as of July 1, 2013, of a new senior administrator to oversee international initiatives (N'gom, 2013). As a result, while Morgan's study abroad program remains small, opportunities for students are growing. However, it remains to be seen whether students will take advantage of these opportunities. With such strong institutional support, the future of study abroad at Morgan State has the potential to be very bright indeed.

Spelman College

Spelman College has offered study abroad opportunities for more than 50 years, beginning with the fully funded Merrill scholarships in

1958 (Robertson, 2010). Over the past 30 years, the growth of study abroad has been astounding, in terms of both program offerings and student participation. While Spelman's office of study abroad operated independently for decades, it has recently been brought under the umbrella of the newly established Gordon-Zeto Center for Global Education. The Center, the establishment of which was made possible by a $17 million anonymous gift, "serves as the institutional focal point to cohere, enhance and lead the College's global strategic initiatives" (Spelman College, 2013a). Within the study abroad office, there is only a single fulltime employee: the program assistant. Dr. Ganz, who has been directing Spelman's study abroad and exchange programs since her arrival at the college in 1981, divides her time between her teaching duties as a faculty member and overseeing the study abroad office. She is able to do this by teaching a reduced course load each semester. In addition, the study abroad office usually employs three to four work-study students per year, at least one of whom is always an international exchange student.

In 1981, only one or two Spelman students went abroad every year; today, around 150 are studying abroad each year for academic credit, participating in semester, year, and summer programs, or as an add-on to a course (Ganz, 2013). An additional 100 students participate in other, non-credit international experiences, such as Spelman's Model UN program, its Student Activities Global Experience Program, and international community service trips. In terms of credit-bearing study abroad, Spelman offers a wide variety of programs. Over the years, it has established a number of true exchange programs, including two in the United Kingdom, one in the Czech Republic, and one with a women's university in Japan (Spelman College, 2013b). During the summer, Spelman also runs short-term, faculty-led programs to destinations such as Spain, France, Turkey, Japan, China, South Africa, and Brazil (Ganz, 2013). Finally, Spelman also works with a wide range of approved third-party providers, for whose programs they offer students in-residence credit. These providers include the Danish Institute for Study Abroad, Arcadia University, the Institute for Study Abroad of Butler University, the School for International Training, and the Council on International Educational Exchange (CIEE), for which Spelman serves as the School of Record (the institution that provides transcripts and records for students whose home schools "require that the coursework completed abroad transfer through an official," accredited US institution (Council on International Educational Exchange, 2013).

While initially, Spelman students studied in traditional study abroad locales in Western Europe, focusing on languages such as Spanish and French, their destinations have broadened significantly over the years. As the college's languages department added new offerings, the diversity of study abroad destinations increased, soon including programs in Latin America, Africa, and Asia. In addition, as students from a variety of academic disciplines began to pursue studies abroad, academic departments at Spelman began to promote particular study abroad destinations. For example, Spelman's psychology department explicitly recommends programs through the Danish Institute for Study Abroad; as a result, a significant number of psychology majors study there each year. Today, the most popular study abroad locales for Spelman students are in Britain, Denmark, Ghana, South Africa, Argentina, and Spain, along with a variety of programs offered through the School for International Training (Ganz, 2013). Overall, while many students are interested in studying abroad in Africa, traditionally considered a heritage destination for many HBCU students, students' program choices do not necessarily align with the specific geographic areas associated with their heritage, which are generally located in West Africa; rather, they often choose to study in locations such as Botswana and South Africa (Ganz, 2013).

As mentioned above, Spelman has seen a significant increase in the number of students studying abroad over the past 30 years; it now has one of the largest study abroad programs among the 105 HBCUs. This can be seen as a result of aggressive outreach through the study abroad office, and the participation of program alumnae in recruiting efforts. Students learn of Spelman's wide range of study abroad programs before they are even admitted to the school; pre-freshman events include programming that provides prospective students and their parents with information regarding the many international opportunities available to them. Further outreach is conducted during freshman orientation fairs, and the study abroad office utilizes posters, e-mails, and postings on the school's e-notice boards to promote Study Abroad 101 sessions, which discuss program offerings and available funding. In addition, individual providers hold recruiting sessions over the course of the school year to promote their programs, with study abroad alumnae participating in the sessions to discuss their international experiences with prospective students.

In order for Spelman students to study abroad, they must comply with a number of requirements. Students must have a grade point average of 3.0 or higher, and must have "at least junior standing when commencing the program" (Spelman College, 2013c), although those with sophomore standing are permitted to participate in summer programs for credit (Ganz, 2013). Students must also demonstrate "emotional maturity," an "adaptability to [the] overseas environment," a "sincere commitment and interest in the host country," and "relevance of the overseas program to [their] academic and career goals" (Spelman College, 2013c). Once students are accepted into their program of choice, Spelman also requires that students enroll in a one-credit orientation course during the semester prior to their departure (Ganz, 2013). During their predeparture orientation, students often talk through issues that may arise while they are abroad, including the fact that they may stand out in nonheritage locations, the corresponding possibility of experiencing racism while abroad, and the possibility that students who study abroad in heritage locations will not be welcomed as long-lost brothers and sisters as they might have imagined (Ganz, 2013). In addition to the orientation course, students must blog while they are away, and must submit a reflection paper upon their return, which faculty across the college will evaluate for essential learning outcomes (Ganz, 2013). Finally, students must agree to participate in round tables and recruiting events once they have returned to campus (Ganz, 2013).

Students at Spelman who study abroad come from a range of geographic and socioeconomic backgrounds. They include local students who have never left their home state, as well as students who have traveled abroad extensively. While the number of students participating in study abroad has increased substantially, much of this increase has been within the short-term programs. At the same time, many students decide to return abroad for semester or yearlong programs. This is likely due to the fact that short-term programs, which allow students to travel abroad with "a cohort of friends who look like them" ultimately enable students to "get their feet wet and gain skills" before they study abroad for longer periods (Ganz, 2013). In addition, while students from all majors are participating in Spelman's programs, there are two majors—Spanish and International Studies—that require at least one semester of study abroad.

For Spelman students, the most consistent and common barrier to study abroad is a lack of sufficient funding or financial aid. This has been especially true in recent years, due to the continuing economic recession. However, the college has taken significant steps in order to enable students from all socioeconomic backgrounds to participate in international experiences. Spelman ensures that all financial aid is available for approved programs. Spelman also provides a number of endowed scholarships specifically for study abroad. The college has an annual scholarship competition for sophomores, as well as a yearly competition for summer money that can be applied to Spelman-run, short-term programs (Ganz, 2013). The director of Study Abroad and International Exchange works with students to apply for external scholarships; to date, Spelman has won more Gilman Scholarships than any other HBCU (Ganz, 2013). Additionally, as the school of record for CIEE, Spelman receives a small fee for every non-Spelman student who utilizes their services. Finally, the Spelman office of study abroad works in conjunction with the development office to raise money in order to support study abroad. Here, the current director's longtime presence at the college has been key to fundraising success; a group of alumnae recently contributed funds to establish an endowed scholarship in her name (Ganz, 2013). These scholarships and financial aid typically cover a significant portion of students' tuition, room, and board. Yet despite a willingness to disburse and seek funding for students, there is still not sufficient money to fund all students who want to go abroad. Consequently, many students who have expressed an interest in study abroad are ultimately unable to participate in international programs.

Throughout Spelman's recent history, there has consistently been strong institutional support for study abroad. Most recently, the institution's strategic plan has emphasized the desire for every Spelman student to have an international experience prior to graduation. While study abroad preceded the development of other international initiatives, it now exists within a broader trend of internationalization at Spelman. As mentioned earlier, Spelman received a $17 million grant for internationalizing its campus. The resulting internationalization efforts include: the recent establishment of the Gordon-Zeto Center and the appointment of the Gordon-Zeto Dean for Global Education; support for Model United Nations, student scholarships, and faculty; and funding for a course that focuses on the African diaspora (Ganz, 2013). The Spelman curriculum further illustrates the college's internationalist thrust, requiring students to select either an approved internationally oriented course or a women's studies course. This international focus is similarly apparent among the student population; International Studies has been one of the college's fastest growing majors in recent years (Ganz, 2013). As the college continues to move toward comprehensive internationalization, it will likely maintain its position as one of the most internationally focused college campuses—both among the existing HBCUs, and in the United States more broadly.

Observations and Best Practices

Based on the existing evidence of current trends in study abroad at HBCUs, it is possible to draw out two major issues confronting HBCUs in this context. First, study abroad opportunities are generally lacking or underdeveloped among the 105 HBCUs. This can likely be explained by the lack of human and financial resources available to these institutions—particularly those that are private. Additional reasons may include HBCUs' commitment to low-income students, who have been historically underserved in the context of study abroad, and a lack of institutional commitment to internationalization. While there are a number of institutions that have a strong global focus, these institutions tend to be the exceptions, rather than the rule.

Second, institutions that do offer study abroad opportunities do not sufficiently facilitate students' access to essential information. Even among those institutions that mentioned study abroad on their websites, few provided comprehensive information regarding program offerings, requirements for participation, the application process, and available funding. In addition, while some schools did mention that they offered school-run pre-departure orientation sessions, many seemed to leave this to third-party providers, who might not address the specific issues that typical HBCU students may face when studying abroad.

In light of the prevailing challenges that HBCUs face in providing their students with opportunities for international study, there are a number of best practices that should be adopted. These practices are prevalent among institutions with well-developed study abroad programs, such as Spelman, and are central to their overwhelming success. HBCUs that are seeking to initiate or expand study abroad offerings at their institutions should therefore take note of these practices, and incorporate them into their current and future study abroad initiatives.

First, enunciate an explicit institutional commitment to study abroad specifically and to internationalization more generally. This commitment must exist at the highest levels of leadership, and must be incorporated into the institution's mission or strategic plan. It must also indicate a willingness to expand study abroad despite the fact that it may have negative financial implications for institutions. By emphasizing its dedication to ensuring that students are internationally competent, an institution can indicate to students, faculty, and staff that it recognizes the importance of international education for students' future success.

Second, provide students with clear and consistent information. This information should be easy to find on the school's website, and should preferably be located on a separate page dedicated to study abroad. It must also be comprehensive; the website should answer questions about the institution's programmatic offerings, requirements for participation, application process, and opportunities for financial aid and scholarships. The site should also emphasize that study abroad opportunities are available to all students, further indicating the institutional commitment to international education. If information is easily accessible to students and their parents, they will be more likely to seek out additional information and counseling, and explore study abroad as a realistic option.

Third, begin student outreach early. Students should have access to information about study abroad opportunities before they enroll at the institution. By planting the seed before students arrive on campus, students will be more aware of the international opportunities available to them. By coupling early information with aggressive outreach once students are on campus, HBCUs may be able to substantially increase the number of students pursuing studies abroad.

Fourth, organize pre-departure orientations for all students travelling abroad, even those working with third-party providers. HBCU students face unique challenges when it comes to study abroad, and schools cannot rely on third-party providers to address issues such as racism during provider-run orientation sessions. Institutions must therefore ensure that students will be sufficiently prepared for the issues that may arise while they are overseas.

Fifth, fundraise. This is particularly important for private institutions, which cannot participate in the study abroad consortia established through state systems of higher education, and which do not receive consistent state funding. While it is understandable that cash-strapped institutions may be hesitant to let go of much-needed tuition dollars, fundraising for student scholarships and other study abroad support can help HBCUs begin to overcome the financial barriers that they and students face in the context of study abroad.

Finally, work together. History has shown that HBCUs can achieve great things when they combine forces and work toward a common goal. While this practice is not yet prevalent, both private and public institutions can pool their resources and work together to promote international education and study abroad for their students. Combined with other best practices, this approach will ultimately enable HBCUs to provide students with the skills that they need to succeed in our increasingly global economy.

Note

1. The author acknowledges that using the term "students of color" can be problematic, as it tends to aggregate many diverse groups into one umbrella category. However, for the purposes of this study and much of the existing research, challenges and trends have been consistent among the many groups of non-White students. Consequently, while keeping in mind the complications that can arise when this term is employed, the author has chosen to use "students of color" as shorthand for those who have been historically underserved and underrepresented throughout the history of study abroad.

References

Akomolafe, O. (2000). Africanizing HBCUs: Problems and prospects of international education in historically black institutions. *African Issues, 28*(1/2), 103–107.

Alabama A&M University (n.d.). *International programs.* Retrieved May 2, 2013 from http://aamu.abroadoffice.net/index.html.

Alamo Community Colleges (2013). *Study abroad.* Retrieved May 3, 2013 http://www.alamo.edu/international/study-abroad/.

Brux, J. M. & Fry, B. (2010). Multicultural students in study abroad: Their interests, their issues, and their constraints. *Journal of Studies in International Education, 14*(5), 508–527.

Burkart, B., Hexter, H., & Thompson, D. (2001). *Why TRIO students need to study abroad!* (N.T. Clearinghouse, Producer). Retrieved March 19, 2013 from http://www.pellinstitute.org/downloads/trio_clearinghouse-opportunity_outlookC.pdf.

Carter, H. M. (1991). Minority access to international education. In *Black students and overseas programs: Broadening the base of participation* (pp. 9–20). New York: Council on International Education Exchange.

Cole, J. B. (1991). Opening address of the 43rd international conference on educational exchange. In *Black students and overseas programs: Broadening the base of participation* (pp. 1–8). New York: Council on International Educational Exchange.

Comp, D. (2008). U.S. heritage-seeking students discover minority communities in Western Europe. *Journal of Studies in International Education, 12*(1), 29–37.

Council on International Educational Exchange (1988). *Educating for global competence: The report of the Advisory Council for International Educational Exchange.* New York: Council on International Educational Exchange.

——— (2013). *Terms & conditions: CIEE college study abroad programs.* Retrieved May 4, 2013 from https://www.ciee.org/study-abroad/terms-conditions/.

de Wit, H. (2002). *Internationalization of higher education in the United States of America and Europe.* Westport, CT: Greenwood Press.

Ganz, M. A. (1991). The Spelman experience: Encouraging and supporting minority students abroad. In *Black students and overseas programs: Broadening the base of participation* (pp. 29–34). New York: Council on International Educational Exchange.

——— (2013, May 4). Study abroad at Spelman College. S. E. Mullen, Interviewer.

Global Learning Semesters (2006–2013). *Abroad office.* Retrieved May 4, 2013 from http://abroadoffice.net/index.html.

Hinds Community College (2000–2012). *International studies.* Retrieved May 3, 2013 from http://www.hindscc.edu/departments/honors/international.aspx.

Institute of International Education (2012). *Profile of U.S. study abroad students, 2000/01–2010/11.* Retrieved March 19, 2013 http://www.iie.org/opendoors.

Institute of International Education (2013). *Benjamin A. Gilman International Scholarship Program | About the program.* Retrieved February 23, 2013 from http://www.iie.org/en/Programs/Gilman-Scholarship-Program/About-the-Program.

Jackson, M. J. (2005l). *Breaking the barriers to overseas study for students of color and minorities.* Retrieved March 19, 2013 from http://www.nxtbook.com/nxtbooks/naylor/IIEB0205/index.php?startid=16#/16.

Kilar, S. (2012, April 19). *Morgan State establishes student exchange program with Chinese university.* Retrieved May 1, 2013 from http://articles.baltimoresun.com/2012-04-19/news/bs-md-ci-morgan-state-china-20120419_1_student-exchange-morgan-state-university-program.

Metzler, J. (2002). Undergraduate study-abroad programs in Africa: Current issues. *African Issues, 30*(2), 50–56.

Morgan State University (2013a). *Center for global studies and exchange.* Retrieved April 4, 2013 from http://www.morgan.edu/administration/academic_affairs/center_for_global_studies.html.

——— (2013b). *Study abroad.* Retrieved May 1, 2013 from http://www.morgan.edu/administration/academic_affairs/center_for_global_studies/study_abroad.html.

——— (2013c). *The strategic plan for Morgan State University.* Retrieved May 1, 2013 from http://www.morgan.edu/Strategic_Plan.html.

N'gom, M. (2013, May 1). Study abroad at Morgan State University. S. E. Mullen, Interviewer.

Oakwood University (1996–2013). *Study abroad.* Retrieved May 3, 2013 from http://www.oakwood.edu/academics/study-abroad.

Perdreau, C. (2002). *Study abroad: A 21st century perspective: Building diversity into education abroad programs.* Retrieved March 19, 2013 from www.aifsfoundation.org/perdreau.htm.

Prairie View A&M University (2013). *Prairie View A&M University study abroad program.* Retrieved May 3, 2013 from http://www.pvamu.edu/PDFFiles/South%20Africa%20flyer%20%20-%20Revised%20Course%20Number%202012-4-12.pdf.

Robertson, L. (2010, September 2). *After 50 years, Spelman continues to cultivate global scholars.* Retrieved May 1, 2013 from http://www.insidespelman.com/?p=2104.

Sebeck, L. (2005). Underrepresented groups in study-abroad programs. *Journal of Student Affairs at New York University, 1*(5), 38–44.

Spelman College (2013a). *About the center.* Retrieved May 4, 2013 from http://www.spelman.edu/academics/gordon-zeto-center-for-global-education/about-the-center.

——— (2013b). *Study abroad destinations.* Retrieved May 4, 2013 from http://www.spelman.edu/academics/special-academic-programs-and-offerings/study-abroad/destinations-program.

——— (2013c). *Study abroad requirements.* Retrieved May 4, 2013 from http://www.spelman.edu/academics/special-academic-programs-and-offerings/study-abroad/requirements.

Universities News (2012, November 8). *Morgan among universities chosen for US-Brazil higher education partnership.* Retrieved May 2, 2013 from http://www.universitiesnews.com.previewdns.com/2012/11/08/morgan-among-universities-chosen-for-us-brazil-higher-education-partnership/.

University of the Virgin Islands (2008–2013). *Student exchange programs.* Retrieved May 3, 2013 from http://www.uvi.edu/sites/uvi/Pages/Counseling_Services-National_student_Exchange.aspx.

Walker, S., Bukenya, J. O., & Thomas, T. (2010). Examining students' perceptions of globalization and study abroad programs at HBCUs. *Southern Agricultural Economics Association Annual Meeting* (pp. 1–20). Orlando.

Xavier University of Louisiana (n.d.). *Center for intercultural and international programs.* Retrieved May 3, 2013 from http://xula.abroadoffice.net/index.html.

CHAPTER TEN

LGBT Centers on HBCU Campuses: Bowie State University

JOSEPH BARONE

It has been asserted that at Historically Black Campuses and Universities (HBCUs), lesbian, gay, bisexual, transgender (LGBT) students implicitly understand that being gay will not win allies, particularly as support services for such students are rarely made explicitly available (Harper & Gasman, 2008). Often LGBT groups are refused recognition due to quotas on new student groups. However, according to one source, "to evaluate the relevance of an LGBT student organization the same way one might a drill team or fashion club is outrageous. The LGBT identity of these students is not a hobby, but represents a part of their lives and directly impacts their ability to succeed academically. What I think is truly problematic is the fact that students are being forced to develop their own means of support in the first place" (Pritchard, 2007, p. 2).

The call for administrative support for LGBT students is inherent in the testimonies of graduates who call for professional guidance for students in need of help to manage converging minority identities. In the words of Pritchard: "The development and sustainment of an affirming and safe space for LGBT students is an institution's responsibility" (2007, p. 2).

This chapter aims to explore the development of LGBT initiatives in recent years and assess their strengths, particularly their ability to help students negotiate their racial and sexual identities and the crucial intersection of the two. In the wake of not only complaints but rising STD infections among African American youth and reportedly unfriendly campus climates for LGBT students of color, how are

HBCUs responding (if at all) and how are they measuring the success of their programs (Sutton et al., 2011; Harper & Gasman, 2008)?

In 2012, Bowie State University in Bowie, Maryland, founded the first LGBT center on a historically Black campus, the "Lesbian, Gay, Bisexual, Transgender, Queer, Intersex and Allies Resource Center." The Center is notable for its administrative support. The LGBTQIA Resource Center boasts two full-time staff members and a relatively robust programming effort in its first year. In addition to detailing the current state of LGBT awareness at HBCUs and discussing the importance of such growth initiatives on campus, this chapter analyzes the work at Bowie State University. Through interviews with facilitators and students who have worked with and used the Center, the chapter discusses the intersection of race and sexual identity as it applies to counseling and programming practice.

While scant research on the application of practices at LGBT centers on HBCU campuses exists, calls for such initiatives abound. Through the testimonies of LGBT students of color one understands that such centers are not only necessary at HBCUs, but perhaps even more necessary than at PWIs. Students report significant discouragement when they find a socially conservative campus perpetuated by religious traditions that inevitably obscure LGBT causes. These campuses are, at times, host to homophobic student bodies and strict administrators and faculty whose practices can marginalize the needs of diverse students in the name of standards and conformity. Antiquated, conservative rules and homophobia often block students from forming a united voice for gays on campus (Associated Press, 2007).

"I felt like I was the only gay person on campus—it seemed like nobody was really out," said a female student of her experience at Hampton University (Associated Press, 2007). Indeed, the creation of welcoming spaces for LGBT students on campuses has become a national trend, one that few HBCUs have followed. While student groups continue to attempt formation, administrator-led initiatives, like resource centers or programs for students exploring their sexual identity, are few and far between. Modeling their authorities, heterosexual students often follow suit, relegating invisible LGBT students to the sidelines (Harper & Gasman, 2008).

While this experience can manifest itself in student-led social justice initiatives, campuses can prove too conservative for such measures to take flight. At Hampton, a panel of students and faculty members denied a student-organized gay support group the charter it required to earn official status in 2001. More recently, a panel denied a second attempt at chartering SPEAK, Students Promoting Equal Action and Knowledge (Associated Press, 2007). While denying such groups an official status on campus does not necessarily indicate a student body's or administration's bias *against* LGBT initiatives, it does not encourage students hoping to make a difference for their peers or looking to explore emerging aspects of their identities. Even when students do take the initiative to create such groups, they are likely to be met with administrative resistance. At eight of twelve HBCU campuses, student participants reported being met with opposition upon trying to create student organizations for LGBT students. Students who were successful in developing a group felt it was ignored and unsupported by the University (Harper & Gasman, 2008). As Pritchard's (2007) call opined, the creation and facilitation of such centers and programming should be the responsibility of the administration, not students.

A student's personal negotiation of their identity in an HBCU without visible LGBT support systems is detailed in "Intercultural (mis)communication: Why would you 'out' me in class?" The student's testimonial cites research that outlines five key components of coming out: LGB activity involvement, development of attitudes toward LGB identity, comfort with that identity, number of disclosures of identity to others, and type of sexual identity (Rosario et al., 2001). Links are presented between psychological functioning, self-esteem, and sexual behavior. Frequency of unprotected sex, for instance, can increase when discovery and development of these dimensions are not facilitated. When sexual identity awareness and growth is administered by practitioners, students learn how to manage their converging identities in oppressive social climates and overcome internalized homophobia (Howard, 2012).

In this way, while HBCUs are considered safe spaces for racial minorities, issues of intersectionality for such students who also identify as lesbian, gay, or bisexual threaten to damage the coming out process on campuses often perceived as homophobic. Indeed, further testimony is invoked, which points to the strong Christian values of many HBCUs and their influence on campuses not particularly welcoming of homosexuality in various subtle ways (Howard, 2012).

While such values can be implicitly understood by students, explicit restrictions on sexual expression are present on some campuses in the form of written restrictions on sexual behavior. Harper and Gasman (2008) cite that at one HBCU, the policy defines sexual misconduct as "sexual intercourse, adultery, rape, sodomy and homosexual acts" (p. 10). Homosexuality is cited as misconduct in documents of other HBCUs as well. One student noted: "This campus is like the rest of

Black society. Black society is not accepting of gay culture. And so, they are definitely on the outskirts of this campus. They're not included" (Harper & Gasman, 2008, p. 10).

Discussing her comfort with peers yet pervasive fear of discrimination from those in power, Howard (2012) states: "I felt the need to conceal my sexual identity around faculty and staff members as I did not want to be discriminated against in any way by those that had the power to deny me a degree...I was even more aware of the image of the Black community as homophobic" (p. 124). Howard describes her choice to conceal her sexual identity during her graduate experience at an HBCU due to her inability to sense whether an environment was safe. Her academic career may have depended on it.

The differences of experience in varying communities can lead to incongruous approaches and understandings of sexual identity. These conflicts demonstrate the importance of a "safe space" for the discussion and exploration of LGBT identities, particularly in relation to one's racial identity. For instance Howard, a graduate student at an HBCU, found her classmate, "Jane," explicitly unaware of the management some students face in relation to their sexuality. Jane had attended a predominantly White institution where sexuality was less taboo and the LGB community was integrated in her college experience. Jane failed to consider the difference in these groups and inadvertently outed Howard in class, embarrassing Howard and leaving her afraid of losing status and advocacy from her academic mentors (Howard, 2012).

A communication gap between students and administrators at HBCUs is a common theme. Testimonies provide insight into the inconsistencies students face when developing their identities on campus as they navigate the differing rules among spaces that may or may not feel safe for them. Students report feeling subordinate and recognizing the need to stay in their "child's place" rather than start difficult conversations with those in power (Harper & Gasman, 2008). Students feel they have no agency in creating safe spaces for these conversations and the sense of conservatism is often perpetuated by vigilant authority figures.

Explaining her preconceptions of the unfriendly campus climate for LGB students, Howard states: "The strong Christian values within the HBCU experience gave me the perception that being open about my sexuality would yield negative reactions...incidences and stories I heard about the treatment of gay men and lesbians at the institution deterred me from coming out" (Howard, 2012, p.131). Though the number of gay and lesbian groups on campuses continually increases, participants sometimes face the consequences of joining or leading these ventures on a conservative campus. In some cases, the consequences are as extreme as death threats (Harper & Gasman, 2008). Some administrators blame the conservative religious roots of many HBCUs. Larry Curtis, Norfolk State University's vice president for student affairs, states: "You've got to recognize the history of HBCUs... most of them were founded by religious organizations" (Associated Press, 2007, p. 1). Norfolk State, however, is home to a relatively new student-formed gay-straight alliance. Reverend William Owens, HBCU graduate and leader of the Coalition of African-American Pastors, argues inclusion of gay students is in the hands of administrators, who can say "no" and not "'have to give a lot of reasons,'" particularly considering homosexuality can be seen as a threat to the traditional family values espoused by many Black students and HBCU leaders (Associated Press, 2007). Family values often contribute to the "underground" nature of LGBT students on historically Black campuses.

The "down low" culture of bisexual men, particularly in the African American community, who have sex with men or women and men, has been perpetuated by religious leaders who oppose gay marriage and combat the comparisons between civil rights and gay rights. Additionally, the trend of Black men who have sex with men on the "down low" has been invoked as potential cause for increased rates of HIV/AIDS in Black men and women (Associated Press, 2007). These happenings provide further motivation for the facilitation of campus conversations on sexual health as it relates to sexual identity. On HBCU campuses, men who have sex with men and women are less likely to self-identify themselves as gay than their nonstudent counterparts (Washington et al., 2009). LGBT resource centers, provide structure for conversations on these challenging identity concepts to occur.

Scholars have examined condom use at HBCUs and noted differences between men who have sex with women and men who have sex with men and women. The latter are less likely to always use condoms compared to men who have sex with women. By addressing the issues of Black LGBT students, practitioners can help students cope with homophobia from members of the church community, fear of family rejection, hiding same-sex sexual activity, and facing rising cases of HIV/AIDS. Historically Black colleges are pivotal in addressing these issues and affecting change (Washington et al., 2009).

Some schools have begun holding campus initiatives that combat the dangers that the lack of conversations based on sexual identity can create. Walter Kimbrough, president of Philander Smith College, remembers his disbelief upon discovering that Black teens comprise 68% of new AIDS cases and are more likely to contract STDs than their White and Hispanic counterparts. Additionally, a 2011 study of HIV awareness at HBCUs found that these campuses were integral to combating the disproportionate numbers of African American young adults affected by sexually transmitted diseases (Sutton et al., 2011). HBCUs are in a critical position to shape and promote sexual health understanding.

To take action, President Kimbrough borrowed an idea from Yale University, which launched "Sex Week" in 2002 to promote sexual health and facilitate discussions about sexuality on campus. Kimbrough invited experts on a range of topics to Philander Smith College's campus and catered the week to the interests of his student body, engaging in frank dialogue on STDs, AIDS, Christian dating, sexual harassment, and domestic abuse and offering free sexual health screenings. Kimbrough was aware of the controversy such an event might cause in the often-conservative community of Black higher education, but wrote that for him, "the controversy is allowing these dreadful statistics to continue to spiral out of control and not attempt to change behavior. Hopefully, the conversations this week will help begin to align beliefs with behavior" (Hawkins, 2011, p. 1).

In that vein, the National Black Leadership Commission on AIDS began partnering with HBCUs such as Bennett College in 2009 to promote HIV prevention with campus leaders (Hawkins, 2011). Initiatives promoting sexual health and facilitating conversations on sexual identity began the work that LGBT centers on HBCU campuses should ultimately house.

Spelman, another trailblazer in LGBT issues on HBCU campuses is on the forefront of promoting LGBT awareness in the African American community (Garcia, 2011). The institution hosted a conference of nine HBCUs to discuss issues of race, gender, and sexual orientation while acknowledging that the issues vary across the 105 HBCUs. Location, religious affiliation, and the presence of alumni mentors can drastically affect the experiences of LGBT students on HBCU campuses. Beverly Guy-Sheftall, a women's studies professor at Spelman asserts that while allowing students to form gay campus organizations, true change will come from administrators learning to facilitate open conversations and address LGBT issues and homophobia: "I think addressing LGBT issues is good for everyone on the campus. Not just LGBT students, but others who are being marginalized or even bullied" (Garcia, 2011, p. 2).

A study of 12 HBCU campuses showed participants reporting a lack of facilitated conversations by professional administrators and faculty. While gossip among students was rampant (with some participants reporting a significant culture of homosexuality on campus that goes unrecognized and ultimately constrains gay male students to the margins), acknowledgment of LGBT issues by university administrators was rare. In all 12 campuses studied, student organizations not only lacked acknowledgment, administrators resisted them (Harper & Gasman, 2008).

Through the analysis of interviews with 76 HBCU undergraduates and examination of documents from 103 schools, the conservatism on Black campuses was evident. The fearful perception students may hold of conservative faculty and administrators in relation to issues of sexuality and sexual orientation was particularly present. Detrimental sociocultural norms contribute to the struggles many students, especially Black males, face in college as they strive for academic and interpersonal success. For instance, respondents to a student survey in 2006 reported troubling perceptions of administrative treatment of gay males, and students witnessed discriminatory treatment of other students based on their sexual orientation and attributed it to the religious conservatism of their professors' beliefs (Harper & Gasman, 2008).

At Morehouse, an all-male HBCU with a significantly large gay community, history does not bode well for the outward expression of one's sexuality. In 2003, after a violent crime between two males (the aggressor perceived an unwanted sexual advance), Morehouse created a task force for diversity and tolerance to make recommendations to administrators. The chairman, Walter Earl Fluker, astutely pronounced that these initiatives would not only combat homophobia, but address "diversity issues that meet us at the intersection" (Petrosino, 2003, p. 1). Although efforts to combat homophobia in response to what was eventually deemed a hate crime at Morehouse were flawed (a questionnaire sent to alumni used implicitly negative language to assess the need for LGBT awareness on campus), the conversation that started was a crucial beginning (Petrosino, 2003). Dillard chaplain Gall Bowman later remarked, bolstering the language of Morehouse's Fluker, that the challenge lies in extending the community's commitment to civil rights to include gay rights: "It's astonishing that Black people don't see the parallel because we use the same language" (Petrosino, 2003, p. 2).

To fight perceptions of homophobia campuses must create an explicitly welcoming climate for LGBT students of color. It should not just be equally, but more explicit and accessible than the climate created at predominantly White institutions (PWIs). Howard (2012) suggests curriculum change, faculty training, and seminars to address issues of sexual identity and diversity. Instilling these practices and trainings makes the classroom an actively accepting environment for students managing multiple identities and beginning to develop the dimensions of their LGB identities (Howard, 2012).

Social structures impeding the development of LGBT students on HBCU campuses are a critical challenge for the current and emerging generations. More and more, students arrive on campus knowing their sexuality, not "experimenting" as they did in generations past. High school is quickly becoming the point of sexual awareness for many students. HBCUs, which may change more gradually than PWIs, have begun to face critical choices that may determine their survival. Brandon Braud, diversity manager for the Human Rights Campaign, has encouraged the development of student groups at over 20 schools through special programs, and more schools' administrations have begun plans to establish their own LGBT programming initiatives and centers, a sign of administrative support and advocacy of student engagement in issues of sexual and gender identity (Associated Press, 2007).

Testimonies find success by appealing not only to the human rights integrity of HBCUs, but to the pocketbooks of campus leaders as well. Indeed, HBCUs have little chance of moving into the twenty-first century without change in this direction, as expensive lawsuits could potentially leech funds while fewer students are drawn to seemingly conservative campus climates (Pritchard, 2007). With resources like the Human Rights Campaign at their disposal, it is now financially feasible for HBCUs to implement modern innovations and keep their campuses attractive to new generations of socially responsible students. As another alumnus points out, promoting the well-being of LGBT students of color on campus is not only an idealistic and economic concern. Black communities have much to gain from the nurturing of talents and skills of LGBT individuals on HBCU campuses and more to lose if these students are educated elsewhere. "Why not do everything possible to nurture the next generation of beneficial Black leadership from all positive and talented students?" (Brown, 2007, p. 1).

Approach

Harper and Gasman (2008) state, "Instead of pretending that LGBT students are not there educators and administrators at Black colleges should intentionally structure conversations and experiences that allow heterosexual and LGBT students to learn from their differences, challenge stereotypes and misunderstandings, and develop a mutually respective social code of conduct that extends beyond avoidance and segregated sexual grouping" (p. 14). With the existing research in mind, I examined a new LGBT center at Bowie State University, and its ability to address the void lamented above and to provide useful programming for LGBT students of color and their heterosexual peers. Through interviews with its charter director, Adrian Krishnasami, testimonials from students, and exploration of the success of its programs in the past year, I will explore how one university addresses issues of diversity and intersectionality on campus. In particular, I will evaluate how an LGBT center may combat the dynamics of coming out discrepancies between social groups, address students who are "passing," ameliorate the perceived homophobia from administrators, and manage the sexual well-being of students in early phases of their sexual identity development.

In the following sections, I will explore findings from oncampus interviews and observations in order to determine recommendations for the success of LGBT centers at other HBCU campuses. My discussion will focus on the implementation and degree of success of campus events associated with the new center, the student response to the center's involvement in campus life, and the history and purpose of the center's founding. Testimonials in this area were collected from the center's founder and director and four of its most involved students. In just a year of existence, data on the success of the center is limited. The testimonials provide qualitative insight, although specific to one institution that is important.

It is important to note the perspective of the researcher and the role this bias could play in this study's findings. I have no affiliation with HBCUs besides the interactions discussed. However, as a member and supporter of the LGBT community, I bring to this research a staunch belief in the value of gender and sexuality centers on campuses. This research assumes such support and, rather than focusing on justifying the existence of such initiatives, aims to provide insight as to how centers can be implemented and supported by HBCUs in an effort to provide guidance to students negotiating the development of multiple identities.

The Center at Bowie

Considering the vital role Bowie State's LGBTQIA Resource Center plays on campus and the attention it has garnered nationally, one would be surprised to know the tipping point that led to the first physical LGBT presence on an HBCU campus was the availability of free furniture.

Krishnasamy asserts that interest in the development of a center had been expressed to him as early as 2007, but the question of "where" stunted such efforts. It is important to note that administrators, not students, initiated such early talks. Although students established a campus group called "Eyes Wide Shut" to program for LGBT students and allies, the establishment of a physical center was the product of administrative support. In 2012, this support led to the creation of a center. Krishnasamy received a call from Bowie State's dean of the School of Education indicating the University of Maryland—College Park was in possession of some unwanted furniture from their LGBT center. Knowing there was administrative support for a Bowie State LGBT center, Krishnasamy gladly adopted the furniture and 400 books from the College Park campus.

At the same time, a floor of office spaces had recently been vacated on campus due to the construction of a new performing arts facility. Krishnasamy was able to secure two rooms to amass the donated books and furniture into an intimate, secure space for LGBT students on campus. Tucked away on the third floor of a large building, Krishnasamy cites the campus culture as necessitating the Center's development: "Being gay and visible is not invited" (Krishnasamy, personal communication, 2013). The director, who students lovingly call "Dr. Adrian," asserts that to combat this lack of inclusion, the Center opened to be a visible character of LGBT identity on campus, yet one that is facilitated and managed by professional staff members equipped to support the needs of students. Explaining the Center's success through administrative backers, he states "top-down initiative was needed...students are afraid to do that at an HBCU, they were meeting in visible spaces, there were threats" (Krishnasamy, personal communication, 2013). In this way, the origins of Bowie State's Center prove it takes a convergence of events, at this point, for such an initiative to take flight. Further, it shows the most important element in implementation might very well be faculty and staff support.

Echoing research previously cited on the conservative backgrounds of many HBCU students, Krishnasamy discussed the need for frank discussions on all vectors of diversity on HBCU campuses: "How do HBCUs define diversity? We fail to look at sexuality, don't want to include it in diversity...because the church is a major part of the Black family experience" (Krishnasamy, personal communication, 2013). To that end, the LGBTQIA Resource Center's plentiful inaugural programming efforts included multiple events focused on facilitating discussions that cleared misunderstandings on religion and sexuality that many students may have held.

Bowie State, a public university, is located between the liberal, metropolitan districts of Baltimore and Washington, DC. As such, the campus benefits from access to diverse area leaders of virtually every race, religion, and sexual identity. In the fall, as Question 6, Maryland's referendum to approve or reject same-sex marriage, headed to the polls, Krishnasamy used local resources to facilitate thoughtful, open debate. The Center sponsored a panel of leaders from various perspectives to discuss the implications of the referendum, including a lesbian minister supporting the approval of same-sex marriage, representatives from the Human Rights Campaign, and fundamentalist representatives. Although the event had only roughly 30 attendees, Krishnasamy remembers the strong reactions of those in the audience. Even his graduate students, he recalls, had never heard the message of marriage equality debated from all sides as the event allowed. Additionally, students had the opportunity to challenge preconceived notions and prejudices. For instance, some in attendance held the belief that if same-sex marriages legalized, every church would be required to administer them. The forum dispelled such myths and allowed students to view LGBT rights in alignment with civil rights (Krishnasamy, 2013).

As the Center invites conversation onto campus, Krishnasamy is able to hone its programming and explore what the focus of upcoming events should be. For instance, he has noticed a significant challenge with the Center's ability to cater to Black male students who may be passing or ignoring the development of their sexual identity. As an out gay man, Krishnasamy believes he may represent a threat to male students not ready to come out or discuss such developments with another gay man. As such, these students are more likely to seek out the guidance of one of Krishnasamy's female peers for counseling rather than using the Center (Krishnasamy, 2013).

The Center aims to become more accessible (a name change to the "Center for Sexual and Gender Diversities" is forthcoming) to all students. In this way, the Center might align itself with efforts like the "Black Male Initiative," conceived by the president, in nurturing the whole person to find success. Krishnasamy hopes to be in position to combat negative behavior patterns of coping that he has noticed in Black males on campus who are on the "DL," such as treating a male sexual partner terribly and not using campus resources to negotiate identity developments (Krishnasamy, 2013).

The Center has excelled in building relationships with valuable national partners. Donna Payne, a key representative from the Human Rights Campaign (HRC), gave a keynote address at the Resource

Center's opening in April 2012. The HRC has continued their support of Bowie State's LGBT initiatives by providing training to students from the Gay-Straight Alliance to administer HIV-testing. In its first year, the center has already hosted testing clinics and partnered with the Wellness Center to encourage sexual health (Krishnasamy, 2013).

Krishnasamy recalls the student leaders of Bowie State's Gay-Straight Alliance, a student-initiated club, having to hide on campus without a home space and legitimate administrative support. In the past year, however, the Center has absorbed the GSA and provided its students a comfortable, safe space for their weekly meetings and programming. The GSA, a group of about 20–30 core members, has taken to studying and socializing in the Resource Center as much as possible. The Center is off the beaten path, which for the GSA students imbues the space with privacy and safety, particularly for their weekly meetings. As a student organization, they are required to facilitate six or more events a semester, so Krishnasamy encourages them to partner with other organizations, like the Wellness Center or political student groups, to gain larger recognition on campus (Krishnasamy, 2013). The Center is able to maintain its privacy for curious and exploring students while promoting campus-wide awareness to those who may not seek out the Center or become a part of the GSA.

For student leaders of the GSA, a student group that recently changed its name from "Eyes Wide Shut" and was absorbed by the LGBTQIA Resource Center, the transition has provided tangible opportunities to grow their presence on campus. In her senior year, one student, Katherine, notes the broad changes that have occurred. Upon joining the GSA two years ago, this student took it upon herself to restructure the weekly meetings. In an effort to increase the organization's legitimacy and create a respectful environment for discussion and discourse, she issued a declaration on the Center's status as a safe space and outlined ground rules for the proceedings (Hockey, 2013).

Katherine, a White female who came to the GSA to support a friend as they explored their sexual identity, is proud of how students were able to come right into the group and grow it, but notes the Center's importance in their success. "It's really good for GSA to have a home" (Hockey, 2013). She, too, finds the remote location to be an advantage. The privacy it encourages allows those students who do seek out the Center to feel safe and not be shy. That being said, she also notes the campus' changing climate. When promoting the Question 6 forum on campus, she notes that almost all who stopped by were supportive, with only one student verbally badgering the students (Hockey, 2013). While one would hope for no such behavior, for a group in its first year of truly public programming supported by the Center, it seems an accomplishment.

Katherine sees her peers starting to change as the Center becomes more known and LGBT issues become less taboo. More and more of her peers are realizing they might know someone who is gay. The Center and the GSA have gained widespread campus recognition in just a year. The Black Male Initiative on campus, an effort to encourage success through development as a "whole person," is, in Katherine's opinion, a more conservative group on campus. So she was surprised when the GSA was given the "Change the World" award by this group of male students. Further, the group's advisor made an effort to assure her it was the students' idea, not any of their supervisors' (Hockey, 2013).

Ultimately, she is proud of her success on campus and in the GSA. "I found a role here. We've been recognized for what we've done and it has made it worthwhile" (Hockey, 2013). Indeed, though Katherine has few metrics to truly judge her and the group's success in its first year with the Center, she can attest to being part of a group that two years ago had no social media presence. Today, she is the proud administrator of a Facebook group for GSA, which counts over 100 students as members. Her peers frequent the Center to study and hang out, and, on average, 15–20 students attend GSA meetings on a weekly basis (Hockey, 2013). In a year of partnership with the Center, the visibility of LGBT students and issues on campus has increased considerably due to the students' passionate belief in their cause and administrative support in planning successful events.

While the Center has encouraged the GSA to be more relevant on campus and increased the physical presence of LGBT issues, students in the GSA find their own ways to adapt to the campus culture, oftentimes subverting expected norms. Like many student organizations, GSA holds annual elections for not only an executive leadership board, but "Mr. and Miss GSA." These students serve as a public representation of the GSA, attending all events and speaking on behalf of the organization. This tradition finds its roots in the pageantry present at many HBCUs, where representatives are chosen through competition rooted in typically gendered activities, and the GSA follows suit with the other student organizations on campus. However, contrary to those groups, the GSA's representatives do not need to be gender binary. Any student is invited to run for the positions and express their gender identity as they choose (Hockey, 2013).

The newest elected "Miss GSA" describes herself as the "most flaming hot lesbian on campus" (Appen, 2013). She ran for the position this year to combat others' opinions of gender norms (Appen, 2013). As a female who chooses to dress and represent herself more closely to "masculine" standards, her status as, essentially, the Homecoming Queen of GSA is a subversive, fun way for her to be involved with GSA and facilitate conversations of gender and sexuality on campus.

When GSA's current president, Jamale Stevenson, joined the group at the end of his freshman year, he was hesitant. He expected the group to be of solely gay men, perhaps like the petty, stereotypical representations he had seen on TV, all just "hooking up with each other like 'The Real World'" (Stevenson, 2013). When a friend took him to a meeting he appreciated the conversations that were taking place. He ran for vice president and enjoyed the experience of being a leader. Contrary to his expectations, it was a nurturing environment that was supportive, not destructive, of gay culture. He found his inclusion in the group beginning to help him grow his self-esteem as LGBT identities were represented to campus in a positive way (Stevenson, 2013).

A junior communications major, Jamale has begun to understand the issues the Bowie State campus faces. For instance, echoing Krishnasamy's sentiments, he laments the prominent "DL" culture among Black men on campus. "It is important to be masculine in Black male culture...Hip Hop, being a dominant provider—it all contributes. It is the same with ultrafemininity for Black females" (Stevenson, 2013).

To that end, Jamale's future plans are inspired by his involvement in the GSA. He hopes to produce films that combat negative perceptions of the Black gay identity and show the variety of experiences and lifestyles present within his culture. Further, he hopes to encourage others to come out, rather than living on the "DL," and fight the notion that all Black gay men have AIDS. The encouragement his campus involvements have given him is apparent: "At this point, I am a prominent leader. Whether you agree or not, I am going to do this kind of advocacy work. I cannot tell you why I was not afraid to do it...I just did it" (Stevenson, 2013).

In its first year, the Center held 14 campus-wide events providing a variety of much-needed discourse for the student body. Events ranged from partnerships with the Wellness Center to combat domestic violence and bullying to a "Sex in the Dark" party where students have questions answered they might be ashamed to ask in public. Clergy for Marriage Equality were invited to discuss same-sex marriage, faith, and justice and HIV testing was administered by trained students in the Center's new space. Though, in Krishnasamy's opinion, student attendance was middling, in his words, "we're still going to have them...I care about the safety of students and mentoring them, without it they are prevented from success" (Krishnasamy, 2013). As with any new initiative it takes time to gain traction and administrators are likely to be more skeptical than their idealistic students. What is evident after the first year of programming and partnership with the GSA, however, is that involved students are continually more confident in their ability to make change with their peers and their self-esteem as they explore their identities.

Conclusion

The case at Bowie State represents a success on many counts. There is a thriving LGBT student community that is taking advantage of the Center. Campus offices have cooperated in providing collaborative programming to help get the Center's name out there as a visible character of LGBT issues on campus. The students attending the events offered by the Center, though not attending in droves, are passionate and committed to the cause. They are learning the appropriate language to discuss LGBT issues and they are finding allies in each other. Indeed, on a brisk morning on campus, one merely needs to stand with two of the GSA's prominent student leaders to be greeted by no fewer than five more members of their thriving community.

As a benchmark for other universities, one must consider that Bowie State has a great deal of advantages. It is located in a suburb between two of America's most liberal metropolitan communities. It is a state school and, as such, maintains relationships with other well-resourced institutions and PWIs like University of Maryland. These relationships, in this example, can, in a roundabout way, initiate rapid change. Finally, Bowie State has a faculty member and administrators willing and excited to support the development of LGBT initiatives on campus.

Given the literature and the example of Bowie State, this final point seems most important. Even without a physical space or in a more conservative environment, a faculty member like Krishnasamy who is willing to have events no matter what and endure comments from peer staff members like "Oh, I have a friend like 'that'" (Krishnasamy, 2013) seems to be the indicator of whether an HBCU can successfully establish a Center. Students, as shown, will convene no matter what. However, their position as a legitimate community on campus requires the advocacy of a staff member.

To this end, it seems the growth of support for LGBT students on HBCU campuses lies in the hands of brave faculty and staff willing to advise students and support what may be unpopular initiatives on campus. And while such administrators might feel they have the most to lose in espousing taboo topics on campuses that are either conservative or just slow to acknowledge the presence of such students, the students themselves surely have more at stake.

References

Appen, S. (April 25, 2013). Personal interview.
Brown, C. (2007). Don't relegate LGBT people to the margins. *Diverse: Issues in Higher Education, 24*(10), 4.
Harper, S. R. & Gasman, M. (2008). Consequences of conservatism: Black male undergraduates and the politics of historically black colleges and universities. *Journal Of Negro Education, 77*(4), 336–351.
Hawkins, B. (2011). Philander Smith brings Ivy League "sex week" to HBCU. *Diverse: Issues In Higher Education, 27*(28), 9.
Hockey, K. (April 25, 2013). Personal interview.
Howard, S. (2012). Intercultural (mis)communication: Why would you "out" me in class? *Sexuality & Culture, 16*(2), 118–133.
Garcia, M. (2011). New rules, old institutions. *Advocate*, (1051), 12.
Krishnasamy, A. (April 25, 2013). Personal interview.
Petrosino, F. J. (2003). HBCUs tackle homophobia with diversity initiatives. *Crisis (15591573), 110*(4), 10.
Pritchard, E. (2007). HBCUs have a responsibility to LGBT students. *Diverse: Issues in Higher Education, 24*(7), 23.
Rosario, M., Hunter, J., Maguen, S., Gwadz, M., & Smith, R. (2001). The coming-out process and its adaptational and health-related associations among gay, lesbian, and bisexual youths: Stipulation and exploration of a model. *American Journal of Community Psychology, 29*(1), 113–160.
Stevenson, J. (April 25, 2013). Personal interview.
Sutton, M. Y., Hardnett, F. P., Wright, P., Wahi, S., Pathak, S., Warren-Jeanpiere, L., & Jones, S. (2011). HIV/AIDS knowledge scores and perceptions of risk among African American students attending historically black colleges and universities. *Public Health Reports, 126*(5), 653–663.
Washington, T., Wang, Y., & Browne, D. (2009). Difference in condom use among sexually active males at historically black colleges and universities. *Journal of American College Health, 57*(4), 411–418.

CHAPTER ELEVEN

Leveraging Honors Programs at HBCUs

CHANNING JOHNSON AND
TYREE WILLIAMS

Honors Programs provide colleges and universities with a way to recruit and retain academically successful students as well as foster the continued academic success of student members. This chapter focuses on how historically Black colleges and universities (HBCUs) can leverage honors programs to attain high-achieving students. In order to develop sound recommendations on how this can be accomplished, we conducted a review to determine the ways in which HBCUs were already doing so. Unfortunately, we soon discovered that there is a dearth of research in general on high-performing Black students, academically successful Black students in honors programs, and even less that focus specifically on Black students who are a part of honors programs at HBCUs. We decided that our research would be expanded to include research on honors programs in general, in order to present a sound argument for the leveraging power of honors programs at HBCUs.

In addition to the literature review, we also conducted an assessment of two HBCUs—Cheyney University of Pennsylvania and Tougaloo College—in order to determine how they were using their honors programs to recruit and retain high-achieving students. These case studies will show firsthand the success of the honors programs on these campuses, the staying power of these honors programs, and ultimately, provide insight into how HBCUs can leverage honors programs to recruit and obtain high-achieving students.

Before proceeding, it should be noted that while we are advocating for the use of honors programs as recruitment and retention tools for

HBCUs, for those that do not currently have existing programs, we are not suggesting that programs should be haphazardly organized just to be able to say that one exists.

What Is an Honors Program?

In order to determine the ways in which honors programs can be used by HBCUs to recruit and retain high-performing students, it is important to get a better understanding of what an honors program is, who an honors student is, and the ways in which Honors programs positively impact students. Honors programs, much like the institutions where they are found, are not uniform. They cannot be neatly categorized into a single box. According to Cosgrove (2004), all honors programs exist in the form of either university-wide honors (general honors), departmental honors (by area of concentration/major), and honors colleges. That being said, all honors programs do have common goals and objectives. Honors programs set as a goal to meet the needs of students shown to be academically successful, by providing an environment and curriculum that serves to nurture and promote the academic talent of said students (Schuman, 1999).

Honors programs attempt to continuously provide their students with opportunities to further strengthen their academic abilities. The common benefits of participation in honors programs include opportunities to participate in honors specific curriculum, study abroad options, designated living spaces for honors students, and scholarships ranging from partial to full to cover costs of tuition, fees, books, housing, and other amenities (Schuman, 1999).

Who Are Honors Students?

Colleges and universities increasingly use their resources to attract students who are labeled as "exceptionally gifted" college students (Rinn & Plucker, 2004). Although the goals of recruiting academically talented students differ across university and college campuses, there seems to be a consensus that these students will enhance the intellectual atmosphere of the college or university and set it apart from other institutions (Rinn & Plucker, 2004).

Just as the definition of an honors program changes depending upon the institution; so does the "definition" of an honors student and how they are selected for their respective program. The typical standards for how students are selected for membership in honors programs are the use of SAT scores and high school GPAs. Some programs will allow students to transfer into the program after their first year at an institution if it is determined that they have met or surpassed the set requirements to do so (Freyman, 2005).

Why Are Honors Programs Important?

As discussed earlier, honors programs are designed to serve a population of students who come with high expectations with regard to the academic rigor and resources that will allow them to continue to flourish academically. Honors programs allow colleges and universities to more effectively compete against other institutions for highly coveted students. However, there are specific traits that further underscore the importance of honors programs and why they are beneficial to students and institutions of higher education.

The biggest benefit associated with the presence of an honors program at an institution is the way in which it can influence recruitment and retention. Top tier institutions heavily recruit students with high GPAs and SAT scores. Many schools are unable to do anything to drastically alter their appeal to prospective students, especially those students who have earned higher GPAs and SAT scores. One way these institutions can increase their level of competitiveness is through creating and maintaining strong honors programs (Seifert et al., 2007). Honors programs often include components that influence college choice decisions such as scholarships, co-curricular programs, as well as programs that stimulate the cultural and intellectual needs of students (Schuman, 1999).

Currently, there are a number of studies that discuss the rates of retention for students participating in honors programs. Slavin, Coladarci, and Pratt (2008) conducted a study to determine if student participation in an honors program was related to retention and graduation rates. This study focused on a comparison between students at the University of Maine; the student groups studied were students in the honors program and students who were not, and followed the students throughout four years of study. The findings showed that the most significant difference in retention between the two groups occurred after the completion of the first year of study, with students in the honors program having a higher retention rate (94%) than non-honors peers (81%). At the end of the four years, Slavin et al. (2008) did find that honors students had a higher graduation rate (64%) than their non-honor peers (4%).

Another study that sought to determine the impact of honors programs on undergraduate academic performance, retention, and graduation (Cosgrove, 2004) found that among their participants (high ability but non-honors, partial honors, and honors completers) selected from the Pennsylvania State System of Higher Education (PASSHE), the group with the highest graduation and retention rates were honors completers, with 77% of members from this group completing their course of study in four years or less compared to 61% (partial honors) and 57% (high-ability students). Even among students who did not maintain membership in the honors program throughout their matriculation, it was found that those who participated at least in the honors programs (partial-honors) had a higher five-year retention rate with only 18% of students in this group withdrawing before graduation compared to 24% of high-achieving students.

Ultimately, Schuman (1999) reports that comparatively, honor programs have been found to be more effective with regard to student retention. This means that while institutions may seek out "ideal" candidates for admission based upon their preferred criteria, students who enroll as honors students as opposed to general admits are more likely to complete their course of study and earn a degree from the institution. Schuman (1999) speculates that the offerings through the honors programs (opportunities to conduct research, study abroad, etc.) motivate students to persist.

Aside from recruitment and retention benefits, honors programs have also been linked to other areas that impact students positively. Seifert et al. (2007) found that students who were members of honors programs reported that they experienced higher levels of satisfaction with positive interactions with peers (course specific "studying"), academic involvement, number of assigned readings, instructor feedback, skill and clarity, and use of high-order questioning techniques. Seifert et al. (2007) also reported that according to their study, honors programs enhanced the level of cognitive growth (especially for math and critical thinking) during the first year of college as a result of a more challenging and academically rigorous curriculum. The mere existence of honors programs have been shown to also provide benefits to students who are not members of honors programs (Seifert et al., 2007).

Honors Program at HBCUs

For HBCUs, securing academically talented students is important for the overall success of institutions. Honors programs are one way in which these students can be recruited. While there is not much literature that focuses on honors programs at HBCUs specifically (Davis & Montgomery, 2011), it is interesting to note that according to Schumann (1999) they are home to some of the largest and most successful honors programs in the country.

HBCUs are, for the most part, open access institutions that pride themselves on providing opportunities, for almost any student that wishes to take advantage, to enroll. As a result of these open enrollment policies, many students are admitted who are underprepared for the academic challenges of college, with lower high school GPAs and SAT scores. This has further perpetuated the myth that HBCUs are inferior to Predominantly White Institutions (PWIs). These issues can be addressed through the strategic use of honors programs to enroll higher performing students.

In addition to the benefits discussed earlier in this chapter, HBCUs are able to capitalize on honors programs in ways that shape long-term academic success (Davis & Montgomery, 2011). HBCUs have a long history of producing leaders in various fields. Davis and Montgomery (2011) reflect this in their findings with leadership development ranked as the top strength on HBCU campuses, followed by mentoring and debate teams.

Other values of importance that that were ranked, which are nurtured and honed through honors program participation, include critical thinking skills, academic/intellectual excellence, and service learning (Davis & Montgomery, 2011). Davis and Montgomery (2011) also found 30% of respondents indicated that their institutions had an honors specific curriculum and about 80% of respondents reported that honors students were required to complete an honors thesis or project.

Providing scholarships is crucial for the recruitment and retention of students at HBCUs (Davis & Montgomery, 2011). With increased tuitions and decreased state/federal funding, loans are becoming a major, if not primary, funding source for students. In 2005–2006, 51% of financial aid was in the form of a federal loan, with approximately 5.4 million undergraduate students receiving a subsidized Stafford loan (Perna, 2004). This shift in funding sources can be detrimental for minority students who are very sensitive to borrowing, and are more inclined to make the decision of if and/or where to attend college based upon institution price points and necessity of borrowing to enroll (Perna, 2004). This is an important factor of honors programs at HBCUs, as the scholarships they provide can directly impact enrollment and retention rates.

The nurturing environment of HBCUs for students is routinely cited as one of the major benefits of enrollment in these institutions. This is also true for the honors programs on their campuses (Mitchell, 2002). Mitchell finds that honors programs at HBCUs allow students to improve their self-development, improve their leadership skills, and increase their levels of self-worth. Self-worth is very important for academically successful students attending HBCUs. For this group of students, it is likely that over the course of their lifetimes being seen as academically successful may not have always been viewed as a positive among their peer group (Fries-Britt, 2004). Honors programs have the ability to counteract the potential "negative" associations of being academically successful, by surrounding students with others that share common interests and goals, specifically pertaining to academic achievement.

Among other benefits associated with enrollment in honors programs at HBCUs, Mitchell (2002) reports that honors students are able to develop close bonds and have close contact with faculty on campus, allowing them to participate in research that interests them and take part in study abroad opportunities. Another major draw of participation in honors programs at HBCUs is the ability to attend conferences for honors students (The National Collegiate Honors conference and the National African American Association Honors program conference, Mitchell, 2002), which give students a chance to present independent research, expand social and professional networks, and be exposed to new ideas and concepts that are presented (Mitchell, 2002).

High-Achieving African American Students

While it is important for HBCUs to recruit and attain high-achieving students, it is equally important for them to note the characteristics of these high-achieving African American students. While there is a plethora of research on African American students who have an intense academic need, there is a dearth of research that focuses on high-achieving African American students in higher education (Fries-Britt, 1998; Griffin, 2006). The small quantity of research that does exist tends to focus on the challenges that these students face being academically gifted African Americans PWIs (Fries-Britt, 1988) or their motivation for doing well academically (Griffin, 2006).

There are many academically gifted African Americans who are accepted to and attend PWIs (Fries-Britt, 1998; Griffin, 2006). While this is something to be celebrated, African American gifted students at PWIs can often feel isolated (Fries-Britt, 1998). This isolation not only stems from being a part of the minority at these institutions, but also from members of their own culture groups who can often ostracize these students (Fries-Britt, 1998). However, Fries-Britt (1998) illustrates that students who participated in the Meyerhoff Program, an honors programs designed for African American students at the University of Maryland, Baltimore County, did not experience this isolation. Instead they felt that being around other high-achieving Blacks helped them establish networks and removed feelings of isolation. Students also reported that it made them feel good to see other African Americans succeed academically, because during high school it was difficult to find other African American students who were also gifted (Fries-Britt, 1998).

These same reasons also influence high-achieving African American students' decisions to attend HBCUs. Freeman and Thomas (2002) show that African American students who attend HBCUs made their decision based on academic reputation, specialized educational programs (which could include honors programs), financial assistance, and low tuition. It would not be cumbersome for HBCUs to capitalize on these reasons, especially since honors programs at many HBCUs showcase high academic achievement, specialized programs, as well as full tuition support and sometimes stipends for other educational experience. In addition to monetary support, high-achieving African Americans have the chance to associate with and connect with other African Americans who are academically gifted. Furthermore, studying at a PWI can make one feel as though there is a small percentage of African American achievers, while studying with a critical mass of African American high achievers can provide "these students with a new awareness and esteem for the intellectual talents of blacks" (Fries-Britt, 1998, p. 563). Attending an HBCU can alter the isolation many African Americans feel at PWIs.

Working with other African American students may also cause students to work harder. Unlike PWIs, HBCUs tend not to aim to create a competitive environment. Instead, the HBCU abounds with a supportive atmosphere. This type of environment nurtures the student while pushing them to be the best. It is for these reasons that many high-achieving African American students decide to attend HBCUs.

Creating an Honors Program

Any HBCU that has or plans to develop an honors program should determine the likelihood of success, and do all that is necessary to ensure this becomes a reality. Before deciding whether an honors program should or could be used for recruitment and retention purposes, there should be both internal and external assessments done to identify the quality of the program; determine if the institution has the capability of dedicating resources to operate the program; the benefits to both students and the institution; and the purpose of the program. General information on the assessment of honors programs can be found in Otero and Spurrier's (2005) *Assessing and evaluating Honors programs and Honors colleges: A practical handbook.*

Otero and Spurrier's handbook provides information on ways in which the administrators of honors programs can evaluate their programs, so that they might identify methods for strengthening current practices and policies or build new ones that would be more useful. This handbook is useful because it acknowledges the wide diversity that exists in the operations of honors programs and colleges across the country. Some of the most useful tools in the handbook are those that center on internal self-assessments and external assessments by a third party.

These assessments are important because they help to show if programs are operating according to a sound plan, that they have a clear mission and well-established objectives, and that benchmarks are in place to determine that these objectives are being met. This is of importance when it comes to issues surrounding funding. Stakeholders want to know that the money being dedicated to these programs is being put to good use (Otero & Spurrier, 2005). The government especially is interested in being able to assess the operations and successes of honors programs. As state and federal appropriations are harder to come by with dwindling state budgets, there are more than 20 states that require institutions of higher education to perform assessments to ensure that set standards are being met (Otero & Spurrier, 2005).

Methodology

The research in this chapter was analyzed using the case study method (Yin, 2003). "A case study is an empirical inquiry that investigates a contemporary phenomenon within real-life context, especially when the boundaries between phenomenon and context are not clearly evident" (p. 13). The case study method allowed us to contribute to the expanding knowledge on honors programs, and honors programs at HBCUs in particular. We used the illustrative case study in this analysis (U.S. General Accounting Office, *Case study evaluations*, 1990). Illustrative case study makes familiar what is typically unfamiliar.

The type of case study method used in this analysis is a holistic multiple or collective case study model (Yin, 2003; Baxter & Jack, 2008). In this model we conducted two separate case studies and then used them to speak to or inform a single larger contextual issue. This model allowed us to analyze two distinct honors programs on two HBCUs campuses within the larger context of HBCU honors programs. Using this method we were able to make comparisons and discoveries about each program that ultimately affect and speak to the larger phenomenon of HBCU honors programs.

The units of analysis used in this case study are two HBCU honors programs housed at Cheyney University of Pennsylvania and Tougaloo College. These two programs were chosen because of our affiliation with the two programs during our undergraduate matriculation, and because their differences (i.e., one is public, the other is private; one is a university, the other is a college, etc.) and similarities (they both serve undergraduate populations that number under 2,000 students). According to Yin, when using the case study method one must employ different sources of evidence to contribute to the analysis of the case (2000, p. 82). For this analysis the researchers used documentation (in the forms of books and other publications), archival records (in the form of newspaper articles), interviews with the current deans of the programs, and participant observation (in the form of the researchers participating within these honors programs). The data from each separate case study was converged to provide an accurate and holistic view of honors programs at HBCUs. Developing case descriptions of each honors program and using those descriptions to inform the literature on HBCU honors programs was the primary form of analysis for these case studies. We analyzed the case studies by identifying patterns and regularities within each case and assessing the importance of these findings (Yin, 2003).

Keystone Honors Academy, Cheyney University

The Keystone Honors Academy is the honors program of Cheyney University. The program was implemented in the fall of 1999, and was developed as a result of a lawsuit initiated on behalf of Cheyney University by a private citizen against the state of Pennsylvania. The lawsuit was initiated because the citizen felt that Cheyney was not receiving adequate state funding as compared to the other state schools within the Pennsylvania State System of Higher Education (PASSHE). This disparity eventually led to the involvement of the Office of Civil Rights, which argued on Cheyney's behalf. The result was an agreement between the state and Cheyney. The state agreed they would provide funding, which would be used to renovate facilities on campus, develop university infrastructure, and fund academic programs. This funding for academic programs led to the creation of the Keystone Honors Academy.

Then-president Clinton Pettus worked on developing the terms of the agreement with the two parties, eventually agreeing on the foundation for what would eventually become the University's centerpiece academic program: the Keystone Honors Academy. The agreement stipulated that part of the goal of the honors academy would be to attract high-achieving students, and provide them with an honors experience that would ultimately contribute to the overall quality of the institution. Expectations were that Keystone Honors Academy student performance would positively influence institutional outcomes including graduation and retention rates.

To ensure that this initiative would be successful, the state allocated $2 million dollars a year for the operation of the honors program. Among the rationale used by the state to provide Cheyney with this funding was that the support would educate and strengthen the future Pennsylvania work force. As a result of this, the recipients of the Keystone Honors Scholarship would have to commit to a year for year service agreement, where for every year funded, they would agree to work a year within the state of Pennsylvania. From the year 2000 up until 2010, Cheyney received the full $2 million a year. During the early years of the program, the full $2 million was not being used due to low recruitment and membership in the honors academy. A surplus began to build. In 2010, the state reabsorbed the balance that had accrued over time and the appropriation decreased to $1.5 million.

In 2011, after the election of Governor Tom Corbett, budgets were cut for a large number of academic programs across the state, which included a 100% cut of Keystone Honors Academy funding. Due to pressure placed on the governor using the data on the outcomes of the honors program, funding was returned, but at the current rate of $1.5 million.

Mission and Objectives

The Keystone Honors program was designed to be Cheyney University's "centerpiece program" for increasing the overall academic profile of the school. The initial intent was to develop this program by inducting a small group of high-achieving, academically successful students and ultimately expanding to the broader reaches of the institution. This idea was met with some push back as some viewed it to be counter to the interpretation of Cheyney's history and mission of being an institution of access and opportunity. Current dean of the Keystone Honors Academy, Tara Kent, shares that she feels this issue may be faced by other honors programs at HBCUs because of the debate surrounding access and perceived elitism of honors programs. Kent expressed sentiments that there is a misperception that these programs are giving student participants access to services and programs that non-honors students do not have. There is also a misperception that as higher-performing students, they are not the most in need. Kent feels that ultimately, as institutions continue to struggle with low retention and graduation rates, they will realize that sometimes shifting the mission and purpose of the institution is a way to address these problems. She feels that honors program at HBCUs and Cheyney, in particular, through a broad array of services in professional development, cultural experiences, and an enhanced curriculum can stay true to their mission of open access while being able to design strategies to bring in higher-achieving students.

Elitism and Preferential Treatment

Overall, as part of the bigger dynamic tension, there is an acknowledgment that the Keystone Honors Academy is something that is separate from the broader campus community. Through participation in the program, students to some degree do have more resources and support available. This is a positive for Cheyney, especially as it relates to recruitment of future students. The honors program is fairly established at Cheyney, so when prospective students are considering Cheyney, the Honors Academy is one of the things at which they are looking. Prospective students know that when they apply to Cheyney, that even if not admitted at time of initial application, they can still qualify for admission into the Academy after their first year of study.

Membership into the honors program is used as incentive and motivation for all students at the university. Many serious students are applying for entry into the program after their freshman year. At the very least students are aware that the honors program is an option for them. Upon initial launch of the program, admission was only allowed for incoming first year students or students transferring in from other institutions. This expansion of opportunities for admission to current students was one of the ways in which the school sought to address claims of elitism or unfair preferential treatment, creating a democratic way of gaining entry that is based upon merit and is the student's responsibility.

Programmatic Offerings

The biggest incentive of the Keystone Honors Academy is the Keystone scholarship. The Keystone scholarship is a full scholarship that covers full cost to attend, fees, books, tuition, laptops, and a commuter stipend for commuter students. Another resource available to the honors students is the living learning center that provides a welcoming space where honors students can work and have social gatherings. It should be acknowledged that the other dorms have the space, and housing and residential life has funding, to provide similar amenities. This was partially the catalyst leading to the development of the University College, a newer initiative on campus that operates as a parallel program for non-honors students at Cheyney.

In addition, to the scholarship and living learning community, the programs that are highly sought out by Honors Academy members are the summer study abroad opportunities. These opportunities allow students to work and take classes fully funded by Keystone. Last, the dean of the Keystone Honors Academy regularly sponsors programs whereby guest speakers are brought in to speak on campus. While these events are organized under the Keystone umbrella, they are open to other students, alumni, and outside members of the community. Yet, because this program is operated by Keystone, it is perceived to be separate and exclusively for honors students.

Successes and How It Is Being Leveraged by Cheyney University

According to Tara Kent, dean of the Keystone Honors Academy, the program is considered to be one of the strongest honors programs in the Pennsylvania State System of Higher Education by the chancellor and the board of governors. One of the major differentiators of the Keystone Honors program from the other honors programs at the schools in the state system is the emphasis on more than just the honors curriculum. At Cheyney, the honors program is more encompassing, with programs designed to engage students' time at the school, including mandated honors courses, additional academic and social programming, designated living learning spaces, internships/fellowships/other professional preparation, preparation for graduate/doctoral level programs, and other ways by which student needs are identified, met, and supported.

Entry into the Keystone Honors Academy is based primarily upon high school GPA and SAT scores, with students needing a 3.0 GPA and at least a 1,000 SAT score to gain admission into the program. Students not admitted into the Academy during their first semester have the option to transfer into the program, if they meet certain criteria and there are available slots and funding to cover them. While transferring in is an option, it is very competitive with only a few slots available for transfer students. Those usually successful in gaining entry carry a 4.0 GPA in college, are active in campus extracurricular activities, and hold leadership positions on campus. This is one of the main ways through which Cheyney leverages the honors program. Cheyney uses the program to recruit students who have an established record of success and involvement, which in turn results in a higher likelihood of continued academic excellence and increased rates of retention and graduation.

In order to recruit students, Cheyney has hired a recruiter who specifically focuses on recruiting honors students. The recruiter develops marketing campaigns, branding, and determines the best way to use images and logos and where they would be most effectively placed. There are also strategies developed using data from lists purchased from the College Board. Using this information, prospective students that qualify are invited to attend on campus events or events organized in their communities. Typically, 90% of students that come to the on-campus event are accepted. At least 50% of students that are offered admission enroll with the scholarship being the biggest incentive. While honors students are typically higher-achieving students than the general student population on Cheyney's campus, they are not necessarily the highest-performing students on a national scale; in fact the students typically admitted into the Keystone Honors Academy are generally on par with national averages for high school graduates in terms of GPAs and SAT scores.

While the numbers for entering honors students mirror the national averages for graduating high school seniors nationally, by the time these students graduate, they are largely exceeding their peers in every category. Looking at six year graduation statistics, the Cheyney University Keystone Honors Academy has a 72% graduation rate, nationally the six year graduation rate is approximately 58% for all students, 38% of African American students complete their course of study in the same time frame, while the rates for HBCUs overall sits around 33%. Most important for the Keystone Honors Academy is the comparison to the overall student population at Cheyney University. Currently, Cheyney students have a six year completion rate of 22%, which essentially means that while seven out of ten students enrolled in the honors program graduate in six years or less, only two in ten students graduate from the university at large.

Due to the success of the honors program at Cheyney, the university has decided to develop a program that would mirror the honors program, but that is open to all students at the school. This program, the University College, was intended for the broader campus community in order to better identify and address the needs of students, so that they too will reach higher levels of retention and graduation. The University College is still a relatively new program, so it is hard to say how, or if, it is in fact contributing to higher retention and graduation rates. Some of the differences between the two programs are the Keystone Honors Academy has lesser students and only one administrator, while the University College works with more students and a larger staff. The selection process for the University College happens after students are enrolled and does not provide scholarships.

Tougaloo College Honors Program

The Tougaloo College Honors program was founded in 2004. Current president Beverly Wade Hogan, and then-provost, Corrine Anderson implemented the program to create an environment that supports, promotes, and enhances the academic excellence of high-achieving students who are enrolled at Tougaloo College. In its initial stages, Tougaloo College received a grant from the Andrew W. Mellon Foundation for $100,000 to aid in developing the honors program. The college then received $230,000 from the Mellon foundation in 2004 in order to implement the program. Since its initial funding in 2004, the honors program received two grants of $500,000 from the Mellon foundation in 2008 and 2010 to support the continuation of the honors program.

Mission and Objectives

The honors program at Tougaloo College was developed for high-achieving students who wanted a rigorous academic college experience, while maintaining the academic prowess for which the institution was past noted. It was also created to provide a superior academic environment in a supporting and accepting space.

The program grooms its participants to be leading scholars, to attend highly ranked graduate school programs, and to receive graduate degrees in a variety of fields. The program strives to prepare African American students to succeed, by enhancing their critical thinking skills, research capability, and most importantly their confidence. In doing this, the honors program at Tougaloo College hopes to create a network of students and alumni that contribute to the ongoing success of the program.

Programmatic Offerings

Participants in the Tougaloo College Honors program are usually recipients of the college's Presidential Scholarship Award. The Presidential Scholarship is broken down into two subgroups; Presidential I scholars and Presidential II scholars. These scholarships offer full tuition coverage, room and board, and a $300 book stipend to students. If students are selected as a Presidential I scholar, they also receive a laptop as an incentive to attend the college.

Students in the Honors program have the opportunity for academic enhancement through two very specific programs designed to challenge students, as well as nurture them in academically supportive environments. The first program consists of academic coursework, specially designed for high-achieving students. Each honors student is required to take one honors course per semester with the other students in their cohort. Students are also required to participate in the Council of Undergraduate Research in partnership with Mississippi College. In this program, students are required to submit and present original research at an annual academic symposium.

The program also offers students the opportunity to engage in traveling and learning experiences. During Spring Break students have the opportunity to travel within the United States to a destination that offers insight into different experiences and cultures. During summer vacation, students in the Honors program travel abroad to gain firsthand knowledge of different countries and cultures. The costs of these trips are greatly subsidized by the honors programs, and students only pay a small amount.

Program Successes

The honors program at Tougaloo College is very successful. Each year it takes in about 20–30 freshmen and these students are the college's top performing students. After graduation the students in the honors program go on to highly ranked graduate programs in an array of fields. The honors program at Tougaloo College not only provides a rigorous academic experience for students but it also provides a supportive environment between faculty and students, and between students themselves.

Although the honors program at Tougaloo College is successful, the college itself has not used the program to leverage its enrollment, graduation rates, or student retention. The reasons are as follows. First, to an outsider the honors program is not a highly visible part of Tougaloo's Campus. For example, when one of the authors of this chapter applied to Tougaloo, she was not aware that the school had an honors program. It was not until a letter arrived inviting her to the honors programs that she realized that the school had such a program. Second, although current students are able to join the program after 24 hours of course work and a GPA of at least 3.5, students do not take advantage of this because it is not advertised highly on campus. Furthermore, Tougaloo does not have a recruiter who focuses on recruiting high-achieving students for the honors program and subsequently for the college. In addition to this fact, statistics are not available on the success of the program. Instead, the success of the honors program is generally spread through anecdotal evidence or through the college's "legacy" of academic prestige.

Findings

We used the case study method to provide unique insights into the workings of two very distinct honors programs. This section will compare and contrast the honors programs at Cheyney University of Pennsylvania and Tougaloo College. This cross-examination will provide a look at the difficulties and triumphs that affect these two campuses. The problems and successes identified on these campuses can be analyzed and used to inform the larger HBCU population, aid in building up honors programs on HBCU campuses, and increase the enrollment of high-achieving students at HBCUs.

Descriptions of both programs illustrate a commonality that exists. Both honors programs offer great benefits and incentives to its students for participating. For example, students in these programs receive financial support in the form of full tuition support, room and board, as well as free laptop computers. Students in these programs take academically challenging courses that allow them to develop critical skills for success. The students also have opportunities to increase their knowledge of other cultures with travel opportunities funded by their programs.

Although different, the programs at these schools have common goals. These programs create spaces for high-achieving students, and give the schools the space in which to recruit and retain high-achieving students. They give HBCUs the leveraging power to compete with PWIs for academically successful students, not only because of the scholarly nature of the programs but also because of the supportive environment in which they exist. These programs prove (1) that HBCUs can compete with PWIs in getting academically successfully students to attend their school and (2) that academically successful students do graduate from HBCUs and go on to achieve great success

While these two programs have a lot in common, there are distinct dissimilarities. The first difference is the funding that each program receives. Cheyney University, a public institution, receives yearly funding from the state that is drastically different from the grant that Tougaloo receives from the Mellon Foundation to run its program. This difference could possibly account for the ways in which each program advertises and tracks the success of their individual programs. As shown in the case studies, Cheyney has a much more robust collection of data that proves the success of the Keystone Honors Academy. As a state-funded program, the Keystone Honors Academy must keep public records to ensure the continued funding of the program. In fact, this data helped the program gain funding after it had been previously cut due to budget cuts. On the other hand, the Tougaloo College Honors program does not have a large collection of data that shows its success. This is not to say that Tougaloo does not have to report its success to the Mellon Foundation; however, as a private institution the data does not have to be public. This lack of data proves to be problematic because there is no factual evidence readily available to account for the success of the honors program. Instead, the success of the program is usually passed around by word of mouth and anecdotal evidence, which is not enough to ensure the continued success of the program.

The programs also differ in the way each is used to leverage success for their respective institutions. The Keystone honors program is used to increase student enrollment at Cheyney University. By hiring a recruiter to target high-achieving students and speak directly to their needs, Cheyney increases the chances of that student entering Cheyney University. Cheyney University has also created a program that mirrors the Keystone honors program to improve the retention and graduation rates of all its students.

Although the Tougaloo College honors program is just as successful as the Keystone Honors Academy, they do not have a dedicated recruiter for honors students. This is not to say that the recruiting system is not successful but that individual attention is not placed on honors students.

Another important difference to be noted between these two programs is the visibility of each program. The Keystone Honors Academy is a staple in Pennsylvania and the Philadelphia community. They are known for their successes, counted as one of the most successful honors programs in the state system, and marketed as such. Keystone Honors Academy has its own webpage with its accomplishments and special events. However, the webpage has not been updated since 2009. Although the Tougaloo College Honors program also has a page on the school's website, the webpage is extremely hard to find. Upon finding the page, there is only basic information and it does not list any of the accomplishments of the program.

Recommendations

HBCUs must develop and implement sound strategies that will successfully market their honors program. This can be accomplished in a variety of ways. For example at high school days and other recruitment events, HBCUs should always talk about and showcase their honors programs. As the research shows (Seifert et al., 2007), students tend to pass up HBCUs in lieu of prestigious academic opportunities at other colleges. If HBCUs show that they too have rigorous opportunities in the form of honors programs, they may be able to recruit these students. In addition to prestige, research shows that college costs and the number of scholarships available to students influences students' decisions in determining what school to attend (Schuman, 1999). By showcasing the financial benefits that they offer students, HBCU honors program would be able to recruit more students.

Furthermore, honors programs at HBCUs should use the research on high-achieving African American students to tailor their programs to this group of students' needs and use this information as a recruiting method. For example, research shows that high-achieving African American students often feel isolated at PWIs and seeing other African American students succeed helped them in their own academic endeavors (Fries-Britt, 1998). Using this knowledge, recruiters can emphasis the familial and supportive atmosphere of HBCUs to entice students to attend their institution.

HBCUs can also use the successes of their honors program to create programs for other students on their campuses. Using the knowledge of what causes students to succeed in honors programs and applying it to fit the institution could result in increased graduation rates and retention for the university. Finally, honors programs on HBCU campuses must use data to back up their successes. Anecdotal evidence is just that, anecdotal; in order to successfully leverage their honors programs HBCU must collect and keep data that proves its success. With statistics, HBCUs would be able to show that their honors programs are indeed successful, and this would result in increased enrollment in the institution.

Conclusions

By offering an in-depth look at two honors programs, this chapter hopes to inform the current literature on HBCU honors programs and provide HBCUs with sound strategies to leverage their honors programs to increase enrollment, retention, and graduation rates. The case studies presented show that through their honors programs, HBCUs have what it takes to be competitive and attract academically talented students. With this information, HBCUs must now create ways to use their honors programs for the overall betterment of their institutions.

References

Baxter, P. & Jack, S. (2008). Qualitative case study methodology: Study design and implementation for novice researchers. *The Qualitative Report, 13*(4), 544–559.

Cosgrove, J. (2004). The impact of honors programs on undergraduate academic performance, retention, and graduation. *Journal of the National Collegiate Honors Council*, Fall/Winter, 45–54.

Davis, R. & Montgomery, S. (2011). Honors education at HBCUs: Core values, best practices, and select challenges. *Journal of the National Collegiate Honors Council*, Spring/Summer, 73–87.

Freeman, K. & Thomas, G. (2002). Black colleges and college choice: Characteristics of students who choose HBCUs. *The Review of Higher Education, 25*(3), 349–358.

Freyman, J. (2005). What is an honors student. *Journal of the National Collegiate Honors Council, 6*(2), 23–29.

Fries-Britt, S. (1998). Moving beyond black achiever isolation: Experiences of gifted black collegians. *Journal of Higher Education, 69*(5), 556–576.

Fries-Britt, S. (2004). The challenges and needs of high-achieving Black college. In M. Christopher Brown II & K. Freeman (Eds.), *Black colleges' new perspectives on policy and practice* (pp. 161–176). Westport, CT: Praeger.

Griffin, K. (2006). Striving for success: A qualitative exploration of competing theories of high-achieving black college students' academic motivation. *Journal of College Student Development*, 47(4), 384–400.

Mitchell, I. A. (2002). Honors programs at Historically Black Colleges and Universities. *Education*, 123(1), 31–35.

Otero, R. & Spurrier, R. (2005). *Assessing and evaluating honors programs and honors programs and honors colleges: A practical handbook*. National Collegiate Honors Council.

Perna, L. W. & Titus, M. A. (2004). Understanding differences in the choice of college attended: The role of state public policies. *The Review of Higher Education*, 27(4), 501–525.

Rinn, A. & Plucker, J. (2004). We recruit them, but then what? The educational and psychological experiences of academically talented undergraduates. *Gifted Child Quarterly*, 48(1), 54–67.

Schuman, S. (1999). *Honors programs at smaller colleges*. NCHC Monograph Series.

Seifert, T. A., Pascarella, E. T., Colangelo, N., & Assouline, S. G. (2007). The effects of honors program participation on experiences of good practices and learning outcomes. *Journal of College Student Development* 48(1), 57–74.

Slavin, C., Coladarci, T., & Pratt, P. A. (2008). Is student participation in an honors program related to retention and graduation rates. *Journal of the National Collegiate Honors Council*, 9(2), 59–69.

U.S. General Accounting Office, Program Evaluation and Methodology (1990). *Case study evaluations* (1995 404–741/20012). Washington, DC: GAO/PEMD.

Yin, R. (2003). *Case study research: Design and methods* (3rd ed.). Thousand Oaks, CA: Sage Publications.

CHAPTER TWELVE

Black Greek Fraternity Experiences on Predominantly White and Historically Black Campuses: A Comparison

DENNIS DALY

In his *Manual of American college fraternities* (1890), William Raimond Baird stated, "college students have always shown a more or less marked tendency to form themselves into societies" (p. 9). Even today, when I reminisce about College I do not think about tests, papers, or classes, but rather I focus on friends, activities, and events, and the larger collegiate experience. I want to explore how these self-constructed "micro" societies and affinity groups impact student development, and how these experiences differ on demographically different campus types. My goal is to provide information on, and discuss the experiences of, Black Greek Fraternity (BGF) members at predominantly White and historically Black institutions through semi-structured interviews of several BGF members and their own personal experiences. It is important to note that the findings of this chapter are in no way meant to be entirely representative of the organizations, the institutions, or all BGFs. Rather, the goal of this chapter is to provide insight into their members' experiences for those who might be unfamiliar with Black Greek Letter Fraternities and explore how those experiences are, in part, shaped by campus demographics. My research shows that although there are some differences in BGF student experiences on predominantly White institutions (PWIs) and historically Black campuses (HBCUs), overall the commonalities outweigh the differences.

Through interviewing participants on both campus types I have found that the fundamentals of BGFs are present regardless of campus demographics.[1] The differences that arise in BGF student experiences in PWIs and HBCUs are merely the result of smaller numbers.

No research is without bias, and as someone presenting research on BGFs at both minority and majority institutions, I feel it is necessary to address my own personal, educational, and professional background so as to alert the reader to any potential researcher bias at the forefront, rather than as an afterthought.

I am a White male who grew up in an upper class, predominantly White, New England town. I attended a predominately White high school and then proceeded to study history at Loyola College in Baltimore, Maryland. Although Baltimore is quite diverse and has a large African American population, Loyola College did not, and would be aptly categorized as a Predominantly White Institution (PWI). In addition to being a PWI, Loyola College did not have any social Greek organizations; therefore any of my prior understanding about predominantly White Greek Fraternities (WGFs) was acquired tangentially through occasionally attending frat parties and interacting with friends who were in fraternities at other institutions.

After college I became a high school teacher in the Baltimore City Public School system, where I first became acquainted with BGFs. While teaching in Baltimore several of my coworkers and friends were members of BGFs, and through my interactions with them I became aware that BGFs were quite different than my notions of WGFs. Primarily, I noticed that BGF involvement went far beyond the college years and young alumni status, and seemed (for some) to be a lifelong component of their social life. Also, whereas WGF seemed to be essentially social in nature, BGFs seemed to be about more than social interaction, and had equally deep roots in community service, racial uplift, and cultural pride.

After spending three years working in the Baltimore City Public School System urban education, minority issues in higher education and Black Greek Letter Organizations became my research interests. I am aware that my own personal background is going to affect the lens through which I view the literature, my research, and the data on BGFs in HBCUs and PWIs. I think this will help my analysis in some instances and hinder it in others. The obvious downfalls are that I have never been involved in a Greek fraternity (either Black or White) and as such I have no knowledge on information that the organizations wish to keep confidential (i.e., ceremonies, particular ideologies, intake process/pledging/hazing). Moreover, any information I glean from resources or research participants is going to be expressly filtered for the public sphere; so any discussion might lack gritty or unflattering information about BGFs. On the other hand, not having extensive fraternity experience will not leave me predisposed to see these organizations without flaw or to view particular organizations through a common stereotype.

Literature Review

Greek Letter Organizations (GLOs) have a long and rich history in US higher education. Phi Beta Kappa, widely considered to the first GLO, was founded in 1776 at the College of William and Mary and eventually became the prototype of what we consider today to be Social Greek Letter Organizations. In the early days of US higher education, students often lived in lackluster housing, ate poor food, and had their power marginalized by both faculty and administration. Therefore students created literary societies and later GLOs to fill the void in social life in institutions that were essentially focused on the academic development of the student. These GLOs grew in number and spread to different campuses between the 1820s and the early twentieth century. Early GLOs, like the institutions they were affiliated with, were designed exclusively for White men. As institutions began to admit African American men, these African American students began to create similar organizations for similar reasons: to provide support and a social outlet for the Black students being marginalized and discriminated against on campus (Torbenson, 2012). Black students who were also servants in predominantly WGFs founded the first BGF, Alpha Phi Alpha, at Cornell University in 1906 (Torbenson, 2012). Their unique perspective as African Americans, students, and servants led to the creation of a system that would take the essential tenets of WGFs and apply them to the needs and challenges that faced Black students (Bradley, 2008; Torbenson, 2012).

As Torbenson (2012) noted, throughout much of American higher education history "the typical college student was male, White and Protestant and from a high economic class" (p. 52). Eventually a select group of students of color began to gain access to a small number of elite historically White institutions as early as the mid-nineteenth century. Despite their academic acceptance, these Black students often faced the same discrimination and marginalization at their institutions as they did in mainstream American culture (Torbenson, 2012). The fact that the earliest BGFs were founded on historically White campuses is important to note when trying to understand their purpose and mission. The fundamental purpose of BGFs can be found in the motto of Alpha Phi Alpha, the nation's first BGF. "First of all; servants of all; we shall transcend all" establishes organizational goals of racial uplift, community service, and cultural heritage (Bradley, 2008). And as Harris and Mitchell (2008) and Gasman, Louison, and Barnes (2008) point out, the fundamentals established in the early twentieth century are still an integral and essential part of modern Black Greek Letter Organizations (BGLOs). The longevity of BGFs special mission is part of what makes these organizations so distinct from their WGF counterparts.

Historical evolution aside, modern WGFs and BGFs have very different organizational purposes and structures, as well as effects on their membership. Fox, Hodge, and Ward (1987) point out that while there has been a considerable amount of academic sociological research on the collegiate fraternalism system, there is, by comparison, relatively little scholarly work that focuses exclusively on BGF members. Gregory Parks (2008) makes similar claims and goes on to point out that the scholarly work (aside from a few individuals) that has been published on BGLOs prior to the most recent literature tended to focus on some of their more high-profile cultural aspects, such as stepping or hazing, rather than being an in depth analysis on the membership or organizations as a whole. Kimbrough and Hutchenson (1998) highlight two major differences between BGLOs and predominantly White GLOs. They claim that unlike predominantly White GLOs, BGLO membership and involvement often extends past the collegiate years and has a heavy emphasis/role on the development of leadership skills. McClure (2006) states that professional connections through BGLO membership, "facilitate job opportunities and supply increased social capital to members, capital that may be particularly important to members form lower socioeconomic backgrounds" (p. 1051).

Black enrollment at PWIs grew after the landmark Supreme Court case *Brown vs. the Board of Education*, which effectively overturned racial segregation in public educational institutions. The increase in Black enrollment in PWIs was accompanied by an increase in BGLO chapters in many PWIs. As discussed earlier, the first collegiate BGLO was created in order to provide marginalized Black students with social outlets and professional inroads on White campuses. McClure (2006) states that today BGLOs on White campuses help integrate Black students into campus culture and facilitate negotiating a predominantly White cultural environment and alleviate pressure to conform to mainstream White culture. Fox, Hodge, and Ward (1987) discuss how BGLOs on White campuses are fundamentally different from their WGLO counterparts. Kimbrough and Hutcheson (1999) elaborate on how membership in a BGLO can help students succeed and excel in both PWIs and HBCUs. There is (as far as I have found) an unfortunate and noticeable gap in the academic literature on how the campus demographic makeup of a particular institution affects the experiences of its BGF members.

Methodology

When I started this project I did not have extensive background knowledge of BGLOs, and therefore I conducted my research with a similar audience in mind, that is, people with no prior knowledge of BGLOs. A number of articles on BGLOs and Black student experiences in higher education have a strong quantitative component, such as Fox et al. "A comparison of attitudes held by Black and White fraternity members" (1987) and Walter Allen's "The color of success: African American student outcomes at predominantly White and historically Black colleges" (1992). However given the size, scope, timeline, and my own personal skill set, using a quantitative analytical approach to come to an overarching conclusion about BGLO members in PWIs and HBCUs would not be prudent. Furthermore, as Strayhorn and McCall (2011) state, "empirical research provides comparatively little information about the BGLO members' experience" (p. 280). The goal of this chapter is to provide the reader with information about that experience through firsthand accounts of BGLO students in fundamentally different campus environments. Rather than provide a lot of quantitative data on student success and campus activity participation to illustrate BGF experiences in HBCUs and PWIs, I decided to take a similar approach to that of McClure (2006), and let students discuss how membership in a BGF affected their experiences.

For my research I conducted a number of semi-structured interviews of undergraduate BGLO members at both PWIs and HBCUs. The participants were informed that the purpose of the discussion was for academic research and they were given a list of topics that would be discussed in advance. The interviews were recorded, typically lasted between 30 and 60 minutes, and spanned a variety of topics, such as personal background, institutional choice, experiences/perceptions of BGLOs prior to college, introduction to BGLOs on campus, and experiences and aspirations as member of a BGLO. Although all participants were given the same topics and were asked the same questions the responses varied greatly based on their own experiences, passions, and view on BGLOs. The recordings were analyzed for common themes about BGLOs, their membership, and member experiences that transcended campus type, or for trends that were exclusive to one particular type of campus.

In order to gain access to participants, I initially reached out to the Office of Greek Life at a local university and the Multicultural Greek Council Advisor arranged interviews with several current undergraduates who were BGF members. After the first round of participant interviews, I relied on BGF and student referrals in order to gain more data on BGF student experience from a college or university that had a different campus demographic. Also, it should be noted that all participants' names, the names of their institution, and the names of their organizations are pseudonymous. This was an option offered to all interview participants in light of the sensitive nature of some questions and in an effort to gain qualitative data that was not skewed due to concerns of scrutiny and an attempt to create a positive public image.

There were three participants who attended a predominantly White institution. Vincent, a senior, is a member of BGF Chi on a White campus. He grew up in an urban upper-middle-class environment and attended a college prep charter high school that was majority Black. His parents were both educated at PWIs, and his mother and sisters were all members of BGLOs. He has secured a job at a major tech company for the fall, but aspires to work in urban education eventually. Michael, a senior and member of BGF Upsilon, also lived on a predominantly White campus. He grew up in a semi-urban upper-middle-class environment and attended a very racially diverse public high school. His parents were both educated at PWIs, and neither were members of BGLOs. He hopes to work in marketing and eventually make a transition to the entertainment industry. Gregory is a senior and nontraditional student who is actively involved in BGF Zeta on a White campus. He grew up in a small predominantly White, lower-middle-class Southern town. Gregory described both his town and high school as having high levels of de facto segregation, overt racism, and racially motivated acts of violence. Gregory's grandmother raised him and does not have a college education. Gregory is a veteran of the Iraq war and is studying history with the hopes of becoming a high school teacher.

Vincent, Michael, and Gregory attended the same predominantly White institution, which will be referred to as Mid-Atlantic University (MAU). MAU is a large, prestigious university that is consistently ranked in the top 25 universities in the nation. It has large and prestigious liberal arts, applied sciences, and business programs. The racial makeup of MAU is approximately 46% White and 40% students of color, with a Black population of approximately 7%. The tuition cost of MAU is relatively high at $40,000; 60% of MAU students receive some sort of financial aid, however only 7% receive federal Pell Grants.[2] MAU is situated on an open urban campus in a diverse neighborhood in a major city.

There were two participants who attended historically Black institutions. Ken is a senior and member of BGF Chi in an HBCU. He grew up in an urban middle-class predominantly White environment. He attended a college prep charter middle and high school that had a very diverse student population. His father also went to the same historically Black institution, although he had no BGF affiliation. Ken is studying communications and education with the hopes of becoming a teacher. Ken attends Middle-State University (MSU), a small historically Black college that is part of a larger state system of higher education. MSU is located in the suburbs of a major metropolitan city. The most popular majors at MSU are business and social science degrees. Of MSU undergraduate populations, 96% are students of color, with 93% self-identifying as Black. Tuition at MSU is approximately $21,000 per year with 78% of students receiving federal Pell Grants.[3] The second participant, Quinn, is a senior and member of BGF Chi in an HBCU. Quinn grew up in a middle-class background and came from a relatively diverse high school. Quinn attends South-Eastern University (SEU), a medium-sized university situated on an urban campus in a major metropolitan city. SEU has large communications, business, and psychology programs and is well known as a major historically Black institution. Of SEU's student population, 90% self-identify as Black, with 8% opting out of ethnicity classifications. Tuition at SEU is approximately $21, 000 with 82% of students receiving need-based grants or scholarships.[4]

Findings

Prior to any research, I speculated that BGF members' experiences would differ significantly based on the given racial demographics of a particular institution. I knew from my own minimal and tangential WGF experiences that WGF student experiences differed greatly from school to school. At some institutions the "Greek Scene" dominated campus culture and social events while on others WGFs were present but really had an impact only on a small niche in a larger non-Greek campus culture. Overall, my research shows that BGFs in PWIs and HBCUs are more alike than they are different, and the minimal differences that do exist are merely the result of smaller numbers rather than campus cultural issues.

All participants, regardless of institutional background or organizational allegiance, had noticeably similar themes when discussing their BGF student experiences. These similar experiences can be loosely grouped together into three major commonalities: fundamental BGF tenets, an emphasis on upward movement and the development of professional skills, and a commonly accepted agreement on organizational "personalities."

When asked to outline the structure and fundamentals of BGF Chi, Vincent noted that his organization's aims were focused around scholarship, community service, and encouraging gentlemanliness. All of the other participants when asked to describe the fundamentals of their organization mentioned similar goals or aims (although the specific language varied from organization to organization). Aside from merely echoing standardized organizational mission statements, most participants reinforced these aims from a personal or experiential standpoint. Four participants (representing both campus types) noted their interest in scholarship and made mention of high academic achievement at their own particular institutions. When asked about their ultimate goals, three participants (representing both campus types) said they wanted to end up in the educational field in order to help those in their community. Furthermore Michael, who attends a PWI, made a note of how his BGF's take on community service is different from WGF's "philanthropy" efforts. He shared his opinion that his organization thinks it is more important to go out into the "community and actually volunteer and help out, rather than just collect money and donate it to a cause." Gregory, from BGF Zeta, even went as far as to say, "I am firmly entrenched with trying to help my community... I thought maybe by joining [a BGF] I can use that as a tool, it was the major reason I joined." Last, Vincent, Michael, and Ken (representing both campus types) all mentioned a commitment to proper behavior, attire, and other "gentlemanly" attributes as a priority. They all explained that ultimately they were representatives of their organizations, and as such they have a responsibility to both look and act accordingly at all times. Most participants mentioned that BGFs emphasized upward social-economic mobility. Based upon participants' responses, it is clear that there are both explicit mechanisms and implicit skill-building in place that reinforced a commitment to success and upward movement. When I asked Michael why he joined a BGF in a PWI, he clearly stated that "one of the things that connected me to [BGF Upsilon] was the idea of being upwardly mobile and using that personal advancement to advance others as well." Ken, who goes to a historically Black institution, says that one of his earliest recollections of BGFs was when his uncle told him "you'll either be a [member of BGF Chi], or you'll wind up working for one," and that he ultimately joined BGF Chi because he thought the competitive nature of BGF Chi would prepare him for success in the working world. Vincent mentioned in his interview that his organization has a national alumni directory. This alumni directory is sorted by both region and profession for the express purposes of networking. BGF members who move to different cities can use this tool to immediately connect into a social pipeline. Furthermore, BGF members who are recent college graduates can search the directory by profession and use BGF alumni as a resource when interviewing for a job or for industry networking.

Aside from the explicit professional development mechanism, BGFs also encourage upward social movement by nurturing the development of nontechnical "soft skills." When asked about what they intended to take away from belonging, most participants mentioned that running an organization was an important developmental experience for them. They noted that skills such as building group consensus, time management, and learning how to navigate organizational structures would help them succeed after college. These explicit mechanisms and implicit skill-building will give BGF members the tools to help increase their social-economic status in the future and enable a clear crossover into the professional world.

Finally, one of the commonalities that I found most interesting was the popularly accepted "personality" of certain BGFs. During the interviews I asked each participant what their impressions were of the different BGFs on their campus and how they ultimately made their choice. Four of five participants (representing both campus types) stated that they ultimately chose their organization because their personality matched well with other members of their organization. When I inquired about the nature of the other BGF personalities, most participants used the same or similar adjectives to describe the same groups. The language that the participants used to describe different BGFs ranged from positive to slightly negative, but was clearly a description of similar things. Afterward everyone made an effort to note that these organizational "personalities" or stereotypes were all in good fun, and went on to reiterate that all BGFs are about similar positive things. Nevertheless, it was surprising that these BGF stereotypes transcended campus type and operated on a national level as opposed to a localized campus or regional level. This reinforces the idea that BGFs, regardless of campus type, have more commonalities than differences.

Despite the overwhelming commonalities in participant responses at both HBUCs and PWIs, there were a number of places where their responses differed. These differences roughly correlated to campus demographic makeup and were mostly centered on the logistical issue of chapter size. Some noticeable topics where participant's responses differed along campus lines were chapter size and recruitment, campus-wide support, and the social impact of being a BGF member.

When asked about the size of their chapters, there was a clear disparity between the PWI participant responses and the HBCU participant responses. At MAU, Vincent's organization had 6 members, Gregory's organization had 2 members, and Michael's city-wide chapter had 7 members. In comparison, on Black campuses, Quinn's chapter at SEU had close to 40 members, and Ken's at MSU had a "somewhere in the mid-30s." Among many things, this most clearly affected recruitment and the path by which people joined BGFs. For the most part people were drawn into BGFs in PWIs through personal relationships with existing or prospective members, and the organizations themselves had to actively recruit new people. Based upon participant responses from HBCUs, the BGF recruitment in HBCUs was much more passive and impersonal as groups marketed their organizations in general and then filtered out the undesirable applicants.

Michael, who attends a PWI, mentioned that he was drawn to BGF Upsilon because his friends were interested in joining a BGF, and he found out that he got along well with the existing brothers. Vincent, also from a PWI, noted that he became involved in BGF Chi because he was involved in other Black cultural organizations, and from having interactions with people in those organizations he was encouraged to look into membership in BGF Chi. The small numbers and low profile of BGFs in PWIs mean that in order to survive, they must actively recruit and create personal relationships with prospective members who are already involved in similar affinity groups. Although the numbers for BGFs on PWIs may be smaller, the smaller numbers might not necessarily be a negative thing. Being part of a BGF at a PWI might allow the students to have a more intimate experience with several peers, rather than a group of 40 classmates where intra-organizational cliques would inevitably form. Also, the low numbers might force BGF students at PWIs to reach out to nearby HBCUs for events, thereby giving them exposure to a different campus type.

Unlike the participants from PWIs, the HBCU participants did not mention existing personal relationships as one of the reasons they joined BGF Chi. When talking about the recruitment process at MSU, Ken said, "[The BGFs] made themselves known in the first few weeks" and individuals ultimately decided to pursue which organizations they found most appealing. When asked about how he chose among the BGFs on campus at SEU, Quinn talked at length about his desire to be part of an organization that had spawned a number of prominent and important African American politicians, academics, and activists. It was clear from talking to him that Quinn was attracted to his organization because of the abstract ideals of the group rather than because of a personal connection of an existing or prospective member. The high-profile nature of BGFs on Black campuses and their large numbers mean that the organizations do not have to solicit for members on an individual basis, and they can rely on marketing rather than personal recruitment.

This issue of size was also apparent in the BGF activities on campus at both HBCUs and PWIs. Ken noted that his chapter and other BGF chapters had officially designated spaces on MSU's campus, in the form of plots of land, where they could hold events, gatherings, meetings, and cookouts. Ken went on to say that when his chapter put on events, they were always well attended by students, both Greek and non-affiliated. Quinn discussed how SEU's entire campus was involved in a lively Greek Week, which received a large amount of administrative support and student turnout. On the other hand, Gregory at MAU noted that BGFs were consistently overshadowed by WGFs during MAU's Greek Week, and that they consistently received little administrative support or publicity around campus. All three MAU participants said that their BGFs events did not enjoy a large turnout, nor did the administration offer their organizations any official spaces (lounges, land, or houses) on or near campus that they could consistently use as their own. If BGFs help Black student development in ways such as increasing professional development opportunities and the nurturing of "soft skills," then schools that have a commitment to diversity and access should fully support these organizations in a broad sense. It is not enough to officially recognize their organization and provide them a seat at the table for Greek affairs and activities. PWIs should fully support BGFs and make sure that they have equal access to the same sorts of resources as the WGFs on campus.

Further, there was a disparity in the responses of participants from HBCUs and PWIs with regard to the social impact of being a member of a BGF. I made it a point to ask every participant what it was they enjoyed about being a member of a BGF. Quinn from SEU talked about the deep and important historical legacy of his organization and the "vibrant nature of BGFs on [his] campus"; he went on to say that he did not think it would be possible to replicate that on a predominantly White campus in the North. When I asked Ken the same question, he immediately quipped, "Ladies love a man in letters." Although his response was obviously in jest, his joke illustrated that merely belonging to a BGF could boost social standing on campus. He went on to express that he believed it would be difficult for certain BGF cultural pastimes, like strolling at a party or step competitions, to have the same impact in a PWI. When I asked the participants from MAU the same questions, they did not bring up the campus social impact of being a BGF member. They discussed the personal relationships they have forged with their brothers or alumni, the community service opportunities they have had on the campus, the networking and professional development aspects, but there was a noticeable lack of discussion about social activities in the PWI of MAU.

Conclusion

BGLOs were created in the early twentieth century in an effort to support Black students at a time when they faced a large degree of overt oppression and marginalization on White college campuses (Torbenson, 2012). I believe the numerous and important similarities that bind these different organizations together today, regardless of institutional size, location, and demographic makeup, are products of the environment that created them. Despite their size, variations, and complexities the American Black population was treated as a monolithic group in the early twentieth century and subject to a high degree of overt oppression and marginalization, even in the higher education sector. Black students who gained acceptance and admission to elite historically White institutions turned to each other, in the form of BGFs, for support and strength to overcome the obstacles placed in their way by various administrations and White students. At their roots, all BGLOs are designed to help their members succeed academically and professionally, and encourage them to help others in their community. I believe that these founding members created such similar organizations because they were ultimately facing similar forms of oppression and required similar types of support. The differences that do exist between BGFs on HBCUs and PWIs are not the result of a fundamentally different student experience, but rather the logistical consequences of smaller numbers.

From my research it is clear that BGFs have a positive influence on their members and provide vastly more than a social experience. They promote academic success among their members and a commitment to community service, while at the same time fostering upward social movement through professional development training, networking groups, and increasing soft skills. If one could dissect the mechanisms by which BGFs developed such a successful model for student achievement, then those systems could be applied to a whole host of other student populations. If we can find out exactly what makes BGFs so successful, we can try and create organizations that would cultivate the same environment to help students from other populations thrive, particularly first-generation college students, "at-risk" high school groups, and students struggling with learning disabilities. It is possible that the answer lies in the marriage of the unique cultural, academic, professional, and social mission of these groups. But we will never know until more research is done and we delve deeper into what makes BGFs so successful in preparing young Black men for the professional world.

Notes

1. Throughout this chapter predominantly White campuses will be referred to as PWIs and historically Black campuses will be referred to as HBCUs. It should be noted that neither of these campus types are racially homogeneous, these descriptors merely describe the dominant racial demographic on campus for the sake of brevity.
2. All data about MAU tuition, size, campus demographics, popular majors, and financial aid were taken from the institutional website, the 2008 *U.S. News and World Report* rankings on Economic Diversity, http://www.usnews.com/education/blogs/college-rankings-blog/2010/09/30/new-rankings-college-economic-diversity, and the College Board's "Big Future" website, https://bigfuture.collegeboard.org/. For the sake of preserving institutional anonymity, the exact websites will not be directly cited.

3. All data about MSU tuition, size, campus demographics, popular majors and financial aid were taken from the institutional website, the 2008 *U.S. News and World Report* rankings on Economic Diversity, http://www.usnews.com/education/blogs/college-rankings-blog/2010/09/30/new-rankings-college-economic-diversity, and the College Board's "Big Future" website, https://bigfuture.collegeboard.org/. For the sake of preserving institutional anonymity, the exact websites will not be directly cited.
4. All data about SEU tuition, size, campus demographics, popular majors, and financial aid were taken from the institutional website, the 2008 *U.S. News and World Report* rankings on Economic Diversity, http://www.usnews.com/education/blogs/college-rankings-blog/2010/09/30/new-rankings-college-economic-diversity, and the College Board's "Big Future" website, https://bigfuture.collegeboard.org/. For the sake of preserving institutional anonymity, the exact websites will not be directly cited.

References

Allen, W. (1992). The color of success: African American student outcomes at predominantly white and historically black colleges. *Harvard Educational Review, 62*(1), 26–45.

Baird, W. M. R. (1890). *Manual of American College Fraternities* (4th ed.). New York: James P. Downs Publishers.

Bradley, S. (2008). First and finest: The founders of Alpha Phi Alpha fraternity. In G. S. Parks (Ed.), *Black Greek letter organizations in the twenty-first century: Our fight has just begun* (pp. 19–39). Lexington, KY: The University Press of Kentucky.

Fox, E., Hodge, C., & Ward, W. (1987). A comparison of attitudes held by black and white fraternity members. *Journal of Negro Education, 56*(4), 521–534. Retrieved on February 8, 2013 from the JSTOR database.

Gasman, M., Louison, P., & Barnes, M. (2008). Giving and getting: Philanthropic activity among black Greek-letter organizations. In G. S. Parks (Ed.), *Black Greek letter organizations in the twenty-first century* (pp. 187–212). Lexington, KY: The University Press of Kentucky.

Harris, J. and Mitchell, V. (2008). A narrative critique of Black Greek-letter organization and social action. In G. S. Parks (Ed.), *Black Greek letter organizations in the twenty-first century* (pp. 143–188). Lexington, KY: The University Press of Kentucky.

Kimbrough, W. & Hutcheson, P. (1999). The impact of membership in black-Greek letter organizations on black students' involvement in collegiate activities and their development of leadership skills. *Journal of Negro Education, 67*(2), 96–105. Retrieved on March 11, 2013 from the JSTOR database.

McClure, S. M. (2006). Voluntary association membership: Black Greek men on a predominantly white campus. *Journal of Higher Education, 77*(6), 1036–057. Retrieved on February 8, 2013 from the JSTOR database.

Parks, G. S. (Ed.) (2008). *Black Greek letter organizations in the twenty-first century: Our fight has just begun* (pp. 19–39). Lexington, KY: The University Press of Kentucky.

Strayhorn, T. and McCall, F. (2011). Black Greek letter organizations at predominantly white institutions and historically black universities. In G. S. Parks and M. Hughey (Eds.), *Black Greek-letter organizations 2.0: New directions in the study of African American fraternities and sororities* (pp. 277–293). Jackson, MI: The University Press of Mississippi.

Torbenson, C. L. (2012). The origin and evolution of college fraternities and sororities. In T. Brown, G. S. Parks, & C. Philips (Eds.), *African American fraternities and sororities: The legacy and the vision* (2nd ed., pp. 33–61). Lexington, KY: The University Press of Kentucky.

PART III

Purpose and Philosophy

CHAPTER THIRTEEN

Black Lesbian Identity at HBCUs

ALEXANDRA IANNUCCI

As a trainer and advocate for the lesbian, gay, bisexual, transgender, and queer (LGBTQ) community, I have gained a strong sense of awareness regarding the identity development of LGBTQ people. However, as a White lesbian I never considered the impact race might have on the identity development of LGBTQ people, specifically Black lesbians. I am a proud alumnus and out professional at the Catholic University at which I currently work. However, I see and feel discrimination every day. After taking a course on Historically Black Colleges and Universities (HBCUs), I was intrigued by the constant comparisons I naturally made throughout the course. This essay is inspired by the personal experiences of being a White lesbian at a Catholic institution and the meaning of being a Black lesbian at an HBCU. This essay explores the intersectionality of identity, the impact of college environments, heteronormative and homophobic behaviors, and acceptance within the Black community. It highlights the specific needs Black lesbians will require as they enter HBCUs.

Reflection

I design "safe space" trainings that give insight into the world of an LGBTQ person. Creating this program has been interesting and challenging. My personal experiences as a lesbian impact the perspective that I bring to a space. As an out professional at a Catholic University,

I cannot walk into a women's restroom on campus without causing a fiasco. I either get stared at because the women think I am a boy who entered the wrong room or the women double check the sign on the door to make sure they walked into the right room. I notice I walk a little faster from the entrance to the stall just to make my bathroom experience a bit easier. When I walk into the student center hundreds of eyes fall on me as if they have never seen a lesbian before. Students are not sure what they are looking at or how my style could be possible.

As a Catholic, I entered college excited and nervous to explore my spiritual journey. I was very aware of the Catholic message on homosexuality. I thought college would be a place of acceptance regardless of the religious influence. I was excited to be at a place where I could feel free instead of feeling invisible. I was naïve in this thought process. The consistent messages of a heteronormative world truly isolated my development as a young student. My experiences coming out in college forced me to look at the world through a jaded lens that challenges me in every moment and experience today. I recognize it was my choice to attend and now work at an institution that fundamentally does not support a same-sex sexual or romantic relationship. However, I feel I have gained awareness from these experiences that would have otherwise never been understood.

As a trainer, it has been my goal to build a program that levels the playing field between people and creates an experience of understanding for people in order to redefine "normal." It has been my mission to develop a workshop that all individuals can relate to simply by reflecting on their own experiences in life. These life experiences help shape the identity of individuals and define the things they value. We do not stop to reflect enough on the things we have experienced.

However, it has been my understanding that people are afraid to reflect on their own lives. They are scared to see things from a different perspective because maybe in some way it means we are in fact all the same. I believe people are afraid to expose the things that make them different with the concern they might be part of a minority—something not normal, less than. American author Mark Twain (1904) said: "Whenever you find yourself on the side of the majority, it is time to pause and reflect." I find myself reflecting lately in my life. As I pause and describe my experiences, I see there are pieces of my identity that are privileged. These pieces, though, have never had to be considered in my life and in my experiences. Being part of a marginalized group of people gives you a unique perspective. This perspective makes you constantly aware of who you are and who society thinks you should be.

It also challenges you to think beyond yourself in moments of strength and in weakness. Being part of the LGBTQ community is not my only identity or community. I am White. Being White provides a perspective in my life I never considered or had to contemplate. As a student and professional working in a Catholic environment, my "Whiteness" is never measured or challenged. Since taking a class on HBCUs, I am faced with the reality that I am part of the majority in my White race. As I reflect on my own identities as a trainer and advocate, it is crucial that I am aware of the intersectionality of my identities and how they not only shape my own environment, but also how I influence the environments of others. Black lesbians at HBCUs will be faced with the intersectionality of their identities. Though I may find many similarities between being a White lesbian at a Catholic school, I will never be able to fully understand the experiences Black lesbians face at HBCUs.

Intersectionality of Identity

As a White lesbian working at a Catholic institution, I see I am different. I recognize the needs I have as a person living in an environment that does not holistically nurture my identities. I remember the things I needed as a student working through my own identity development. I felt nervous and alone as I tried to explore a major piece of who I was and now am. As I reflect on my experiences as a LGBTQ student, I realize the microaggressions and everyday messages I faced. I remember taking different routes to class in an effort to avoid comments. I often wore headphones because I did not want to hear people whispering as I walked by. "Did you see her?" "Is that a boy?" I have tried to relate these experiences as a White lesbian in a Catholic institution to the experiences of Black lesbians at HBCUs. However, when speaking specifically about racial identity, sexual identity, and gender identity, I cannot directly relate to all three. There are aspects of my experiences I can try to parallel. However, as a White lesbian who attended a Catholic school, race, once again, never had to be something I consciously thought about. I have been constantly challenged throughout the material I read about African Americans because no matter how many parallels I try to make, I, in fact, can never understand. As I continue to train people on empathy and personal experience when dealing with marginalized groups of people, I am faced with the reality that empathy might not be good enough and maybe thinking it is good enough is a privilege in itself.

To understand the experiences of Black lesbian identity, we must first reflect on what we value and identify with as people. Torres, Jones, and Renn (2009) describe identity as one's personal beliefs about oneself in relation to social groups such as race, ethnicity, religion, and sexual orientation (p. 577). People have specific identities that help shape and mold them into the people they are. These identities define the values and perspectives we have. They help shape the way we respond to situations, environments, and people. As a lesbian identified White woman who also identifies strongly with being a daughter and a sister, I see and value the world in a specific way. I have faced many hurdles of discrimination as a sexual minority and felt gender bias as a woman. I have been called a dyke in front of my brothers. I have been addressed as "sir" in public and am often not asked to get a mani/pedi with my friends because they assume I would not be interested. My experiences as a minority have shaped my tone and my stance as a professional and as a person. However, as a White individual, I have noticed I have an advantage in a space even if my sexuality is "different" from the norm. As a White person I do not have to consider my racial identity. I always see people like me and I am never reminded of the history of our oppressive past. As a White person, I have had time to develop my sexual identity without having to focus on race.

Identities define us whether we choose to accept that or not, or rather, whether we have the privilege to accept that or not. As a trainer, I encounter many people who say they do not like to define themselves. They do not like labels. I find these people are able to have this perspective because they have the privilege to not have to define certain parts of themselves. The majority is able to move in the world without ever having to think about what they are, or how their identity is influenced every single day. As a White lesbian I do not have to think about my racial identity. I can spend a great portion of my development working through my identity as a sexual minority who faces gender bias. But, Black lesbians do not have that privilege.

Black lesbians are not just a racial minority. As lesbians they are a sexual minority and as women they are a gender minority. These identities are impacted by the opinions of the greater society in which we live. Jewell explains:

> Black women still find themselves confronting sexism and sexual violence on Black college campuses, despite the ubiquitous presence of an official rhetoric that preaches respect for Black women, and are often forced to choose between what are considered to be mutually exclusive loyalties of race and gender. (2002, p. 18)

Jewell describes HBCUs as institutions impacted by the discrimination of the larger society creating a problem for the management of diversity (p. 17). This type of impact creates a campus environment accepting of some and exclusive of others. This can be a problem as our students embark on their college careers and their personal journeys. The intersectionality of race, sexuality, and gender plays a significant role in the development of Black lesbians.

The "American norm" culture of racism, heterosexism, and homophobia challenges Black lesbians every day. These cultural norms give Black lesbians a very specific perspective of the world. Identity defines who we are, what we value, and where we want to go in life. As a White lesbian who identifies strongly with being a daughter and a sister, I value family. As a person that struggled immensely during my coming out process, I compromised my sexual identity for years with the worry and concern that I might in fact lose my family. I might jeopardize my identity as a daughter and sister with my identity as a lesbian. So I compromised. I hid. I chose to not develop my identity as a lesbian. I chose to introduce my girlfriends as friends to my family. I only held their hands in private. I chose to avoid wanting to express my gender through bow ties and ties. I stared at the invisible line in all clothing stores for years before I decided to tiptoe over. W 29 L 30 in men's pants was made for my body. But, I hid those needs in my own life because I thought I needed to salvage the relationships in my life that meant everything.

Hiding parts of my identity hindered the development of my whole self. I felt discrimination for being a lesbian at my Catholic school. This discrimination creates a negative and intimidating attitude on a college campus. It is crucial for our colleges to realize students cannot choose to represent pieces of their self. It is an institution's responsibility to cultivate safe environments for all types of students. Racial identity is part of a person's holistic identity. Racial identity will be developed at HBCUs, but other pieces are present in our student's lives that need to be recognized.

> Although the African American experience with discrimination and inequality has produced a certain amount of progressivism on racial issues at HBCUs, certain categories of people have been and continue to be discriminated against because of their gender, national origins, social class, sexual orientation, religion, race, or ethnicity. (Jewell, 2002, p. 18)

I believe Black lesbians are confronted with these compromising positions as they experience the intersectionality of identity. They begin to negotiate who they are based on the environments around them.

The battle of homophobia in a heterosexual and heteronormative society will play a part in the self-worth, personal engagement, academic advance, and identity development of a LGBTQ student. According to Battle and Ashley heteronormativity is explained as heterosexuality being the standard that all other genders, sexualities, and sexual expressions are supposed to follow (2008, p. 1). Anyone or anything outside of this standard is considered different. As Black lesbians enter an academic setting they will be challenged by prejudices and privileges of our American society and very well may struggle to find their own place within their institutions. It is critical for colleges and universities to be aware of the needs of all of their students. This institutional awareness will foster a sense of self-worthiness and commitment in students as they engage academically and socially.

Black lesbians will be faced with the intersection of race, sexuality, and gender. Harley, Nowak, Gassaway, and Savage state that racial minority LGBT students are faced with integrating at least two central identities (2002, p. 530). "There is a constant negotiation between different cultures causing students to feel they are caught in between" (p. 530). This sense of compromising, in some cases, forces students to under develop pieces of who they are. It is necessary to identify these separate identities and synthesize them in a way that forms a holistic perspective. Without an institutional awareness of these issues, Black lesbians can be developing pieces of who they are but not the entirety. These central identities of race, sexuality, and gender shape the experiences of Black lesbians and the people they will become.

HBCUs and Black Lesbian Identity

HBCUs were historically created to educate Black Americans in safe and united environments. In a segregated society it was critical to have a place where Black students could find camaraderie and not fear being Black. HBCUs gave Black students a place to learn and advance without feeling the racial discriminations of the society around them. As I stated before, as a White lesbian, I rarely ever considered being White or the impact it had on me. At HBCUs race is celebrated and becomes the norm for students that decide to attend. It is a time to value race, to find a place equally in society, and to be part of a greater community of likeminded people.

HBCU environments create a safe space to explore racial identity in a positive way. Many Black Americans wanted a safe experience and many Black Americans chose HBCUs because of the racial benefits. It was a chance to learn, to live, and to prosper in a Black community. This still holds true today. Van Camp, Barden, Sloan, and Clarke confirm that many of the students who attend HBCUs indicate race played into the college choice (2013, p. 458). This decision allows Black students a potential opportunity to be empowered by their racial identity. HBCU communities allow Black students a space to relate to the academic rigor, social lifestyle, and cultural identities within the institution. HBCUs afforded room for personal development, learning, and change without the pressure of racial discrimination.

HBCUs are designed to cultivate safe spaces for the development of their students. However, not all students identify with the mission and vision of the institution. There is in fact diversity within the student bodies of HBCUs. It is essential for an institution to realize different types of students are selecting their school to help shape the people they want to become. College choice is important to student development. According to Van Camp et al., "the choice of which college to attend is one of the most critical decisions that young people face which have enormous implications that resonate through the rest of their lives" (2013, p. 458). This college decision will play a large part in the development of a person's mind and person's identity. HBCUs, like any institution, need to be prepared for all types of students. It is possible students are choosing colleges or universities to support one piece of their identity. However, students that have layered perspectives might not be developing holistic perspectives as people.

Yes, racial development is essential as a young Black lesbian develops her own mind and sees her own place within a society. However, if an institution assumes their students only need support in their racial identity, Black lesbians might feel invisible as lesbians. Every school must be aware of the underlying message its mission could be sending to its community. An LGBTQ identified student might receive the message they are not welcome. A heterosexual student might interpret the message that it is ok to discriminate against an LGBTQ student. Institutional messages can create oppressive tendencies for their campus communities. Torres et al. state, "This majority view can be seen as oppressing identities that are non-majority and therefore not consistent with definitions of the norm" (2009, p. 584). Messages come in all forms and are perceived in many ways.

As a student at a Catholic school, the campus climate was generally not accepting of LGBTQ people. There was no center, there was no student group, and there was no inclusive language in classrooms or around campus that supported the issues of LGBTQ students. A community picks up on these messages. They subconsciously act in accordance with these institutional messages to create a community standard. These institutional messages and expectations can be interpreted as the standard the community lives by. This can also be interpreted as homophobia.

The Influence of Heteronormativity

Institutional forms of homophobia create fear and hatred within a campus climate. This fear and hatred can be created unintentionally without even considering the impact it might have on an environment. Wickens and Sandlin define homophobia as the fear or hatred against individuals who have a non-heterosexual orientation deriving from personal opinions or beliefs (2010, p. 653). This type of hatred plays a large role in the heterosexist society we live in. This heterosexist society forces homosexuality to either become invisible or is repressed and stigmatized by the outside culture and society (Wickens & Sandlin, 2010). According to Wickens and Sandlin, "these two terms ground recent discourses on *heteronormativity*, which presumes and privileges heterosexuality and monitors 'proper' and accepted gender identities through regulation of sexual arrangements" (2010, p. 653). Anyone or anything outside of this standard is considered different. Heteronormativity and homophobia are overlapping ideas focusing on the notion that people hate and fear those not "normal" (non-heterosexual). When I walk on campus I feel this fear from people. I sense lingering eyes as people forget to close their mouths when they realize I am a woman wearing a bow tie. Heteronormative responses shape everyday experiences. Whether being questioned for entering the wrong bathroom or being called sir at a restaurant, I am constantly confronting heteronormative expectations and behaviors.

This type of norming is the most difficult to combat in all aspects of society. In education specifically, gender bias as well as sexual identity discrimination is present from a very young age. We see these very clear gender binary identities in all aspects, from bathrooms (Men and Women) to college applications (checking female or male). We see sexuality discrimination and heteronormative behavior in most religions, TV commercials, and songs on the radio. This behavior is expressed constantly. Whether it is subconsciously putting another person's identity in a box or blatant discrimination against an individual's sexual orientation, homophobia plays a large part in educational settings. Often times we do not notice the subtleties of hatred within our communities. However, a person who is LGBTQ will feel these homophobic behaviors immediately as they are trying to find a place in the culture and community of which they are a part.

I felt discrimination every day as a student attending a Catholic university. The overall assumptions that I would marry a man, I would have a family, and being gay was not accepted were constant messages I felt from my campus community. I paired these messages with the very insecure person I was. I felt very isolated in this Catholic environment because I truly wanted to be there; however I was only in the beginning stages of my development. I needed help and support. I was drawn to the dedication the institution had to social justice. I wanted to explore service immersion trips and I wanted to be close to home. At a time where I was discovering my own sexuality, I did not pick the university because I was gay. I was not fully developed or confident in my lesbian identity. I picked the university based on the things I knew to be true. My older brother went there. It was close to home.

People of the LGBTQ community are aware of the societal norms with which they interface. LGBTQ people realize the forms of discrimination that will influence their daily lives. Because of these surrounding pressures, LGBTQ people are able to identify who they are in relation to their environment. When a person is pressured to identify with or deny parts of who they are, it becomes very clear what becomes "worth it." As a White lesbian, I never once considered compromising my White identity. But, a Black lesbian might feel the need to pick. She might feel that her Black community will not accept her if she were to identify as lesbian.

Black lesbians will be faced with multiple forms of discrimination that make them question who they are. These women will decide whether to accept all of their identities holistically or whether they will compromise parts of their overall identity. Black lesbian poet Audre Lorde talks about this feeling of compromise in describing how society around her tried to define her. Lorde explains: "There's always someone asking you to underline one piece of yourself—whether it's Black, woman, mother, dyke, teacher, etc.—because that's the piece that they need to key in to. They want to dismiss everything else" (2004, p. 31).

The Impact of Community

As Black lesbians begin to explore and combine multiple forms of identity they will also gravitate to environments and communities that continue to support their entire person. However, if faced with a community that does not accept one piece of their identity but does in fact support another, a person might decide to neglect parts of who they are. Based on racial oppression, the Black community is shaped by its unique social, economic, and cultural position in the United States (Phillips, 2005). Community is important in a person's development. There is a commitment one has to bettering the communities of which they are a part. According to Robinson and Biran: "Level of commitment to the Black community is defined as the extent to which persons feel responsible for positively contributing to the Black community" (2006, p. 52). A Black lesbian might find safety and security racially but might be fearful she will not be accepted or might not be contributing positively to her community because of her sexual identity. She will stay in the environment that feels safest to her. If that safety means compromising her sexual identity she could choose for that identity to become "invisible." Not all lesbians are able to pass as straight women. Sexuality, gender, and gender expression all fall on a spectrum. Some Black lesbians might find safety in compromising parts of their identity, but others might not have that privilege.

I attended a conference once where the panelists were asked to give advice on being "out in the work place." The overarching message was essentially not to come out. Be invisible. The panel said it could jeopardize you professionally. As a young professional I was very offended by this message, mainly because I do not have the privilege of "hiding" and becoming "invisible." As a professional my appearance is a startling force in my Catholic environment. My gender identity is female. My gender expression leans masculine. I wear a tie or bowtie to work every day. My men's pants are perfectly tailored and I have refined the sweater and shirt dryer shrink to fit my petite body. My feet are too small for men's shoes, so finding the androgynous women's shoe has been a headache. My hair is cut into a "Mad Men" fade every week, yet I wear a full face of makeup. I wear perfume and cologne and find the mixture of the two is just right. Men and women stop to ask me what scent I am wearing, where I got my clothes, or where I get my hair cut. I worry often this will be interpreted as a costume, however; it is genuinely how I see myself—a perfect combination of the two.

Sexuality, gender, and gender expression are all interesting things. They are not always binary and they are not just as simple as straight or gay, male or female, and masculine or feminine. These ranges vary within the LGBTQ community. From childhood we are grouped according to cultural norms. Boys like girls, they prefer blue, and have short hair. Girls like boys, they prefer pink, and have long hair. We see these trends throughout all institutions in almost everything we do. Yet, we all do not have the privilege of hiding behind or defining all aspects of who we are. It is not always so clear.

When students choose HBCUs they are choosing an institution that will cultivate an experience of positive racial interaction. However, not all Black students are looking to develop just their racial identity. Black lesbians will find security at HBCUs as members of the Black community, however; Black lesbians will face challenges as women and as lesbians as they make the transition into this environment. Patton and Simmons explain that sexual identity can become invisible as these students face prejudice and rejections (2008, p. 198). These feelings of rejection can lead to failure in academics, personal emotional development, as well as forming a holistic identity. Cohen and Garcia explain that people find value and identity from the groups they belong to (2005, p. 566). They go on to explain that a person who is victimized by discrimination can be significantly impacted (p. 566). If Black lesbians feel isolated from their institution because of their identity they will be less engaged in the campus's academic and social settings. There are many different dimensions of identity that influence a student's engagement with their surroundings

According to Abes, Jones, and McEwen college students have an intense relationship with their identity. In this relationship, each identity dimension must be embraced in unison instead of in isolation (2007, p. 3). There are many external factors that contribute to an individual's holistic identity. At HBCUs specifically, campus climate and community expectations will greatly affect a Black lesbian's identity development.

Oftentimes the argument surrounding sexual identity is that it is only a piece of the overall person. But all pieces contribute to the entirety of anything. All experiences and interactions contribute to the overall development of a person's identity. This contributes to the way individuals interact with their surroundings. The way someone perceives their own identity in relation to other dimensions, such as gender, religion, race, etc., will greatly impact the engagement that one has with these factors. Pike and Kuh explain that a student's positive experiences are essential to creating successful student engagement (2005, p. 186). Without student engagement, student development cannot happen. One learns when they are interested, engaged, or fueled in some way. Without addressing issues, opinions, and differences there is no room for explicit engagement to occur.

Being a White lesbian that attended a Catholic institution in some ways parallels being a Black lesbian attending an HBCU. The barriers of religion, culture, and gender are all very apparent. Black communities are shaped greatly by their religious affiliations. Ward states that Black churches are significant in the social aspects of the Black community and are considered the most influential institution in Black communities (2005, p. 494). Constant disapproval from their church communities reinforces homophobic perspectives. Ward attributes religious beliefs, historical sexual exploitation, and racial awareness during slavery to the homophobic perspectives within Black churches (p. 494). Based on Lewis's study, the majority of Black people believe that homosexual relations are generally wrong and some believe AIDS might be God's punishment for this sexual behavior (2003, p. 75). These messages are powerful and can have a lasting impact. There is also pressure to be a positive representative of one's community. Cohen and Garcia explain this as collective threat. This concept explores the idea of "I am us," which defines an overall group on the way it is perceived (2005, p. 566). This can cause a great deal of stress when deciding to explore parts of an identity that might negatively impact an overall group.

Summary and Recommendations for HBCUs

Black lesbians need support as they enter college. This support is bigger than physically seeing a center for LGBTQ people. There needs to be education for LGBTQ people, specifically Black lesbians, as well as the entire campus community. Black lesbians need to know their institution will partner with them as they find ways to develop holistically. Patton states that HBCUs rarely offer resources (student organizations, offices, centers) for LGBT students (2011, p. 77). This means the dialogue is not happening in classrooms and in social settings. Identity plays a very important role in the success of students. Student engagement and success is critical to a student's connection with their identity and their university. Kinzie explains that student engagement creates a positive and successful college experience (2009, p. 471). Our students' engagement will come from their connection and dedication to their institution. If Black lesbians feel isolated from their institution because of their identity they will be less engaged in the campus's academic and social settings. There are many different dimensions of identity that impact a student's engagement with their surroundings. Without the proper resources students are not supported and guided through their own struggles and experiences. When a university does not have resources like a student group or center it is saying these students are not significant. These messages will make students feel like they are not important or worthy. This type of neglect or avoidance will force a student to abandon the parts of their identity that are not supported by a university or community.

Resources such as training, centers, and programs help communities of people learn the importance of inclusion. If HBCUs do not foster this type of learning, these students will be left out of the equation. Patton and Simmons explain that racial identity development complicates the identity of LGBT people (2008, p. 198). Dealing with multiple identity developments can lead many students to feel abandoned and unsupported by their surrounding environments. They will feel confused and unsure about how to fuse identities to become one. The pressures of academic success alone are intimidating. But, when a culture indirectly sends the message that you are not accepted, students internalize and avoid certain aspects of who they are, and essentially become incapable of forming holistic identities.

I felt this way at my university. As an LGBTQ person, I felt extremely underrepresented and undersupported as I was working through my central identity as a lesbian. I never heard conversations in my classroom surrounding issues of LGBTQ people and I rarely heard people in my campus community talking about these issues. Language was very heteronormative. Religion played a major role in the opinions of the community. I recognize I signed up for that experience. However, I do not believe this is a valid argument. We cannot assume the identities of all our students regardless of what the majority is. As educational institutions, it is critical to pledge to be part of the developmental process with each of our students. We cannot pick and choose who we think we want them to be.

All experiences and interactions contribute to the overall development of a person, the way they interact with their surroundings and the reactions they have to their environment. Identity development has a direct relationship with the level and quality of one's engagement. Without student engagement, student development and success cannot happen. Without addressing issues, opinions, and differences there is no room for explicit engagement to occur. The focus should be on having the freedom to act and being able to authentically learn. Learning in a biased environment could lead to disconnect between students, disconnect from the self, and disconnect from the university.

Writing this essay was difficult because I constantly tried to relate my experiences to the material. Trying to relate to the material made me feel guilty. I never wanted to trivialize the experiences of Black lesbian identity development with a comparison to my experiences of spiritual and sexual identity. However, as a person who attended a Catholic institution for my undergraduate and graduate careers, I was assumed to be many things and normal was not one of them. I felt isolated and different every single day being part of a campus community that subtly yet consistently sent messages of heteronormative and homophobic opinions.

All colleges and universities have an obligation to their students. Regardless of their identity, students should be provided resources to support their identity development. I recommend all educational institutions should be required to train their communities (faculty, staff, administration, students) on creating safe spaces. Schools should have centers that provide resources to raise awareness of the issues LGBTQ people face. There needs to be an obligation to the entire student body and institution to support the personal growth, development, and exploration of all their students. Having resource centers, fulltime professional employees, training, fully operating student groups, and class curriculums focusing on the inclusivity of all people will create environments that motivate our students to thrive. It is our responsibility to cultivate these safe environments for all people.

All I can confirm are my own experiences. I would be wasteful if I did not think about my own journey and wonder how it has contributed to my overall person. After reflecting on my own journey, I never felt unsafe or the pressure of having to choose between being White, or being gay. In having the privilege to focus solely on my sexual identity I believe I had an advantage. Having the freedom to focus on my sexual identity gave me a voice and a confidence I never truly valued until recently.

Identity shapes us. It makes us define our surroundings. Identity does not mean that we are clearly defined in who we are. It could actually mean the opposite. The invisible. Bingham states: "Our identity is partly shaped by recognition or its absence, often by *misrecognition* of others, and so a person or group of people can suffer real damage, real distortion, if the people or society *mirror back to them* a confining or demeaning or contemptible picture of themselves" (2006, p. 325). Identity plays a fundamental part in the development of students. It is a college's responsibility to create safe environments for students to feel connected and appreciated within their communities. Black lesbians are faced with layers of oppression, doubt, and concern as they choose an institution. Black lesbians at HBCUs will be challenged with gender bias, and heterosexist and heteronormative behaviors. It is crucial for our institutions to be committed to their students, to want the best for their students, and to help them define their holistic selves. HBCUs have provided educational opportunities and social equality to Black students by creating safe places to combat racism. As diverse students continue to attend HBCUs, it is up to the institution to pledge to create environments of acceptance for all of their students.

References

Abes, E., Jones, S., & McEwen, M. (2007). Reconceptualizing the model of multiple dimensions of identity: The role of meaning-making capacity in the construction of multiple identities. *Journal of College Student Development, 48*(1), 1–22.

Ashley, C. & Battle, J. (2008). Intersectionality, heteronormativity, and black lesbian, gay, bisexual, and transgender (LGBT) families. *Black Women, Gender + Families, 2*(1), 1–24.

Bingham, C. (2006). Before recognition, and after: The educational critique. *Educational Theory, 56*(3), 325–344.

Cohen, G. L. & Garcia, J. (2005). "I am us": Negative stereotypes as collective threats. *Journal of Personality and Social Psychology, 89*(4), 566–582.

Harley, D. A., Nowak, T. M., Gassaway, L. J., & Savage, T. A. (2002). Lesbian, gay, bisexual, and transgender college students with disabilities: A look at multiple cultural minorities. *Psychology in the Schools, 39,* 525–538.

Jewell, J. (2002). To set an example: The tradition of diversity at historically black colleges and universities. *Urban Education, 37*(1), 7–21.

Kinzie, J. (2009). Student engagement in higher education: Theoretical perspectives and practical approaches for diverse populations. *Journal of College Student Development, 50*(4), 471–474.

Lewis, G. (2003). Black-white differences in attitudes towards homosexuality and gay rights. *The Public Opinion Quarterly, 67*(1), 59–78.

Lorde, A. & Hall, J. W. (2004). *Conversations with Audre Lorde.* Jackson, MI: University Press of Mississippi.

Patton, L. & Simmons, S. (2008). Exploring complexities of multiple identities of lesbians in a black college environment. *The Negro Educational Review, 59*(3/4), 197–215.

Patton, L. (2011). Perspectives on identity, disclosure, and the campus environment among African American gay and bisexual men at one historically black college. *Journal of College Student Development, 52*(1), 77–100.

Phillips, L. (2005). Deconstructing "down low" discourse: The politics of sexuality, gender, race, AIDS, and anxiety. *Journal of African American Studies, 9*(2), 3–15.

Pike, G. & Kuh, G. (2005). A typology of student engagement for American colleges and universities. *Research in Higher Education, 46*(2), 185–209.

Robinson, J. & Biran, M. (2006). Discovering self: Relationships between African identity and academic achievement. *Journal of Black Studies, 37*(1), 46–68.

Torres, V., Jones, S., & Renn, K. (2009). Identity development theories in student affairs: Origins, current status, and new approaches. *Journal of College Development, 50*(6), 577–596.

Twain, M. (1904). *Mark Twain's notebook.*

Van Camp, D., Barden, J., Sloan, L. R., & Clarke, R. P. (2009). Choosing an HBCU: An opportunity to pursue racial self-development. *Journal of Negro Education, 78,* 457–468.

Ward, E. (2005). Homophobia, hypermasculinity and the US black church. *Culture, Healthy & Sexuality, 7*(5), 493–504.

Wickens, C. & Sandin, J. (2010). Homophobia and heterosexism in a college of education: A culture of fear, a culture of silence. *International Journal of Qualitative Studies in Education, 23*(6), 651–670.

CHAPTER FOURTEEN

Not in My Backyard: Puritan Morality versus Puritan Mercantilism and Its Impact on HBCUs

TIFFANY N. DECKER

In the antebellum period, as well as during the Civil War, Northern Whites used Southern slavery as proof of their moral and economic superiority over Southern Whites. As tensions between the North and South grew, Northern and Southern Whites adopted disparate racial identities in response to their differing perspectives on the morality of slavery, and the economic realities of agricultural slavery versus industrialization, to justify disunion. Southern Whites labeled Northern Whites as "Puritans" overcome with religious fanaticism and greedy mercantilism. After the Civil War, Southerners believed that the stereotypes about Northerners held true, as during Reconstruction, religious Northern abolitionists sent teachers and money southward in an effort to educate free Blacks. However, this benevolence toward the former slaves was not without its disturbing side. While these missionaries believed that former slaves were persons deserving of freedom, they also believed that slavery corrupted their character, and therefore, post-bellum, they needed to "save" Blacks from their moral "savagery" (Watson, 2008). The Northern White educators believed that education served as the primary method to eradicate the moral deficiency of the former slaves and to help Blacks obtain the knowledge that would allow them to fully enter White "civilized" society.

While the religious mission to educate Blacks held sway until the turn of the twentieth century, post-Reconstruction, industrial Northern White philanthropy began to overtake religious philanthropy as the primary means of funding Black education. Northern White industrialists, as exemplified by the General Education Board (GEB), became the primary donors to Black education and instituted programs focusing on industrial and agricultural education in an effort to foster Black economic security in the South. These industrialists ultimately agreed with the Jim Crow caste system of the South, and, through their donations to primarily industrial Historically Black Colleges and Universities (HBCUs), illustrated that their interest in Black education was to create an economy that functioned efficiently, rather than to foster equality. These industrialists demonstrated that it was more important to keep Blacks as cheap labor in the South and live up to the part of their "Puritanical" ancestry that promoted economic interests, rather than to respond to their forbearer's religious and humanitarian interests in equality.

Antebellum Race Mythology

Race mythology started long before differing ideologies led to conflict and Civil War. The first racial taxonomies were primarily derived from skin color. In 1735, Carolus Linnaeus, in his essay *Systema Naturae*, "divided people into White, Black, Red, and Yellow" (as cited in Watkins, 2001, p. 27). These different colors hypothetically differentiated groups in terms of their intellectual and behavioral characteristics. Whites were deemed to be "innovative" and intelligent; Blacks were deemed to be "lazy and careless" (p. 27). Beyond intellectual and behavioral characteristics, racial taxonomy also determined the moral fitness of each race. In the Babylonian Talmud, "a collection of oral traditions of the Jews, appear[ing] in the sixth century A.D.; it states that the descendants of Ham are cursed by being black, and depicts Ham as a sinful man and his progeny as degenerates" (Sanders, 1969, pp. 521–522). Over time, further accounts detailed the supposedly sinful nature of Blacks. In the Middle Ages, one rabbinical scholar expanded upon the Genesis account as follows: "Canaan's [a son of Ham] children shall be borne ugly and black!...Men of this race are called Negroes, their forefather Canaan commanded them to love theft and fornication, to be banded together in hatred of their masters and never to tell the truth" (p. 522). Therefore, even prior to the "scientific" racism of the nineteenth and twentieth centuries, the philosophy of White supremacy in terms of intellect, behavior, and morality was already clearly established. These notions were combined in the effort to justify enslaving Africans.

Southerners and Northerners united during the Revolutionary War. Whether one was of Dutch, English, German, Irish, Scottish, French, or Welsh descent, each united under the banner of "American" to defy British authority. However, within the promise that "all men are created equal," the looming question of the place of Blacks within a republican nation still plagued the burgeoning country. In fact, "the central paradox of white American society was to think equality but to practice inequality—a succession of English monarchs had been replaced by the equally divine-right aristocracy of skin color" (Quarles, 1976, p. 229). The United States "was a nation of liars" (p. 229). Frederick Douglas declared that "in her Declaration of Independence, and the gateway to her Constitution, she proclaims 'all men are equal,' while she holds in bondage three millions and half of her subjects" (p. 229). Slavery revealed the hypocrisy of a nation founded upon the ideals of liberty for all, elevating and differentiating various White ethnicities while also stripping Blacks of any notion of their African ethnicities.

While ostensibly forgotten today, the perceived racial differences between Northern and Southern Whites greatly influenced the trajectory of Black education. During the Revolution, Whites united from various ethnic backgrounds into a cohesive group. However, even within a simplistic racial system where one was either "White," "Black" or "Red," or "Yellow," there were small indications that Whites below the Mason Dixon line, and those above it, were beginning to think of themselves as different peoples shortly after the Revolution. In 1785, Thomas Jefferson wrote that those in the North were "cool, sober, laborious, persevering, independent,...chicaning, superstitious and hypocritical"; while, those in the South were "fiery, Voluptuary, indolent, unsteady independent...generous, candid" (Boyd, 1953, p. 468). While many still subscribed to the notion that Whites were a united people, fractures within this ideology came to the fore in the 1850s as the question of the "peculiar institution" of slavery took on increasing prominence (Watson, 2008, p. 26).

The "Science" of Race

As the nineteenth century progressed, the "science of race" was used as a method to justify conflict and separation. Where discrimination based upon skin color was a long-standing custom in the United States, the scientific community contributed to notions that there were inherent "biologically heritable, moral and intellectual characteristics" even between those of White ancestry (Watson, 2008, p. 38). Race took on increasing importance as new states joined the union as either slave states or free states. As Southern and Northern Whites found themselves at an impasse about the economic—agricultural or industrial—future of the United States, as well as the morality of slavery, perceived racial divisions among Whites were co-opted as a method to justify conflict. The scientific community contributed to the illusion that there was a moral hierarchy among races—not just between "Black" and "White" and "Red" and "Yellow"—but between sub-races of Whites as well.

The "Norman" and the "Anglo-Saxon"

As the conflicts over slavery in the 1850s increased, these perceived racial differences between Whites of the North and Whites of the South took on mounting significance—a significance that overtly and subtly influenced the funding of Black education in the decades to come. Southern Whites "eagerly embraced the notion of a racially determined nationalism" as a way to justify their different perspectives from Northern Whites (Gilpin Faust, 1988, p. 10). The notion that there was a taxonomy even among Whites served to further place Blacks at the bottom of this taxonomy and to reinforce Southern superiority—not just over Blacks—but over other Whites as well. Southern Whites united through the myth of a "Norman" ancestry; Northern Whites united under an "Anglo-Saxon" ancestry. "Norman" Southerners claimed that they could trace their roots back to aristocratic ancestors in England who would have been a part of the Norman Conquest of England in 1099. Those of "Anglo-Saxon" descent in the North also hailed from England. These two "racial" groups were chosen by the opposing sides in an effort to illustrate long-held differences in perspectives deriving from their supposedly different racial origins. Normans, as aristocratic conquerors, believed that society functioned better through hierarchy. The Anglo-Saxons, prior to the Norman Conquest, practiced a more egalitarian form of government. Thus, the thinking went, aristocracy was in the blood of the Norman; whereas, democracy was in the blood of the Anglo-Saxon. These perceived differences, while seemingly forgotten by the twentieth century, continued to play a role in the fate of Blacks in the South.

The "Cavalier" and the "Puritan"

Each of these two racial groups adopted the terms "Cavalier" and "Puritan" to represent the philosophical underpinnings of their different races. Those of supposed Norman descent adopted the term "Cavalier" to represent their heritage. For the most part, these English Cavaliers were Anglicans, supported the state religion, and relied upon a caste system to ensure the viability of their agricultural estates, much like those in the South. Southern Whites felt a kinship with this "Norman Cavalier" heritage and felt that the conflicts with Northern Whites illustrated how Northern Whites wanted to ruin their economic system, which was based upon slavery, with their mercantile economy and abolitionist morality. Much like their English forbearers they felt that they understood and adhered to the true nature of the country and their religion by continuing with agricultural slavery. Even after their defeat in the Civil War the underpinning "Norman Cavalier" myths continued and ultimately resulted in Jim Crow laws that tried to keep Blacks tied to the land and continue the "aristocracy" of Whites in the South.

Northern Whites, on the other hand, were labeled "Puritans." Historically, the Puritans represented those in opposition to England's hierarchical society and opposed kings Charles I and Charles II. Puritans practiced a religion vastly different from the state-sanctioned religion and were often merchants. These Puritans stood for everything that the Cavalier abhorred. Thus these "Norman Cavaliers" and the "Anglo-Saxon Puritans" were different in terms of religion, ideal economic systems, and views of government. Southern Whites and Northern Whites rallied under these supposed racial identities in an effort to illustrate their vastly different perspectives about religion, the future of agricultural slavery versus industrial economies, and the role of government. Southern Whites felt that Northern Whites were "Puritans" fueled by religious and mercantile fanaticism. To Southerners, Northern religious zeal and devotion to industrial pursuits demonstrated that they were of a race wholly different from the refined, aristocratic Southerners, and while the use of "Puritan" and "Cavalier" rarely appeared after the Civil War, the economic and moral differences were not forgotten.

"Race" and Religion

Slavery was justified under a system where those in the South, of "noble" Norman heritage, stemming from their supposed aristocratic

English ancestry, were destined and morally justified to hold "the depraved and fallen" Blacks in bondage (Watson, 2008, p. 41). The "Cavalier" gentleman planter further utilized the idea of biblical slavery to demonstrate that slavery could fit within Christian morality. While all men were "fallen," Blacks were "most inferior and deeply fallen" and it was through their contact with civilized Whites that they would learn of Christianity, and, thus, the slave master could act as a guiding father-figure protecting his childlike slaves from their baser natures (Watson, 2008). While upward of three-fourth of White Southerners did not hold slaves and very few, even of those of the planter class, were actually of "Norman" descent, the myth prevailed as a way to unite White Southerners and to give credence to the feelings of poor Southern Whites that they too were superior to Blacks. The notion of a shared "Norman Cavalier" ancestry also gave poor Southern Whites a way to feel kinship with the Southern aristocracy, which had just as much a hand in keeping those Southern Whites poor as it did in promulgating slavery. By essentially co-opting poor Whites to the slaveholder's cause through this fiction of shared ancestry, the aristocratic planter elite tried to ensure that their worldview would prevail, while in fact these poor Whites would otherwise have very little incentive to prop up the system. Southern Whites also promulgated a literal interpretation of the Bible in an effort to justify slavery and felt that Northerners with their "puny vision" were trying to "dictate to the Almighty where, how, and when He shall do His own work" to determine when and if the slaves should be freed (Dawson, 1978, p. 605).

While Southerners relied upon the philosophical and religious traditions of their communities, Northerners, with their Puritan heritage, subjected "everything...to the test of the reason of the individual" (p. 605). The new religious thinking in the North, Transcendentalism, aligned itself with abolitionist views. Whites in the North also believed that Blacks were morally debased; however, they believed that it was slavery itself, and not their inherent nature, that created their immorality. These "Puritans" also referred to the Bible; however, rather than relying on the slavery of the Old Testament, the abolitionist Whites used New Testament doctrine and declared that all were equal in the eyes of God. The "Puritan" believed that the only "saving" Blacks needed was from the ravages of slavery upon their virtue and that could only be done through emancipation.

The Cavalier and Puritan Make Peace

While literature supporting the myths of "Norman Cavalier" and "Anglo-Saxon Puritan" dramatically increased in the decade prior to the Civil War, after the war, the supposed racial differences between these two groups was ostensibly forgotten (Watson, 2008). While many in the South proclaimed that the American Civil War was "the final act of the English Civil War" and thus, in the end, the Puritans had won, each quietly began to reunite under the idea of a universal "Anglo-Saxon" race in the United States to represent Whites, while still acknowledging that there were cultural differences between Whites of Northern and Southern roots (Dawson, 1978, p. 608). Rather than being inherent, biological differences, these differences were referenced in terms of differing cultural perspectives primarily on religious and economic values. The reuniting of the two different "races" of the North and South dangerously reestablished a White racial identity to be contrasted with Black identity.

This unification did not mean that there were no vast differences in terms of how Northern and Southern Whites viewed the future of the United States. Since the North had won the Civil War, Northern Whites were able to use their economic resources to illustrate their moral superiority to both Southern Whites and Blacks through Reconstruction. Applying the logic of medieval trial-by-combat, the victory of the North illustrated that Northern perspectives, economic systems, and religions were more "enlightened" than, and superior to, that of their Southern peers. The term "Anglo-Saxon" may have once again represented all White Americans—North or South—but only because "Puritan" religious and economic ideology won the day and cleared the field of the "Cavaliers."

Toward Education for Blacks

Education Is Freedom

Blacks were not without agency in their desire to obtain education; however, post-Emancipation, they, for the most part, lacked the economic capital to supply their own schools. Thus, "when local black teachers could not be identified, the freed people appealed to northern missionary organizations to send trained teachers to meet their needs"

(Williams, 2002, p. 373). While Blacks attempted, and in many cases were successful in their endeavor, to control their own schooling, they also had to rely upon the benevolence of Northern religious and industrial philanthropists to fund and staff the vast majority of their schools. Blacks had little access to literacy prior to Emancipation. Laws prohibited Whites from "instruct[ing] Negroes in reading in writing" for fear that education could lead to "Negro unrest and make white control more difficult" (Roucek, 1964, p. 164). Prior to the Civil War, "all Southern states employed statutes called the Black Codes which strictly forbade the schooling of black slaves" (Peeps, 1981, p. 253). Even in the North, the education of Blacks often focused on rescuing "black heathens" (Roucek, 1964, p. 162). While the primary focus in educating Blacks was on religious education as a means to salvation for "savage" Blacks, even as early as 1693, Quakers "advocated religious training as a preparation for emancipation" (p. 162). Northern religious sects were the first to establish higher education institutions for the education of Blacks. In contrast to the Black Codes of the South, religious abolitionist groups in the North, specifically Presbyterians, Methodists, Episcopalians, and Quakers, established tertiary institutions for the education of Blacks. Three institutions—Lincoln, Cheney, and Wilberforce—were founded by these groups and were all located north of the Mason Dixon line. The establishment of these schools illustrates abolitionist religious sects believed in the educability of Blacks, even as their primary focus may have been on saving their souls.

After the Civil War, as Blacks "attempted to take control of their own lives, many freed people wanted one thing more than all others: to learn to read and write" (Williams, 2002, p. 372). Education was particularly important to those who had been denied it for so long. These newly freed people understood that illiteracy "would impede their ambition for full participation" in the "public" and the "political sphere" and "therefore education took on added significance" (p. 373). They thirsted for the knowledge that would make them citizens who were able to exercise their hard won rights. Many went to extremes in their quest to acquire an education. In November 1866, an American Missionary Association employee in Beaufort, South Carolina, observed: "All around us the Freedmen are struggling hard against poverty, some against actual starvation, yet they beg harder for school than for food or clothing" (p. 376). Others, like John Alvord, superintendent of education for the Freedman's Bureau, were equally impressed by the hunger for knowledge that the newly freed Blacks exhibited. Just after the war ended and the South was still in shambles, he observed:

And yet here is a people long imbruted by slavery, and the most despised of any on earth, whose chains are no sooner broken that they spring to their feet and start up an exceeding great army, clothing themselves in intelligence. What other people on earth have ever shown, while in their ignorance, such a passion for education? (p. 376)

Former slaves flocked to schools, clamoring for knowledge, knowing that it was only through education that they would truly gain their freedom.

Post-bellum, Northern religious groups extended their programs to educate former slaves into the South, where the vast majority of Blacks resided. While these Northern missionaries "may have been paternalistic" they never "had any doubt about the ability of black men to master the standard liberal arts curriculum of the day" (Peeps, 1981, p. 253). These missionaries believed that "blacks were equal to whites but for the debilitating effects of slavery" (p. 254). Former slaves were hungry for the education that had been denied them for centuries. Education "came to be one of the great preoccupations of Negroes; and enlightenment was viewed by many as the greatest single opportunity to escape the proscriptions and indignities that [Southern] whites were heaping upon blacks" (Franklin, 1974, p. 271). While these missionaries expanded educational opportunities, they still believed that, along with instilling the basics of a liberal arts curriculum, it was their duty to provide Christian instruction and correct the "moral character" of slaves, as slavery had "morally, spiritually, and culturally bankrupted Blacks" (Brazzell, 1992, p. 31). Their paternalism also extended toward Southern Whites. There was no system of public education for either Whites or Blacks in the South. By providing education for Blacks and not the Whites of the South, Northern missionaries were defying the Southern White establishment and illustrating that they were morally superior to their White "peers." By establishing colleges for freed slaves, Northern Whites attempted to provide an example of the "right" type of Christianity—a Christianity that believed in the basic humanity of all God's creatures, Black or White—while demonstrating the immorality of Southern Whites who denied this basic fact.

The "Great Detour"

While Southerners no longer persisted in the notion that Northern Whites and Southern Whites were a separate race, they continued in the belief that Northerners still held a "Puritanical" zeal for religion and industrialization. Northern *industrial* philanthropy began to overtake Northern *religious* philanthropy at the turn of the twentieth century. White Northern industrialists, while still paternalistic toward Southern Whites, embraced notions of Black inferiority in an effort to further their economic interests. Rather than embracing the egalitarianism of their religious forebears, the industrialists were comfortable reestablishing a caste system with themselves at the top, the "backward" Southern Whites below, and the former slaves back at the bottom.

While missionary philanthropists believed that Blacks could eventually be equal to Whites, industrial philanthropists may have inadvertently been harkening back to the philosophies of their English Puritan forbearers who believed that "rich and poor, everyone is exhorted to labor in his calling and to keep his station in life" (Seaver, 1980, p. 48). To confirm the notion that everyone must labor according to their "station," conveniently, the caste system that denigrated Blacks was being reestablished by Southern Whites through Jim Crow laws, just as Social Darwinism became an increasingly popular "scientific" justification for White supremacy. This change from Northern missionary philanthropy to Northern industrial philanthropy thus forced a "great detour" in the future of Black education, from a liberal arts-based approach focused on creating an informed citizenry to an industrial one interested only in training future workers.

Social Darwinism

Social Darwinism gave a scientific gloss to the systemic discrimination of Blacks. While Darwin, himself, never equated his research on evolution to humans, many others soon used his theories to promote social stratification. Herbert Spencer (1874) was the first to use the phrase "survival of the fittest" and to extrapolate that the Darwinist principles of natural selection could also be applied to human societies (Dennis, 1995, p. 244). Some Social Darwinists, like William Graham Sumner, even went as far as to reason "that because slavery permitted superior groups the leisure to construct and develop more refined cultures, it actually advanced the cause of humanity" (p. 244). Therefore, as Blacks had previously been subjugated, it stood to reason under these theories that they were subjugated due to the natural inferiority of their race to the White race, and that the new caste systems created by Jim Crow furthered the aims of civilization.

Social Darwinism also aligned with capitalist ideology as it gave reason for exhorting capitalism over those of supposedly inferior race and civilizations, and thus "Social Darwinism was directed... toward both race and economics" (p. 249). Hofstadter found that "in the decades after 1885, Anglo-Saxonism... was the dominant abstract rationale of American imperialism... The Darwinist mood sustained the belief in Anglo-Saxon racial superiority" (1992, pp. 172–173). The wish to suppress others "speaks volumes about the tangible political and economic gains accrued to those doing the subjugating. Attacks on the abilities of the subjugated can thus be seen as merely an attempt to morally justify actions that often run contrary to the stated democratic principles of the subjugators" (Dennis, 1995, p. 249). Social Darwinism provided the moral justification for the Jim Crow caste system while forging an alliance between Northern and Southern Whites through their ostensibly superior White racial heritage, all the while furthering their economic objectives.

Thanks to Social Darwinism, many Northern Whites abandoned their previous belief in Black equality and began to accept Southern notions of White supremacy. Even Dr. Wallace Buttrick, one of the executive heads of the General Education Board stated: "The Negro is an inferior race" (Peeps, 1981, p. 267). Uniting racially with his Southern White brethren he proclaimed: "The Anglo-Saxon is superior. There cannot be any question about that" (p. 26). These Northern philanthropists no longer defied White Southerners in their view of Blacks as an inferior race, and rather they tried to fit their economic objectives into the systematic racism of the South. Through Jim Crow laws, Blacks were, for the most part, retied to the land through sharecropping. Whereas Northern missionaries defied Southern White supremacy through their belief that Blacks were essentially the same as Whites, but for the moral corruption of slavery itself, Northern industrial philanthropists were much more obliging to the desires of Southern Whites to maintain a caste system based upon skin color, if it furthered their economic interests.

The Morality of Industry

Despite the "great detour" in terms of how Blacks were educated under Northern missionaries versus Northern industrialists, and their new embrace of the Southern caste system, the industrialists still found a way to fit their mercantile pursuits within their religious heritage. In fact, they discovered, industrialization and morality were not entirely separate. John D. Rockefeller Sr. "accepted the puritanical and equally popular notion that godliness was in league with riches" (Watkins, 2001, p. 120). While both John D. Rockefellers, *père et fils* (founders of the GEB), were Northern Baptists, many of the tenants of Puritanism had found themselves enshrined in other Protestant denominations, especially in evangelical creeds like the Baptists. In equating wealth with God's grace, John D. Rockefeller Sr. was not much different than a seventeenth-century English Puritan, Nehemiah Wallington, who believed that it was through "the love and kindness of God in giving me six days [to work] and taking but one for himself" that he was able to build his empire (Seaver, 1980, p. 42). Working hard and acquiring wealth did not detract from one's salvation. In fact, one's wealth may have demonstrated that he was one of God's "elect" and that by denying wealth one was, therefore, denying God's will, for "if God show you a way in which you may lawfully get more than in another way...if you refuse this, and choose the less gainful way, you cross one of the ends of your calling, and you refuse to be God's steward" (Weber, 1958, p. 162). "Handy (2002) suggests that the success of American capitalism rests on the combination of the Puritan traditions (wealth as a symbol of worth, being well-off through one's own efforts as a sign of God's approval)" (in Porter, 2004, p. 430). While Northern industrialists were more accommodating to Southern White perspectives, and, in many cases, agreed with segregation, they still found a way to align their mercantile pursuits with their religious heritage. In fact, they may have considered the continued subjugation of Blacks as morally justifiable as early English Puritan ministers admonished that "poverty might well be God's punishment for sin" (Seaver, 1980, p. 36). Thus, the poverty of Blacks may well indicate their sinful nature, just as the wealth of the industrialists demonstrated their moral superiority.

"Attach the Negro to the Soil"

This did not mean that the industrialists had to let go of "Puritan" paternalism toward Southern Whites peers as they attempted to further their economic objectives. In fact, George Foster Peabody declared, privately: "We cannot afford for the present generation of the South to control negro education" (Anderson & Moss, 1999, p. 16). While it may seem that this statement illustrates the benevolence that Peabody felt toward Blacks and the underlying belief that Southern Whites would halt any progress toward equality, Peabody's use of the word "afford," implies a belief in the importance of Blacks in terms of their economic value, not in humanitarian terms. His statement could just as easily mean that he did not trust the "backward" Southern Whites to control and train the workers necessary to support the new industrial economy.

In fact, Northern philanthropists like Robert C. Ogden openly declared that the "great problem is to attach the Negro to the soil and prevent his exodus from the country to the city" (Roucek, 1964, p. 374). Philanthropists continued to support the Hampton-Tuskegee model of industrial education for Blacks, even while Blacks advocated for a liberal arts curriculum. Northern philanthropists "regarded an economically efficient and politically stable agriculture as a necessary underpinning for national industrial life," as "high agricultural productivity lowered food prices, dampened workers discontent and resulted in a general quickening of the wheels of industry" (p. 374). Another GEB chairman, Wallace Buttrick, felt that it was necessary that Blacks become "common laborers and servants in the South's caste economy" (Anderson, 1988, p. 134). Jones (1917) considered "manual training mandated by 'modern educational practice,' for example, was 'even more necessary for the Negro than for the white," he declared, "since the Negro's highly emotional nature requires for balance as much as possible of the concrete and definite" (Franklin, 1974, p. 208). Thus the great hopes for equality that many Northern abolitionists fought for were quashed under the wheels of their own descendants' industrial aspirations.

Placating Southern Whites

While Northern industrial philanthropists forged ahead with many of their programs for educating Blacks, they remained acutely aware of Southern White sentiment. In fact, "fear of Southern White opposition played an important role in the structuring of northern philanthropy" (Anderson & Moss, 1999, p. 9). The GEB openly endorsed, in 1911, the "policy of cooperating with the white people of the South in promoting Negro education" (p. 9). While ostensibly the GEB was founded to fund Black education, "in the end only 19 percent of the board's gifts went to black education" (p. 9). The GEB "always stated that it supported Southern education, not Black education" (Watkins, 2001, p. 129). This shift in focus illustrates that Northern industrial philanthropists had accepted the Southern caste system under Jim Crow and would only invest in ventures that furthered the domination of Whites by relegating Blacks entirely to physical labor. While Northern industrial philanthropists were still paternalistic towards their Southern White neighbors, they did believe that they shared a common bond through their race and that it was important to foster education for White Southerners in an effort to propel the White race forward, and, more importantly to continue their capitalistic expansion into other parts of the country.

The First Great Migration

With the establishment of Jim Crow laws and seemingly greater economic options for Blacks in the North, a great exodus from the South to the North ensued. Rather than support Blacks in the North, the hypocrisy that Thomas Jefferson pointed out with regard to the Northern character came to the fore. Unlike their missionary predecessors, many Northern industrial philanthropists accepted Social Darwinism and believed that Blacks were an inferior race. Rather than work against the system of White supremacy as many Northern missionaries had, these industrial philanthropists worked through systemic racism to achieve their economic objectives. The "verification [that Blacks were inferior] was especially important in the United States during the first two decades of the 20th century. Indeed racial chauvinism provided a philosophical and moral rationale for differentiating 'native' Anglo-Saxon Americans from the...millions of African Americans who were then migrating en masse from the South to other parts of the country" (Dennis, 1995, p. 246). Thus, as the industrial philanthropists aligned themselves more with Social Darwinist ideology, their desire to keep "undesirable" Blacks working productively for their economic gains, while simultaneously keeping them from migrating North where there was the possibility of infiltration into their superior Anglo-Saxon race, and, additionally, "punishing" White Southerners by forcing them to continue to live in close proximity to a supposed sub-race of people, provided compelling incentives for continuing to support Black agricultural and industrial education in the South.

The Pull North

Even while Northern philanthropic money continued to flow South, Blacks began to move North. Freed from the bonds of slavery, Blacks were finally able to determine their own fate and follow their economic and social interests. With Southern Whites and Northern philanthropists working to economically retie Blacks to the land, and many "noneconomic grievances," like lynching, political disenfranchisement, and other social restrictions, increasingly threatening their lives and livelihoods, the North appeared to be a viable option for those who could make the journey (Tolnay, 2003, p. 215). In 1900, only approximately 740,000 Blacks lived north of the Mason Dixon line (Gregory, 2005, p. 18). By 1930, the Black population in the North and Midwest exploded to over 2.4 million (Gibson & Young, 2002). This mass migration North presented new problems for Northern cities and Southern Black migrants.

Problems in the "Promised Land"

Moving North was not a panacea for those members of the Black population who were able to make the journey. Tolnay found that "in virtually all [Northern] destinations, the Southern migrants were greeted with suspicion and hostility" (p. 218). Blacks in the North blamed for causing "crime, alcoholism, venereal disease, and illegitimacy" (p. 218). Blacks, in many cases, traded the caste system of the South for one in the North. Employment prospects in the North were "restricted by a racially and ethnically defined occupational queue that channeled them [Black Southern migrants] into the lowest-status, least remunerative positions" (p. 218). Additionally, "black neighborhoods often were situated in the least desirable sections of the city and offered dilapidated dwellings with substandard facilities" (p. 219). Therefore, there were plenty of social and economic ills facing the Black population that provided opportunities for Northern philanthropists to aid the plight of this new Black population right in their own backyard.

Ignoring Northern Black Needs

The GEB was founded in 1902, just as the first Great Migration of Southern Blacks to the North began. That this powerful organization continued to fund education in the South while ignoring the needs of the newly expanded Black population in the North demonstrates that the organization hoped that, by continuing to support Black education in the South, they could create a stable work force there that would stem the tide of Blacks moving North. As over two million

Black people moved North from 1900 to 1930, the heyday of the GEB's philanthropic pursuits, and not one new Black college was formed for this population, even while Blacks were barred from most Northern Historically White Institutions, demonstrates the desire of Northern philanthropists for Blacks to remain in the South. While the majority of the Black population still remained in the South, and thus it remained important that philanthropic efforts be focused there for the sake of expediency, that the vast Black Northern migration was virtually ignored by Northern philanthropists demonstrates their desire to keep the South just economically viable enough to maintain its racial caste system and create incentives for Blacks to remain in the South rather than migrate North.

Conclusion

Where Northern missionary philanthropists used their Puritan religious heritage to further the education of Blacks, Northern industrial philanthropists tapped into their Puritan mercantile heritage to align themselves with Southern Whites in creating a Black underclass to support their economic interests. Combined with the teachings of Social Darwinism, Northern industrial philanthropists abandoned the notions of equality that their forbearers championed and, instead, worked with Southern Whites due to their supposedly shared "Anglo-Saxon" heritage to relegate Blacks, again, to an inferior caste. Tragically, as one Black Northern missionary teacher, Charlotte Forten, wrote:

> One cannot believe that the haughty Anglo-Saxon race, after centuries of such experience as these people [enslaved Blacks] have had, would be very much superior to them. And one's indignation increases against those who, North as well as South, taunt the colored race with inferiority while they themselves use every means in their power to crush and degrade them, denying them every right and privilege, closing against them every avenue of elevation and improvement. (Williams, 2002, pp. 379–380)

Thus the "great detour" in philanthropic pursuits changed the trajectory of Black education in the South, and also illustrated the inherent racism of Northern industrial philanthropists as they worked to keep Blacks in the South and out of their own backyards.

References

Anderson, E. & Moss, A. A., Jr. (1999). *Dangerous donations: Northern philanthropy and southern Black education, 1902–1930.* Columbia, MO: University of Missouri Press.

Anderson, J. D. (1988). Northern foundations and the shaping of southern black rural education, 1902–1935. *History of Education Quarterly, 18*(4), 371–396.

Boyd, J. P. (Ed.) (1953). *The papers of Thomas Jefferson.* Princeton: Princeton University Press.

Brazzell, J. C. (1992). Bricks without straw: Missionary-sponsored black higher education in the post-emancipation era. *Journal of Higher Education, 63*(1), 26–49.

Dawson, J. C. (1978). The puritan and the cavalier: The south's perception of contrasting traditions. *Journal of Southern History, 44*(4), 597–614.

Dennis, R. M. (1995). Social Darwinism, scientific racism, and the metaphysics of race. *Journal of Negro Education, 64*(3), 243–252.

Franklin, J. H. (1974). *From slavery to freedom.* New York: Knopf.

Gibson, C. & Young, K. (2002, September). Historical census statistics on population totals by race, 1790 to 1990, and by Hispanic origin, 1970 to 1990, for the United States, regions, divisions, and states. *U.S. Census Bureau: Population Division.* Accessed on May 2, 2013 from http://www.census.gov/population/www/documentation/twps0056/twps0056.html.

Gilpin Faust, D. (1988). *The creation of confederate nationalism: Ideology and identity in the Civil War South.* Baton Rouge, LA: Louisiana State University Press.

Gregory, J. N. (2005). *The southern diaspora: How the great migrations of Black and White southerners changed America.* Chapel Hill, NC: University of North Carolina Press.

Handy, C. (2002). Tocqueville revisited: The meaning of American prosperity. *Harvard Business Review, 79*(1), 57–63.

Hofstadter, R. (1992). *Social Darwinism in American thought.* Boston, MA: Beacon Press.

Peeps, J. M. S. (1981). Northern philanthropy and the emergence of black higher education—do-gooders, compromisers, or co-conspirators? *Journal of Negro Education, 50*(3), 251–269.

Porter, G. (2004). Work, work ethic, work excess. *Journal of Organizational Change Management, 17*(2), 424–439.

Quarles, B. (1976). Antebellum free blacks and the "spirit of '76." *Journal of Negro History, 61*(3), 229–242.

Roucek, J. S. (1964). Milestones in the history of the education of the Negro in the United States. *International Review of Education, 10*(2), 162–178.

Sanders, E. R. (1969). The Hamitic hypothesis: Its origin and function in time perspective. *Journal of African History, 10*(4), 521–532.

Seaver, P. (1980). The Puritan work ethic revisited. *Journal of British Studies, 19*(2), 35–53.

Tolnay, S. E. (2003). The African American "great migration" and beyond. *Annual Review of Sociology, 29,* 209–232.

Watkins, W. H. (2001). *The White architects of Black education: Ideology and power in America, 1865–1954*. New York: Teachers College Press.

Watson, R. D, Jr. (2008). *Normans and Saxons: Southern race mythology and the intellectual history of the American Civil War*. Baton Rouge, LA: Louisana State University Press.

Weber, M. (1958). *The Protestant work ethic and the spirit of capitalism*, T. Parsons (trans.). New York: Scribner Library.

Williams, H. A. (2002). "Clothing themselves in intelligence": The freedpeople, schooling, and northern teachers, 1861–1871. *Journal of African American History, 87*, 372–389.

CHAPTER FIFTEEN

Searching for Whitley Gilbert: Pluralism, Belles, Bourgeoisie Activism, and HBCUs

CHRISTIAN EDGE

Bewitched, Bothered, and Bewildered

"I think you hurt Black people," she said.

For a moment, my ears failed me. I felt as if I were submerged under water. The voices of the waiters, the clanking of the silverware as they greeted the plates, and conversations of the other patrons in the restaurant all appeared to be on mute. Worryingly, for the first time in my life, my tongue refused to budge in my defense. I must have misheard my best friend of two years.

Finally, I did the impossible. I summoned speech. "Huh?" Pretty impressive.

"I think you hurt Black people," she repeated obliviously, without missing a beat. It unnerved me to see my friend so calm and determined in her convictions. It was disturbing.

"How?" I asked busily occupying myself with my burger to avoid looking at her directly which was becoming increasingly difficult.

"Well, Christian, it's the way you dress. It's the way you talk. It's the way you look. It's who you are."

I felt like someone dropped an anvil on me like in one of those Looney Toons cartoons. I looked down at myself to ensure that my torso had not just transformed into an accordion.

"What are you talking about?" I asked, flummoxed. "You just described my whole being."

"Yeah, it's who you are," she confirmed, popping a helpless fry into her mouth. I could relate. I felt like she was devouring me, too.

"What do you mean?" I was turning into a parrot and growing tropical feathers, incessantly repeating a version of the same question.

"I mean you're an assimilationist."

She might as well have lit firecrackers in my ears. A cocktail of cognitive dissonance and past experiences rang in my ears like the bells of Quasimodo's tower in Notre Dame. This was not the first time someone had called me an assimilationist, an indictment of the perception that somehow I was not living up to my end of the mythological Black bargain. This bargain states that I must somehow demonstrate my Blackness through speech and fashion, despite the fact that the color of my skin is not going anywhere. Apparently, I was not Black enough for my dear friend.

The sound of the bells in my ears receded like a tide, and she continued. "You dress the way you do to let White people know you are their equal, and to let other Black people know that you're better than them."

I nearly fell off my stool. Thank goodness for the chunky and sturdy young man seated next to me, or I may have chipped one of my teeth. Twice in one day, my words failed me. This had to be some kind of record. No matter, she kept coming for me like a line of linebackers from the NFL.

"You confirm for White people that we want to be just like them, which isn't true. But, they see you and they think it is."

That is funny. All this time, I thought I was just being myself. It turns out I'm actually a self-hating sadist who supports racist beliefs about his own people. While I will save the motivations and intentions of my friend for my memoir, I will share this: I think *her* opinions are hurting Black people.

Her scope of Black people is narrower than the straw holes on top of juice boxes. Black people are not a simple monolith composed of natural hair and Kente cloth. Black Americans come in all shapes, sizes, hair textures, colors, and economic classes. Black Americans make their own personal choices concerning fashion, hair style, and physical carriage. To paint Black Americans with a broad brush is sheer folly.

Though my friend's assault on my being was a sneak attack of the highest order, I, unfortunately, cannot say I had not heard it previously. My education, especially middle and high school, was filled to the brim with teachers and peers attempting to cram all Black people into the tiniest box imaginable. With all that hard work, it is a real shame Black people do not fit into anyone's box. Of course, that fact did not stop them from trying. The majority of my public school education surrounding Black American history went a little something like this:

"Who were the slaves?" the teacher would ask, raspy voiced, popping gum.

"Black people," the class would answer confidently. By now, we had that answer down pat. The teacher could not fool us with that question.

"Who freed the slaves?" she countered.

"Abraham Lincoln," the class resounded. We really do owe him a lot, you know.

"Then, what happened?"

This part was always tricky. Apparently, after I began to do my own research around the seventh grade, I discovered quite a bit had happened. Let's see, there was a little Reconstruction, some sharecropping, lynching here and there, and don't forget political disenfranchisement. I soon learned, however, teachers were not really interested in all of that. I knew what they wanted.

"Dr. Martin Luther King, Jr. arrived and freed us from all racism, and now the United States sings a never ending loop of 'Kumbayah My Lord.'" The class inevitably always gave this answer in some form or another.

So, by the time I was in eleventh grade, I was all but finished with this spotty recollection of half-formed facts about Black history perpetuated by my schooling. I should have stayed tuned, however. This was not to be my last experience with the cramming of Black people into a box.

In college, a Black professor labeled me an assimilationist for the first time in my life. How dare I applaud Frederick Douglass' commitment and persistence in trying to work within racist paradigms to transform them for the betterment of Black Americans? Then, another Black professor informed me, had he been younger, he would have thrown paint on my clothes and keyed my car. It was a stellar year in my life!

It appeared that White Americans possessed a certain frame for Black Americans, and Black Americans possessed a certain frame for themselves. Apparently, I did not fit into either of these frames. However, I fit into the frames I constructed and valued for Black Americans. I identified with my mother's frame. I identified with Michelle Obama's frame. I identified with Leontyne Price's and Harry Belafonte's frame, among countless others. These individuals represented the connected, yet highly variable experiences of Black Americans.

I grew increasingly frustrated. I wanted to see my reflection in the tapestry of Black America. I did not appreciate others' attempts to cut me from that great piece of fabric. Sadly, the few images of Black Americans that inundated me at school and college appeared to be cut from the same cloth: bleak and singular. Along with the stereotypical phenotypes in these depictions, these images neglected to include the life I knew and that of my mother's. It appeared that the entire scope of history for Black Americans in this country had been squeezed into three words: slavery, poverty, and thug. There had to be more. Much more.

"I'm Not Most People": There's Something about Whitley Gilbert

Fortunately, there was. Miraculously, I discovered *A Different World*, a television show set within the fictional realm of an HBCU in Virginia called Hillman College. Though my mother attended LeMoyne-Owen College, a HBCU in Memphis, TN, watching *A Different World* acted like the Blue Fairy in Pinocchio, transforming the wooden and removed world of my mother's experience into flesh and blood. The cast of the show presented a three-dimensional sketch of Black life in the United States, unlike anything I had ever witnessed in the media or at school. There was the medically minded Kimberley Reese from Ohio, spoiled lothario Ron Johnson, the frog-turned-prince Dwayne Wayne, and biracial, free-spirited activist Winifred "Freddie" Brooks. These characters lived, worked, and studied in a completely unique space, where diversity could be seen among and *within* various Black communities.

None of these breathing characters, however, captured my attention like Whitley Marion Gilbert. Whitley's southern lilt spewed bourgeoisie fireballs of comedy like an uppity dragon. She said anything that was on her mind, and made scant few apologies for it. When she sashayed across the television screen wielding credit cards and haute couture like toys, she completely changed and challenged the perception of the one-note Black history myth, adding complicated layers to what so many believed to be a simple and somewhat bland narrative.

Whitley possessed no ordinary origins, possessing good looks, fine antiques, and the pedigree of a distinguished family tree ("Faith, Hope, and Charity," 1992). She was the daughter of two Hillman College alumni, Judge Mercer Gilbert and socialite Marion Gilbert, who taught Whitley how to sell "Evian to a drowning man" ("May the Best Man Win," 1992). Whitley's presence at Hillman cements a long and proud tradition of Gilberts attending Hillman College. In "May the Best Man Win" (1992), the Pit, which serves as Hillman's eatery and primary gathering place, Whitley mentions Mr. Gaines, the owner of the Pit, has been feeding her family for generations. "Conflict of Interest" (1992) showcases the arrival of prospective freshmen. One of them deems Whitley royalty, noticing one of the dormitories, Gilbert Hall, is named after Whitley's grandfather.

The episode entitled "Mammy Dearest" (1991) explores much of Whitley's rich and diversified" family background (1991). The Gilbert Archives at Hillman College contain Whitley's unique family history, which yet again speaks to the historical prestige her family holds. In the episode, viewers learn that Whitley is the most recent descendant of freed slave Jeremiah Gilbert, her great-great-great grandfather, who gained wealth by manufacturing cotton gins. A young, underclassmen upstart portrayed by a nascent Jada Pinkett named Lena discovers that Jeremiah added to his wealth by investing in Black chattel, owning slaves himself.

After this information is revealed, a mortified Whitley finds herself feeling a spiritual and physical schism from her friends and schoolmates. Interestingly, "Mammy Dearest" (1991) sheds a light on the history that separates Whitley from her peers. While the differences in Whitley's class and upbringing from the other students always hovered above the characters on the show, frequently used for comedic effect through her romance with Dwayne, this episode addressed them somberly. In addition to Whitley's elite class status, this episode also intimated at historic issues concerning Whitley's perceived beauty in contrast to that of her best friend, the future doctor Kimberley Reese.

Whitley becomes adamant about including the historical figure, Mammy, into a media exhibit in celebration of the construction of a new dormitory on campus. The controversial figure haunts Kimberley, who demands that Whitley remove the piece from the exhibit. Whitley refuses, prompting Kimberley's desire to ask her friend, "Who does this (Mammy) look like? Me or you?" ("Mammy Dearest," 1991).

Still, no matter Whitley's vaulted pedigree, fair complexion, or hair texture, it must be noted that Whitley existed as a solid and consistent part of the Hillman College family. While Hillman did not quite ground the winged Whitley completely, the college allowed Whitley to experience and confront issues never before presented to her.

Whitley confronted the issues of poverty facing Black Americans and the urban community when she volunteered at a local youth center ("To Have and Have Not," 1989). There, she befriended a young boy, who misguidedly stole her wallet. Whitley was forced to confront her preconceived notions about people raised in poverty. Interestingly, she also taught ballet at the youth center, proving to many of the young students that Black Americans perform ballet, and excel greatly at the art form.

In "Monet Is the Root of All Evil," Whitley hosts an art exhibit at a local gallery (1991). When a young, starving artist's work portrays the problems facing the Black community, including drug abuse, the piece is deemed too provocative to hang in the exhibit. Whitley must choose between protesting by closing the exhibit and continuing the exhibition without the artist's work. As a testament to the character's growth, Whitley chooses to stop the exhibit, protesting the exclusion of the artist's piece. Whitley's appreciation of the piece and recognition of its importance expertly showcases the merging of Whitley's background and her present experiences at Hillman. She begins using her appreciation of art, cultivated from privileged trips to the Louvre in Paris, to support the work of Black, urban artists. Whitley explains, "When you silence the artist, society suffers and culture dies."

She even joins the inner workings of the political process in "May the Best Man Win" (1992). Whitley bolsters the campaign of Byron Douglas for State Senator, throwing her support behind a man she feels will sincerely fight for minorities and impoverished people. In the process, she learns about the feelings of disenfranchisement and powerlessness young, Black voters experience during election season.

Whitley herself describes the powerful presence Hillman College holds in her life and its transformative power in "Rule Number One" (1991). When Lena begins to fall in love with her professor, Dwayne, due to loneliness, Whitley empathizes with young Lena. Whitley draws a sharp contrast between her depiction at the start of the series, where she wore her differences like armor, and her current open heart due to embracing the world of Hillman College. Forever true to herself, Whitley does not fail to remind inner-city Lena that each of them come from "vastly different cultural backgrounds, lifestyles, and upbringings" ("Rule Number One," 1991).

While Whitley's eventual husband, Dwayne, readily pointed out that his bourgeoisie wife embodied her racial and cultural identity, warning others that she knew perfectly well "who she was" ("Faith, Hope, and Charity," 1992), Whitley's presence and image continued to be perceived as somewhat anomalous on the Hillman College Campus. While debating the ills of Apartheid in South Africa, and how the Hillman student body should respond, Whitley commented to transfer student, Kobe, that her mind refused to even fathom the horrible treatment Black South African people faced. Kobe responds by saying that he never imagined Black Americans like Whitley. Dwayne, comically, supports Kobe's assertion, agreeing that no one possibly imagined someone like Whitley ("A World Alike," 1990).

Much of the United States appears to share Kobe and Hillman College's opinion. In a National Public Radio (NPR) interview, even Jasmine Guy, the actress who expertly portrayed Whitley Gilbert for six seasons, stated:

> And her whole demeanor and poise was really, I thought, made up until I really met other Whitleys [sic] later in my life—real black Southern belles. I thought, what's a black Southern belle? Black people were picking cotton when there were Southern belles, you know, is there such a thing? But there is definitely an upper, middle-class black echelon that Whitley represented that I didn't realize at the time, that has rarely had a voice on television or anywhere else, you know? Blacks, sometimes, they're depicted in one way, and I think "Cosby" and "A Different World" gave great variety to who we are as black people as far as class and background. And Whitley was fun to play because she was always, to me, a fish out of water going to an all-black college. I always assumed she had gone to prep schools. (Conan, 2009)

Whitley Gilbert often appears to be somewhat of an anomaly at Hillman College. Even Jasmine Guy did not fully realize or understand Whitley's place in society or an HBCU upon taking the role. In actuality, Black Americans like Whitley Gilbert do indeed exist in and attend HBCUs. Whitley's presence at Hillman was not at all anomalous. It was a tradition. In reality, "old families among the black elite have selected certain colleges for their children and descendants" (Graham, 1999, p. 66), just as Whitley's storied family selected Hillman College, an institution where the Gilberts possessed a long and rich lineage.

Exploring the lives of three Black women who attended HBCUs illuminates the tradition of the Black bourgeoisie and pluralism inherent on HBCU campuses, as well as the transformative powers HBCUs possess in their lives. Cora Catherine Calhoun, her sister Lena Leo Calhoun, and Diane Nash each possess traits often ignored in the stereotypical story of Black Americans. Each of the women blossomed in the garden of the Black bourgeoisie, surrounded by financial stability and social activities unavailable to other Black Americans. The presence of these women at these institutions factors greatly into the lexicon of HBCUs, contributing to the holistic painting of Black American history.

Far too often, society squelches the voices of Black Americans such as these in the discourse of American history. It is far easier to depict Black Americans as beaten, victims of a racist ideology from which they will never recover. In truth, industrious Black Americans have carved out opportunities and cultural practices for themselves since arriving in the United States. Furthermore, their voices must be heard if society is to ever expand its definition of Blackness, allowing Black Americans to burst from the box in which so many in the United States seek to enclose them. There exists no one definition of Blackness, and, as a testament to these women's lives, there never has.

A Rare Breed: Cora Catherine and Lena Leo Calhoun

Contrary to Jasmine Guy's previous beliefs, some Black, Southern belles like Whitley did indeed reside throughout the South and attend HBCUs. Though rarely discussed or spotlighted like some little known prehistoric discovery, these unique women witnessed their heyday during the "Mystic Years" of Black American history, 1867–1877 (Buckley, 1986, p. 19). Sisters Cora and Lena Calhoun, ancestors of the legendary Lena Horne, exemplify and embody the lives of these Black belles, as they skated at the privileged edges of Black life in the South.

These "Mystic Years," a period during Reconstruction after Emancipation, allowed the sisters' father, Moses Calhoun, to "*make it precisely because, for a brief decade, the American Dream was color-blind*" (p. 19). During this period, though only a "very few" Black Americans received these privileges, many former slaves possessed the right to "vote, go to school, live where they wished, work as they wished, and marry whom they pleased—regardless of color" (p. 19). Moses Calhoun may have been helped by the fact that he could read and write (Buckley, 1986), as he was the son and slave of his former master. As the plantation owner's son, Moses Calhoun possibly received benefits and privileges other Black Americans were not granted during this time:

Fair-skinned Blacks and mulattoes were more likely to gain well-paying employment, receive a formal education, travel internationally, and be moderately accepted by Whites in the general population. In addition, the benefits given to the generations of fair-skinned slaves gave their successors a significant advantage over dark-skinned freedmen in creating a "normal life." (Taylor, 2008, p. 194)

Yet and still, a person of color in the South, Moses put his fickle advantages to good use. He, alongside his Louisiana Creole wife, named Atlanta, was able to flourish, first opening a grocery store, perhaps thanks to the loans available to Black Americans during the "Mystic Years" of the South (Buckley, 1986). With "great energy and ambition" (p. 23), Moses had established a prosperous household on Atlanta, Georgia's Fraser Street and booming business, soon opening a restaurant and fruit stand to accompany the grocery store. Moses savored his success, as his family began to bloom with Cora Catherine born first in November of 1865 and Lena Leo following in February of 1869 (Buckley, 1986).

Their family, firmly entrenched in the Black bourgeoisie society of Atlanta, the lives of Cora and Lena included a "whirligig of parties, picnics, and flirtatious soirees" (p. 25). The pictures of Cora and Lena see them draped in glamorous dresses, parasols in hand. The fabrics of their dresses fold and flow down to the floor in these posed photographs, Lena's gloved, petite hands grasping the ivy gazebo serving as supplemental décor for the photograph. Their straight hair is pulled back, orchestrated into complex knots, highlighting their aquiline features. A lacey hat adorns the head of Cora. Images such as these usually remain reserved for White women of the time period (Buckley, 1986). However, these photographs speak to the status and position held by the Calhoun Sisters in Georgia.

Yet, "the black upper classes could not afford to be full-time social butterflies" (p. 26), as they embraced a righteous duty to fulfill their collective destiny of navigating the rough waters Black Americans faced during this period in history. A wide "gulf" existed between "brown and black" (p. 26), and "black" could not be trusted to lead. As the talented and privileged, the Black bourgeoisie believed they were destined to lead all Black Americans into their free future.

To accomplish this goal, education must be paramount. And, "of all the bourgeois symbols beloved of the black bourgeoisie, the college degree was the most important" (p. 29). Consequently, Cora turned to her studies at Atlanta University, one-half of the schools presently united to form Clark-Atlanta University. Clark-Atlanta often ranks among other schools "as [one of the] influential institutions in the making of the Black upper class" (Taylor, 2008, p. 197). An educational institution of the highest order, Cora welcomed "its stiff academic regime, as well as the relative prosperity of its student body" (Buckley, 1986, p. 29). Cora graduated from Atlanta University in 1881, and, like her fellow graduates, "admitted no superiors—and very few equals," even White Americans, "most of whose education was inferior to theirs" (p. 29).

Cora's younger sister, Lena, chose to attend Fisk University in Nashville, Tennessee. The illustrious Fisk University offered courses in Greek and German, as well as chemistry, physics, and philosophy (Buckley, 1986). The institution drew the attention of a young W. E. B. Du Bois, who summarized the power and diversity of Black Americans encompassed by HBCUs:

> I was thrilled to be for the first time among so many of my own color or rather of such various and extraordinary colors... Never before had I seen young men so self-assured and who gave themselves such airs, and colored men at that; and above all for the first time I saw beautiful girls. (p. 32)

Thanks to Fisk University, for the first time, Du Bois experienced the beauty of the Black American rainbow, and the pluralistic nature of Black American life. Additionally, Du Bois fell in love:

> Of one of these girls I have often said, no human being could possibly have been so beautiful as she seemed to my young eyes that far-off September night of 1885. She was the great aunt of Lena Horne and fair as Lena Horne is, Lena Calhoun was far more beautiful. (p. 32)

One can clearly imagine the "small, bookish lad" Du Bois chasing the glamorous Lena Calhoun for affection much like Dwayne Wayne pursued Whitley on *A Different World* (p. 32). While collegiate Lena did enjoy "young 'Willie' Du Bois' attention" despite the protests of some of her classmates at Fisk (p. 32), their relationship never bloomed into a happily ever after.

Though Du Bois was impressed by the beauty of Lena Calhoun, he nevertheless expressed displeasure, as he perceived Lena and her classmates as "appearing to be interested only in boys, chewing gum, and spring bonnets" (p. 32). While his words may have been a result of a heart never fully healed, Du Bois' words do reveal that many of Black bourgeoisie society, such as Cora Catherine and Lena Leo, who attended HBCUs faced criticism of vapidity and superficiality.

Truth to Power: Diane Nash, the Later Life of Cora, and Bourgeoisie Activism

On *A Different World*, Whitley Gilbert faced many of the same criticisms hurled by Du Bois and others at the members of the Black bourgeoisie. E. Franklin Frazier's critique of the Black bourgeoisie may exist as one of the most scathing. Frazier deems the lives of the Black bourgeoisie "a world of make-believe," where the Black bourgeoisie "attempts to escape the disdain of whites and fulfill its wish for status in American life" (1957, p. 25).

While Franklin's assertion that the Black bourgeoisie created a world of some insulation, the fact remains that the Black bourgeoisie still existed as Black Americans in the United States, with all "rights" and "privileges" thereof fully intact. Historian Carl Degler sums these sentiments best, stating: "There are only two qualities in the United States racial pattern: black and white. A person is one or the other; there is no intermediate position" (Toplin, 1979, p. 186). Consequently, that insulation, while important, only temporarily isolated the Black bourgeoisie from the Black collective consciousness experiences of racism and discrimination. Due to her attendance at Hillman College, Whitley inevitably confronted many of the pressing social issues from which Black bourgeoisie society may have shielded from her at a younger age.

Whitley's presence at Hillman allowed her to uniquely process the circumstances in which she found herself, offering a system of support that allowed her to work through these racist encounters. Whitley tackled overt racism at an expensive jewelry store when a nasty sales clerk treats her disrespectfully in "Pride and Prejudice" (1990). Unable to reconcile the situation alone, Whitley's peers, who have all experienced similar incidences, are able to help her successfully cope with her mistreatment. Finally, Whitley becomes empowered to stand up to the clerk. When Dwayne is involved in a racist incident at a football game, Whitley is mortified ("Cats in the Cradle," 1992), able to extend a strong shoulder to Dwayne. Whitley truly finds her voice to discuss systemic oppression when her honeymoon with Dwayne lands them in the middle of the Rodney King Riots in Los Angeles ("Honeymoon in LA," 1992). Whitley literally shouts out for justice during a live news interview documenting the riots, citing the cloud of delusion under which she previously lived concerning Black equality in the United States ("Honeymoon in LA," 1992).

Diane Nash, too, found her voice at an HBCU. Parallel to Whitley, Nash lived under a cloud of pretense, blocking the light of reality emanating from the world around her. Born in 1938, Diane Nash and her family acted "as if race in America did not really exist because they willed it not to exist" (Halberstam, 1998, p. 145):

> Diane Nash had been the most sheltered of black children; she had lived in a home which downplayed all talk of race, and tried consciously to think of itself as an American home, not a black home...Diane Nash's family was the most middle class and least radical of black families. (p. 145)

The Nash family travelled during the Great Migration to Chicago from Mississippi, where they "prospered" (p. 145), and Leon Nash, Diane's biological father, studied dentistry. Nash's stepfather, John Baker, worked as a waiter on a Pullman car, a "prestigious job in the black community" (p. 147), enabling Nash's mother, Dorothy Bolton Nash, to remain at home.

The product of a "rather privileged" upbringing in Chicago (p. 145), Diane Nash participated in activities not normally undertaken by many of her peers. Fair skinned with sparkling green eyes peeping underneath long lashes, Diane Nash became a beauty queen, competing for the Miss America pageant while in high school in 1956. In the pageants, she sang and danced to Broadway show tunes like "Take Back Your Mink" from *Guys and Dolls*, something not every Black teenage girl was doing in her spare time (Halberstam, 1998).

Still, her experiences at Fisk University struck a chord in Diane Nash, uniting her with many other Black Americans facing the Jim Crow South. Before attending Fisk, the world of segregation seemed unreal and almost mythic to the young Nash:

> My stepfather was a waiter on the railroads and he would make trips to the south [sic]. He would tell about the segregated facilities down there. I believed him and listened to the stories, but I think it was an intellectual understanding. But when I actually got down there and saw signs, it really hit me that I wasn't "supposed"

to go to this restroom or use this particular facility, then I understood emotionally as well. (Mullins, 2007, p. 15)

At the Tennessee State Fair, Nash felt humiliated and scorned by the "colored only" signs adorning the restrooms. Worse, Diane Nash felt that many of her friends blindly accepted the circumstances around them, never attempting to change them (Mullins, 2007). Interestingly, Diane Nash's privileged background allowed her to feel an outrage that many of her Black classmates did not feel (Mullins, 2007). Nash stated that being told to "'go around to the back door where you belong,' had a tremendous psychological impact on me. To begin with, I didn't agree with the premise that I was inferior, and I had a difficult time complying with it" (p. 16). Whitley appears to take her cue from Diane Nash during her encounter in the jewelry store. Whitley's pride finds her flabbergasted at the mistreatment, yet ultimately guides her in making the right choices by confidently confronting the racist saleswoman.

Nash's position at Fisk allowed her to take action against the laws of segregation. At Fisk, Nash "met people her own age who had comparable experiences" and had also heard about the workshops being developed by local minister, Revered James Lawson (p. 16). At the university, beautiful Diane Nash discovered an "unknown courage" that transformed her into more than a society beauty queen (p. 17). In approximately 1960, Diane Nash would initialize her transformation into a "black student samurai" (Halberstam, 1998, p. 8), battling racism with the ferocity of a lioness during sit-ins and protests during the 1960s. Whether fighting a racist judge in Mississippi while six months pregnant or holding on to the principles of nonviolence taught to her while at Fisk University, Diane Nash fully combined her two selves, merging her bourgeoisie, middle-class upbringing with her zeal for social justice. She commanded attention using the sophistication, charm, and beauty of her bourgeoisie heritage, and kept that attention by drawing upon the power of the lessons taught to her at Fisk University (Halberstam, 1998).

After leaving Clark-Atlanta University, Cora Calhoun transformed herself into a "community activist of warrior determination" (Gavin, 2009, p. 10). Cora no longer existed as the pristine Southern Belle. A chilled and willful woman with "austerely pulled-back salt-and-pepper hair, steel-rimmed glasses, and [a] near inability to smile" took her place (p. 10). Her sister, Lena, pursued a well-worn path, marrying Frank Smith, a doctor, and settling down with two children (Gavin, 2009).

After her university years, though, something changed in Cora. The picture of her after her marriage to her, then new, husband, Edwin Horne, finds her in stark contrast to the parasol-wielding belle. In this picture, Cora is somber, unsmiling. In their twenty-fifth wedding anniversary photograph, Cora continues her somber streak, complete with a severe visage and furrowed brow (Buckley, 1986). Though little evidence exists, Atlanta University's rigorous regimen and academic elitism may have infused Cora with a commitment to social activism.

After moving to Brooklyn to raise the Horne sons, Cora threw herself into a "dizzying array of community causes" (Gavin, 2009, p. 11). Cora counted herself among the members of the Urban League, National Association of Colored Women (NACW), and the National Association for the Advancement of Colored People (NAACP) (Gavin, 2009). She raised the banner of suffrage, leading demonstrations to fight for women to gain the right to vote (Gavin, 2009).

She took "hookie-playing Black youths" to task for skipping their studies and bringing shame to the Black community (p. 11). Cora took action to ensure that young, Black people pursued their education just as her father, Moses, had done for her. She secured scholarships for Black youth to attain higher education, including a young Paul Robeson, who would never have attended Rutgers University without Cora's tireless work ethic (Gavin, 2009).

Fertile Ground: A Conclusion

The power of the histories of these women must not be contained. Like Diane Nash and Cora Calhoun Horne, these stories fight for life amid the common and stereotypical monoliths plaguing Black Americans in the United States. Cora Catherine and Lena Leo existed among the "first black college students, with their ante-bellum manners and New England values, [who] would be the founding mothers and fathers of the twentieth-century black bourgeoisie" (Buckley, 1986, p. 29). Because Black people like the Calhoun Sisters thrived, the seeds were sewn for the middle-class generation of Diane Nash.

Diane Nash acted as the fulfillment of the Black bourgeoisie dream founded during the time of the Calhoun Sisters: weaponizing the privilege of the Black elite to help lead Black Americans to true equality and freedom. Because all of these women existed, more Black Americans like Whitley Gilbert should grace the television screens and pages of America's cultural records. The fact remains that Whitley and those like her are not anomalies, but valuable and contributing members of the patchwork blanket that is the Black American people. More research must be done to excavate the multifaceted and varied lives of Black Americans. Highlighting more of the different hues of the Black experience in America will force the box cramming the spirited lives of Black Americans to burst open in a flood. When that happens, no one will dare to question the amount of Blackness one's soul possesses. Because I began to unveil these hidden stories and histories for myself in middle school, I know who and what I am. Thanks to Cora, Lena, Diane, and Whitley, no one can ever tell me differently—ever. Never entertain anyone who dares question the Blackness of one's being. Simply follow these steps: politely check them for signs of fever or stroke, seek medical help if necessary, and rapidly locate the nearest exit.

References

Allen, D. (Producer) (1987). *A different world* [Television series]. Hollywood, CA: National Broadcasting Company.
Buckley, G. L. (1986). *The homes: An American family.* New York: Alfred A. Knopf.
Conan, N. (Host) (2009). The different worlds of Jasmine Guy [Radio episode]. Washington, DC: National Public Radio. Retrieved from http://www.npr.org/templates/story/story.php?storyId=112856561.
Frazier, E. F. (1957). *Black bourgeoisie.* New York: The Free Press.
Gavin, J. (2009). *Stormy weather: The life of Lena Horne.* New York: Atria Books.
Graham, L. O. (1999). *Our kind of people: Inside America's black upper class.* New York: Harper Collins.
Halberstam, D. (1998). *The children.* New York: Random House.
Mullins, L. (2007). *Diane Nash: The fire of the civil rights movement.* Miami, FL: Barnhardt & Ashe Publishing.
Taylor, B. (2008). Color and class at the black college: The promulgation of elitist attitudes at black colleges. In M. Gasman & C. Tudico (Eds.), *Historically black colleges and universities: Triumphs, troubles, and taboos.* New York: Palgrave Macmillan.
Toplin, R. B. (1979). Between black and white: Attitudes toward southern mulattoes, 1830–1861. *Journal of Southern History, 45*(2), 185–200.

CHAPTER SIXTEEN

A Place at the Table: Etiquette and Invalidation in the Quest for Cultural Capital at Spelman College

TIFFANY N. DECKER

Placed on the auction block, women of African descent have been scrutinized since the first slave ships arrived at North America. While their personal identities did not begin or end with slavery, to the outside world slavery turned these women into chattel—bought and sold, stripped of their autonomy, hypersexualized, deemed morally corrupt. With the end of slavery came the legal recognition of these women as persons, but it did little to alleviate the stereotypes created during slavery. Denied rights because of their sex, many used their newly won freedom to create economic and social capital for themselves and for their children. Education provided the foundation for their efforts. Many looked to Historically Black Colleges and Universities (HBCUs) as a means to create economic and social prosperity. These institutions provided the cultural and social capital to propel former slaves into the middle class. While many descendants of HBCU graduates now attend Historically White Institutions (HWIs), HBCUs retain their mission to advance lower-income students into a different economic and social reality (Graham, 1999). These schools continue to create the embodied and institutional cultural capital necessary to move their graduates into the middle class.[1] While these institutions serve as a nurturing haven for underrepresented students, their very attempt to create cultural capital may invalidate the experiences of African American low-income women, as well as those who do not ascribe to hegemonic forms of femininity and heteronormativity. In an effort to erase the negative stereotypes inherited from slavery, activities on HBCU campuses, notably those at Spelman College, may disproportionately target female students in an effort to "polish" them and make them "respectable." These activities, namely dress codes and pageants, may create an atmosphere that invalidates the very students who HBCUs are trying to help.

History of African American Women

Slave masters and slave traders had a long history of racism to draw upon for justification of their inhuman practices. Yancy (2008) found that "the normative construction of the Black body as evil had already begun as early as the fifth century" (p. xx). John Cassian wrote in the fifth century that the devil was "'in the shape of a hideous Negro'" (p. xx). Blackness was equated with corruption. Through the system of American slavery Whites believed that they could enlighten their chattel through their own example, while coincidentally economically exploiting the very persons they sought to save.

While the Black body—male or female—was portrayed as evil and closer to the "savage," animal passions, the woman of African descent faced a double bind. First, her color denied her any hope of freedom; compounding that misery, her sex placed her in an inferior role to all men, Black or White. Sojourner Truth's question "Ain't I a Woman?" demonstrates the "racialized configuration of gender under a system of class rule that compelled and expropriated women's physical labor and denied them legal right to their own bodies and sexuality" in the American South (Higgenbotham, 1992, p. 257). Slavery not only made "clear the role of race in shaping class relations of the South's peculiar institution," but also served to consolidate the "power of men" (p. 257).

The South's dependence on enslaved women's reproductive capacity placed these women in a situation where their gender was always at the mercy of its economic value. Gender for enslaved women was always in flux. In a society that "enforced strict adherence to sex roles, only enslaved women were compelled to labor consistently across gender boundaries" (Davis, 2002, p. 107). The gender of enslaved Black women was manipulated by slavery. Female slaves were "male when convenient [laboring in the fields, doing other work that, at the time, was considered in the purview of men] and horrifically female when needed" (Davis, 2002, p. 119). Enslaved women's reproductive ability was central to the sexual economy necessary to maintain the labor capacity crucial to sustain slavery. In 1819, Thomas Jefferson wrote, "I consider a woman who brings a child every two years as more profitable than the best man on the farm; what she produces is an addition to capital" (p. 109). To continually reproduce an economy relying on slave labor, the capacity for enslaved women to breed was essential. Frederick Olmstead (an observer of the South) "concluded from his travels that 'a slave woman is commonly esteemed least for her working qualities, most for those qualities which give value to a brood mare'" (p. 110). While both Black men and women suffered the chains of slavery, the visceral attacks on a Black woman's sexuality and gender identity was a burden solely hers to bear. In fact,

> white men and black men (free or enslaved) could father children either free or enslaved, and white women could only give birth to free children. Laws of race and gender merged with *partus sequiter ventrum*'s ["that which is brought forth follows the womb"] status to condemn the wombs of enslaved black women. This is a point about race and gender: only black women could give birth to enslaved children, and every black woman who was enslaved and gave birth did so to an enslaved child. (p. 113)

While slavery, at times, rendered Black women "genderless," the economic expediency of reproducing an economy based upon slave labor exploited the female body at whim.

In order to justify the exploitation of Black women in slavery, Black womanhood was juxtaposed with the notions of White women as "'light,' 'divinity,' and 'goodness'" (Yancy, 2008, p. xx). During slavery "sexual access to enslaved women was central in the creation and maintenance of this repressive ideology of white femininity [being delicate and asexual]. Black enslaved women were excluded from, yet central to, the gender ideology of white masculinity and femininity" (Davis, 2002, p. 115). Even after Emancipation, Black women faced similar social stigmas. Higgenbotham (1992) found that "as gender roles for white women in the years following Emancipation dictated devotion to family and employment solely in the home, it was considered 'unnatural,' in fact 'evil,' for black married women to 'play the lady' while their husbands supported them" (p. 260). While White women were encouraged to remain at home and represent the "cult of true womanhood," Black women were burdened not only with their own responsibility to lift themselves, but also the lifting up of their entire race (Perkins, 1983, p. 183). Black women were not seen as "ladies" due to their race, and they often subsumed their sex for their race, as many deemed racial oppression a more pressing issue than gender discrimination (p. 183). Often these women ignored their status as women and "spoke of their oppression as a result of their race and not sex" (p. 184). While "'race uplift' was the objective of *all* educated blacks," after Emancipation, "the implementation of this philosophy was placed primarily on the shoulders of black women" (p. 185).

Black women sought to change the trajectory of their race through education. Slavery had stripped away the opportunity to obtain an education, as "education for blacks was viewed as dangerous," thus, after the Civil War, the majority of African Americans, regardless of their gender, clamored for the opportunity to receive an education and achieve economic and social stability. However, even as the burden of racial uplift fell primarily on Black women, these same women faced discrimination within their race due to their gender. Anna Julia Cooper, in 1892, wrote: "I fear that the majority of colored men do not yet think it worthwhile that women aspire to higher education" (p. 75). Although Black women faced an uphill battle to obtain an education, many knew that it was through education that they would improve their own futures and that of their race.

The Role of HBCUs

HBCUs provided the primary method to further the economic and social aims of the newly emancipated Black population. Whether institutions focused on industrial or liberal arts curriculum, they shared the goal of creating a new class of freed Blacks. While Booker T. Washington, the main proponent of industrial education and W. E. B. Du Bois, the main proponent of liberal arts education, disagreed on many matters, they each sought to "lift up" African Americans and create a class of prosperous persons (Gasman, 2002). Du Bois, through his "Talented Tenth" philosophy demonstrated his objective to create "an intellectual elite that could advance the civil rights of all black people" (p. 494).

HBCUs served the small portion of middle-class Blacks who enjoyed some economic security; however, their primary constituency was lower-income newly free African Americans.

As Blacks were barred from attending White institutions, excepting a small few, HBCUs served as the primary means to create cultural, social, and economic capital for newly freed slaves. Prior to the *Brown v. Board of Education* decision, most African Americans who sought a way to move out of poverty accessed HBCUs for their tertiary education. Many Blacks continued to value the academic rigor, inclusive environment, and nurturance that HBCUs provided and continued to access them even after the *Brown* decision opened up a wider array of tertiary options.

While most HBCU campuses were founded as coeducational institutions, women still were grossly underrepresented in terms of enrollment on these campuses. By 1890, "only 30 black women held baccalaureate degrees, compared to over 300 black men" (Perkins, 1983, p. 187). Black women struggled to access tertiary education. However, even as they struggled to obtain a place in higher education, several institutions, notably Spelman Seminary, were founded to educate Black women.

The Atlanta Baptist Seminary, later Spelman Seminary and then Spelman College, was founded in 1881 by two White missionaries—Sophia B. Packard and Harriet E. Giles, representatives of the Woman's American Baptist Home Mission Society (Brazzell, 1992, p. 28). While White missionary societies believed in the intellectual capability of Blacks, they also believed that slavery had "morally, spiritually, and culturally bankrupted Blacks" (p. 31). Just as those in the South believed that slavery was necessary in order to "save" the savage African, Northern missionaries believed that it was through education that they would save Blacks from the "depravity" of slavery (p. 31). Although Black women were not considered "ladies" like White women, the "cult of true womanhood" still applied to them in some instances. Since this philosophy dictated that women were the moral and spiritual leaders of their homes, there was a greater imperative that the moral stain of slavery was stripped from these women so that they could foster virtue within their households. The Atlanta Women's Baptist Seminary fashioned itself as a "home and the students were children to be trained morally and spiritually" (p. 35). It was through this training that the "children" (i.e., Black women) were also to gain an "appreciation for the ideals and precepts of White American culture" (p. 35). It was through this exposure to White middle-class culture that women would be "purified" from the stain of slavery and would be able to fulfill their role as female protectors of morality (p. 36). Unlike the roles prescribed for White women, these Black women would need to also earn a living, thus it was vital that they be provided with the practical and academic skills necessary for them to realize their roles as workers, as well as examples of virtue within their homes. While providing the foundation for cultural and social capital in the quest for economic capital, it was thought essential that these Black women be provided with the cultural capital necessary to erase the corruption of slavery and make them morally upright citizens.

Cultural Capital

Cultural capital, coupled with economic capital, is essential for movement into a different sphere in society. Bourdieu (1986) defines three types of capital, each necessary to access power. While economic capital is "immediately and directly convertible into money," cultural and social capital are more discrete (p. 46). Used in this way, cultural capital can exist in three forms: the embodied state, the objectified state, and the institutionalized state. The embodied state is, essentially, "cultivation, *Bildung*" (p. 48). Etiquette, elocution instruction, and dress codes attempt to create embodied capital. The objectified state contains "cultural goods" like art, musical instruments—physical items that represent a cultural knowledge and refinement (p. 48). The institutionalized state is often recognized in the form of "academic credentials" that confer a certain status upon the recipient. Combined, these forms of cultural capital create social capital—networks that provide the possessor access to economic capital.

Often cultural capital is used as a "weapon" in social class "struggles in which the agents wield strengths and obtain profits proportionate to their mastery" of this elusive form of capital. As the "social conditions of its [cultural capital's] transmission and acquisition are more disguised than those of economic capital, it is predisposed to function as symbolic capital, i.e., to be unrecognized as capital and recognized as legitimate competence" (Bourdieu, 1986, p. 50). In the United States, those who have greater access to economic capital, as well as cultural and social capital, have, historically, been White, heterosexual, middle- and upper-class men. Through structural racism, perpetuated classism, homophobia, and institutionalized patriarchy, those who are not born as White, heterosexual, middle- and upper-class men must work harder to acquire the dominant cultural competence in order to break into social networks and access an economic apparatus traditionally held by this exclusive group.

As their slave sisters before them, lower-income Black women are often portrayed as corrupt "welfare queens" who need to be saved through the introduction of middle-class White values (Cassiman, 2007). Certain values, such as desiring a higher socioeconomic status, owning a home, accessing higher education, appearing "respectable" by speaking and dressing a certain way, displaying manners that are deemed "cultured," and displaying physical articles, like cars and other objects of objectified cultural capital, are often claimed as necessary for middle-class membership. However, Carter (2003) demonstrates that even students who are often found to be "lacking" in cultural capital by the dominant culture have formed their own forms of capital within their social groups. Lower-income students often use language, music, and clothing as markers of "authentic" Black identity and to position themselves within their social and economic group (p. 140). While the creation of cultural capital within lower-economic Black society demonstrates that these students are not entirely devoid of their own sources of capital, "full reliance on non-dominant capital to maintain one's cultural status position does provide a challenge to socioeconomic mobility, since dominant cultural capital facilitates success within mainstream institutions and organizations" (p. 139). While lower-income students and those who do not ascribe to heteronormative and patriarchal systems are not devoid of cultural capital, it is much more difficult for them to access the resources held by the middle and upper classes without shedding some of their own cultural capital and obtaining capital that is respected by the middle and upper classes.

The hegemonic notion that only middle-class Whites value institutionalized cultural capital through education, as well as other forms of cultural capital that can be obtained, for example, through music lessons and other cultural activities illustrates the extent of systemic racism and ignores the long-established Black middle and upper classes. Due to institutionalized racism and hurdles placed in the way of social mobility for low-income Blacks, many scholars posit that this group does not hold the same values as the dominant society (Carter, 2003). However, this notion is both racist and classist; it assumes that lower-class status and ethnicity other than that of the dominant culture equals "rejection of commonly shared values regarding social, economic, or educational attainment" (p. 139). Conversely, the Black community has a long tradition of valuing education. The existence and success of middle- and upper-class Blacks demonstrate the long-held importance of obtaining an education.

The Creation of the Black Middle and Upper Classes

While the hierarchy between Whites and Blacks was clearly demarcated both in the North and the South before and after the Civil War, the Black community had its own class distinctions. The most obvious distinction was between free Blacks and those in bondage. Many, if not most, free Blacks had White ancestry, often due to the rape of female slaves by their White masters (Yancy, 2008). This community lived in a gray area in American society—they were not afforded the privileges of White citizens, and often forced to carry papers proving that they were, in fact, "free," yet they were still free to economically benefit from their own labor and create social connections, unlike enslaved Blacks.

Within slavery also there was a class hierarchy. Those who worked in the house were often afforded opportunities denied to slaves in the fields. Often, again, these "house slaves" were of a lighter complexion and were the offspring of slave masters (Graham, 1999). These slaves worked in close proximity to the family. In some instances, these slaves were even taught to read and write so that they would be more useful in the household. Female slaves in the house were often stripped of their sexuality, portrayed as "safe" "mammy" figures; while the female slaves in the field were often portrayed, due to their darker complexion, as closer in proximity to the "savage" African—hypersexualized and dangerous to the morality of the master's house (Yancy, 2008). Slaves in the field occupied the lowest rung on both social ladders. Placed far from the seat of power in the master's house and due to their darker complexion they were deemed morally inferior but physically superior. They were often worked like animals and treated as such.

After emancipation, many of these markers that differentiated the hierarchy to the White community remained with the Black community. While ostensibly granted their freedom and equality through the 13th, 14th, and 15th Amendments to the Constitution, all those of African ancestry were still deemed socially, economically, and politically inferior to Whites. However, within the Black community the same class distinctions established during slavery prevailed (Frazier, 1957). As these Blacks were barred from attending White institutions under Jim Crow, they accessed HBCUs as a means to further their economic and cultural capital.

After the *Brown v. Board of Education* decision—where separate schools were deemed inherently unequal—gradually, and generally through court order, historically White tertiary institutions reluctantly opened their doors to Blacks. Over time, the Black middle and upper classes began to attend Historically White Institutions (HWIs), as many believed that these institutions were superior to HBCUs (Graham, 1999). Even with the exodus of Black and middle-class students to historically White institutions, some HBCUs, namely Fisk, Morehouse, Spelman, Dillard, Howard, Hampton, and Tuskegee, were deemed the "Black Ivy League" and continued to attract students of greater financial means (Fleming, 1984).

Today, HBCUs continue to serve low-income Black students. Many students who attend HBCUs are eligible for Pell Grants, even students attending one of the "Black Ivy League" schools, like Spelman. While more students at Spelman qualify for Federal Student Aid compared to their similarly ranked liberal arts peers, it admits relatively fewer Federal Student Aid recipients than other HBCUs. For example, while 51% of Spelman women received Federal Aid in 2011, 82% of the students at

Bennett College, also an HBCU enrolling only women, qualified for Federal Student Aid (IPEDS Bennett College, 2011; IPEDS Spelman College, 2011).

Additionally, "[HBCUs] enroll 16 percent and graduate approximately 20 percent of all Blacks who attend college" (Gasman, 2009, para. 2). These students cite "the empowering, family-like environment of small classes, close faculty–student relationships, and life without the daily racial tensions experienced off campus" (para. 2). Surrounded primarily by other underrepresented students, Black students feel like they can freely speak their minds and remove "the mask" that they present to the dominant culture (Carter, 2003). However, even within this nurturing environment, there can be instances where certain students are invalidated. The practices of dress codes and pageants, while attempting to create cultural capital for students, may create an environment that is invalidating to Black students who may not ascribe to heteronormative notions of femininity and/or come from a low socioeconomic background.

Microaggressions

A woman who attends Spelman is under great pressure to represent "a *bonafide* woman" (Fallon, 2009, para. 1). Much like the Black woman who shouldered the burden of lifting her entire race, former president Florence Read reiterates that a Spelman woman "must go forth from college and share to the full with their fellows what they have gained" (Guy-Sheftall, 1982, p. 280). Thus, a Spelman woman acts as the purveyor of all that is necessary to "lift" the Black community. She is the model Black woman and becomes a member of what Du Bois called the "Talented Tenth." However, by becoming *the* model for Black womanhood, Spelman women must also ascribe to certain social and behavioral practices. As an alumnae recounts, "We understood from the very beginning who could and could not be called a Spelman woman and by default who could and could not be called a real Black woman. In many ways, the *social practices* at Spelman defined black womanhood as feminine, heterosexual, smart, non-promiscuous, have [sic] good relationships with Morehouse men, Christian, and class privileged" (para. 2). Thus, merely attending the institution was not enough to confer "bonafide" Black woman status on the student. A "Spelman woman" had to ascribe to certain forms of embodied cultural capital. Those who did not fit into this "ideal" form of Spelman womanhood may have been invalidated by the social practices used to create this cultural capital. Unintentionally, the keepers of traditions at Spelman may be inflicting microaggressions on many of its students.

Microaggressions are often "hidden messages" that "may invalidate the group identity or experiential reality of target persons, demean them on a personal or group level, communicate they are lesser human beings, suggest they do not belong with the majority group, threaten and intimidate, or relegate them to inferior status and treatment" (Sue, 2010, p. 3). Microaggressions are, at times, difficult to identify, as they are often "delivered by well-intentioned individuals" and "may on the surface appear quite harmless, trivial, or be described as 'small slights' "; however, "research indicates that they have a powerful impact upon the psychological well-being of marginalized groups" (p. 3).

There are three types of microaggressions—microassaults, microinsults, and microinvalidations. Microassaults are much easier to identify because they are committed by those who consciously are aware of their biases and prejudices. They often present themselves as "'old fashioned racism, sexism, or heterosexism,'" and, this chapter posits, overt classism, as well (p. 9). Microinsults are different because the perpetrator is often unconscious of his or her bias and he or she may actually believe that he or she may be doing or saying something positive about the victim or the victim's group. For example, when Black or Latino students do well in class and are told by their professor that they are "a credit to their race" this positive statement contains an insulting statement that not all Black or Latino students do well in school and that they are "an exception" to "their people" (p. 9). Microinvalidations are often the most insidious type of microaggression, as "microinvalidations directly attack or deny the experiential realities of socially devalued groups" (p. 10). For example, the notion that we live in a "post-racial" society and that race is no longer a factor in terms of access to power negates the experiential reality of those who have suffered overt and covert systemic racism. These forms of microaggressions can combine to create hostile environments for those who are not members of dominant groups.

The impact of microaggressions goes beyond making the victim feel badly. Microaggressions have "major consequences for marginalized groups" (p. 15). Microaggressions may lead to emotional issues, such as feelings of anxiety, alienation, and exhaustion, common to those experiencing these types of overt and covert acts (p. 15). Microinsults and microinvalidations are often hard to identify, explicitly leading to negative cognitive consequences (p. 15). These microaggressions leave marginalized people to wonder if their perception of reality is actually real. Many may wonder, "Did that just happen? Did I hear them correctly? Are they implying what I think they're implying?" The inability to achieve clarity, vis-à-vis others' perceptions, leads only to doubt on the part of students from nondominant groups. Where microassaults are easier to identify, and therefore, address, microinsults and microinvalidations serve to undermine the reality of marginalized people. Each of these impacts illustrates the deleterious effect microaggressions can have on those of nondominant groups.

Validating Women at Spelman

As Black women often face microaggressions due to both their color and gender, Spelman deserves credit for being an environment that promotes a "special sisterhood" and a refuge from discrimination in the larger society (Guy-Sheftall, 1982, p. 280). In many ways, Spelman validates Black women and provides them with the nurturance necessary for each woman to grow into "a Spelmanite: a woman of excellence" (Spelman Orientation Guide, 2012, p. 6). Spelman has a long history of cultivating "Black women for leadership roles" (Guy-Sheftall, 1982, p. 280). Not only does Spelman provide the institutional state of cultural capital by conferring degrees, but many traditions at the school and other practices serve to create embodied cultural capital for the women to utilize in their quest to create their own social and economic capital. As an HBCU devoted to educating Black women, this environment allows women to cultivate cultural and social capital in an environment that is devoid of many of the microaggressions that often target Black women.

Within this nurturing environment, women are allowed to confront the racism and sexism that permeates society. Confronting racism issues begins at orientation. One activity called "Skin Deep" asks students to "reflect on race and ethnicity and the anger, pain, confusion, and hope as they address the United State's racial divide" (2012 new student orientation program, 2012, p. 15). All students are also required to take the "African Diaspora and the World (ADW) class where black feminism and intersectionality are thoroughly discussed" (Johnson, 2012, p. 80). Spelman fosters students' racial and gender identity. Another event that Spelman students attend during orientation is a discussion led by a faculty member on "Becoming a Free Thinking Woman" ("2012 new student orientation program," 2012, p. 8). Spelman students are taught "to be neither victims nor passive observers of unjust treatment but active and proud claimants of our American birthright"

(Edelman, 2000, p. 121). In fact, Spelman was "in the forefront of curriculum development in women's studies on Black college campuses" (Guy-Sheftall, 1982, p. 282). Spelman has a long history of addressing issues relevant to women of color. "Even as early as 1944... Spelman was the site of a 'Conference on Current Problems and Programs in the Higher Education of Negro Women'" (p. 282). Through its Women's Research and Resource Center, Spelman demonstrated its commitment to furthering "research on Black women" while "sponsor[ing] outreach activities," as well as "develop[ing] courses in women's studies" (p. 282). In 1970, Spelman also opened the Margaret Nabrit Curry Collection on Women at the Quarles Library. The example of high-level faculty and staff at Spelman also demonstrates the leadership potential that all Spelman women may aspire to. Former college president Johnetta Cole and current president Beverly Daniel Tatum exemplify to Spelman women that they may aspire to high-level leadership roles. Spelman also boasts a "notable record in awarding bachelor's degrees in STEM fields to Black women" (Perna et al., 2009, pp. 6–7). There is no doubt that many of Spelman's institutional strengths validate and cultivate women of color. As alumnae Marian Wright Edelman (2000) writes, "As an all-black women's college it [Spelman] gave me the latitude and safe space—one not defined by male or white folk's expectations... to dream my dreams and to forge my own path" (pp. 1818–119).

Microaggressions at Spelman

Although there are many instances where Spelman serves to validate women, certain activities ostensibly aimed at creating cultural capital for the women at Spelman College, often through "traditions," may, in fact, be invalidating. Marian Wright Edelman (2000) writes, "Spelman had a reputation as a tea-pouring very strict school designed to turn black girls into refined ladies" (p. 118). While many of the practices that Marian Wright Edelman details—parietals, compulsory chapel attendance, and strict curfews—have changed, many vestiges of these old traditions remain. Traditions that survived may invalidate some women who do not ascribe to heteronormative structures, notions of feminine "respectability" or are from low-income backgrounds. Tice (2012) finds that "patrolling, training, assessing, and assigning value to student appearances through dress codes, etiquette training and beauty pageantry" serve to place limitations on what is considered feminine and acceptable behavior (p. 7). While it would seem that in the nurturing environment of both a women's college and a Historically Black College and University (HBCU) women would be free from the restrictions of the dominant culture, "there is still a great deal of apprehensive attention [to] girls' manners and worry over deviations from cut-and-dried conventions" (p. 36). Under the guise of "traditions," certain cultural practices are used to enforce adherence to racial, heteronormative, patriarchal, classist, and dominant cultural values. Requirements like dress codes, the Morehouse Maroon and White Pageant, and the Miss Spelman Pageant serve to further the aims of the dominant culture while hiding under the pretext of tradition. While campus pageants and other activities used to "polish" women are often protected under the guise of "'girl power,'...and self-improvement," these practices, in reality, serve to subject women to middle-class stereotypes of femininity and to heterosexual norms (p. 5). While these practices might also serve the function of allowing Blacks to "rewrit[e] powerful texts about their presumed immorality and inferiority," they also serve as microaggressions toward Black women who do not ascribe to traditional notions of femininity, who are heteronormous, or who are from a lower-income background (p. 17).

The Spelman Dress Code

The "White Dress Tradition" and Orientation Dress Code

Spelman has a long-standing dress code tradition. Until the 1920s, Spelman "demanded adherence to a strict dress code...with rules about acceptable colors, skirt widths and lengths, collar height, and decoration" (Gordon, 2004, p. 77). While these rules have changed, there are still vestiges of this strict dress code instituted at various campus events. Today, each student at Spelman must meet the "obligatory commitment...to have a 'respectable and conservative' white dress" ("The white dress tradition," n.d., para. 2). Students and alumnae wear this white dress on Founder's Day, Class Day, Baccalaureate, Commencement, alumnae events, and for the March through the Alumnae Arch (para. 2). Much like the strict dress codes listed until the 1920s, the requirements for the white dress are very detailed. The white dress must be:

> A solid white dress or skirt suit. The dress or suit should be "true" white—not off-white or cream. For graduating seniors, when wearing academic regalia, the white dress or skirt should range

from calf length to two inches above the knee, so that the dress does not hang lower than the gown. Pants are not allowed. For first-year, sophomore, and junior students, the white dress or skirt can range from ankle or calf length to two inches above the knee. Pants are not allowed. Flesh-toned hosiery. Black, closed-toe shoes. Functional jewelry only, which consists of a wrist watch and rings worn on the hand. ("The white dress tradition," n.d., para. 4)

Even beyond the White Dress Tradition, in the "New Student Orientation" section on dress, students are asked that "in honor of the first students of Spelman College, new students wear dresses or skirts rather than slacks during orientation activities" ("New student orientation," n.d., para. 7). These dresses and skirts must be "presentable enough to wear to a service" (para. 7).

Dress Codes Counteracting Racial Narratives

Dress codes have often been defended by claims that "others form[ed] their opinions of a woman" by the way she dressed (Gordon, 2004, p. 77). While dress serves as a means to convey class, modesty, and propriety for all women, due to the specific nature of past and present racism aimed at Black women, it is even more important that Black women convey messages about their cultural capital through their clothing. Often dress codes for Blacks were used to "enforce a virtuous sobriety by requiring 'simple, suitable, and healthful clothing'" (p. 77). As the decency of Black women has often been called into question, it remained vitally important to educators that the dress of their students "announce[ed] the professionalism and respectability" of those students (p. 77). Since Black women's bodies were often stereotyped as hypersexual, it was imperative that their clothes demonstrated their propriety. Gordon finds that as there was a "trope that African American women were sexually available, modesty in dress was paramount" (2004, p. 74). In order to demonstrate adherence to the "cult of true womanhood," "elite black women in the United States have a long history of adopting a politic of respectability, adhering to hegemonic Victorian gender roles in an effort to resist stereotypes of black women as sexually and morally deviant" (Johnson, 2012, p. 83). Decent dress was especially important to Black families. These families "hoped that extremely upright behavior would ward off dangerous attention and counteract the negative stereotypes of African Americans that were common throughout white America" (Shaw, 1996, p. 15). That the

Spelman white dress must be deemed "respectable" harkens back to fears that Black women may, in fact, not be "respectable" by default and that they must dress to illustrate their decency. By wearing a "conservative" dress they demonstrate their modesty and allay any fears that their sexuality may be threatening. The white dress serves as a symbol—reminding those within and outside of the Spelman community that a Spelman woman is the "respectable" lady its founders hoped to create.

Dress Codes and Class

Dress codes also require that one prove her status as a member of the middle or upper classes. Spelman's White Dress Tradition began around 1900, as, at the turn of the century, "a white dress was the attire most often used for formal occasions" ("The white dress tradition," n.d., para. 2). This notion presupposes that a woman who attends Spelman has a white dress on hand to attend formal occasions and demonstrate her membership into a certain class of society. As it was generally debutantes or other women who had the means to purchase a white dress specifically for their wedding at the turn of the century, a white dress serves as a signifier of economic security. A white dress may only be used for special "formal" occasions—everyday use would render it soiled and useless. As white clothing is more difficult to keep clean, ownership of a white dress further illustrates that one has the means to afford multiple sets of clothing, including at least one dress kept purely as a luxury. While dress codes also offer a way for educators to provide guidance about the correct form of dress for professional situations, and thus increase students' access to cultural capital, the required white dress, along with the skirts and dresses required for the ten days of orientation, may prove a financial hardship for women of lesser means and serve as a microinvalidation of their experiential reality.

Coupled with the white dress students and alumnae must wear for certain events, students are also required to wear "black shoes" ("The white dress tradition," n.d., para. 2). At the turn of the century, black shoes were a part of the basic clothing requirements which also consisted of having a pair of "sensible black shoes," for Spelman students. This recommendation was made in an effort to "avoid overwhelming students and parents with the cost of having to provide more than one pair of shoes" (para. 2). It is notable that in the "White Dress" requirements, the black shoes, basically, represent the humble origins of the original Spelman students. This connection to those of lesser means may be validating to students who also hail from lower-income backgrounds, even while the requirements for this outfit may be difficult for those of limited economic resources to meet. The dress code also requires that the women wear "functional jewelry only, which consists of a wrist watch and rings worn on the hand" (para. 2). This requirement, in its restriction of ostentatious display, may also validate lower-income women who may not be able to afford extra jewelry. While the black shoes and the restriction on jewelry remind Spelman students of the modest backgrounds of the original Spelman students, the most costly part of this outfit remains the dress itself, which is unlikely to be an item that every student can easily afford. While somewhat invalidating in an economic sense, these dress code traditions may also serve as a way for students and alumnae to all look the same, thus bonding in their shared sisterhood and creating social capital. Many traditions exhibit such a duality and can thus neither be considered an unalloyed good nor a pure disservice to the students.

Dress Codes and Hegemonic Femininity

That students are required to wear a dress may also illustrate the importance of hegemonic femininity. The White Dress Tradition dress code reiterates twice that it is unacceptable for women to wear pants. Women must conform to the normative image of femininity, even within a setting that challenges notions of hegemonic femininity in its curriculum. Keia Martin, a Spelman alumnae, in her 2008 senior thesis writes, "Although some feminist views of womanhood, such as independence, empowerment, and equity, are still present within the student body at Spelman, the focus of becoming the ultimate [feminist, independent, and empowered] young woman gradually fades from existence at certain social events and promptly reappears afterwards" (Johnson, 2012, p. 81). Thus, while women are guided in feminist principals, there are certain traditions, like the White Dress Tradition, that by their nature, depress the women's attempts to live the principals of empowerment that the school exhorts. The guidelines also make it very clear that women are not to wear shorts or slacks during orientation. Women who may feel uncomfortable conforming to the requirements that they must wear a dress may be invalidated by being forced by tradition to do so.

Dress Codes and Morality

The color white has tremendous symbolic significance. Around the turn of the twentieth century, when the White Dress Tradition began, it was common for debutantes to wear white, as "white is used to express the pure" (Bastide, 1967, p. 314). Along with proving their respectability, femininity, and class status by wearing a dress, wearing a *white* dress illustrates that the women of Spelman are unsullied and are "pure" of body and soul. Additionally, the "symbolic wearing of white" often has a "link to matrimony" (Harrison, 1997, p. 501). The white wedding dress has historical ties with the Victorian notion that a bride should possess a virtuous mind and body by remaining a virgin until marriage. Thus, the wearing of the symbolic white dress serves to illustrate to those within and outside of the community that a Spelman woman is a woman of good morals.

Creating Social Capital

However, "instead of challenging the White Dress Tradition as limiting gender expression, it is largely valued and cherished" by students and alumnae (Johnson, 2012). One may surmise that this tradition remains because, by dressing alike, the students in some ways lose their individual identity and become a part of the group. In this action, they make connections with each other and become a part of each other's network. Beyond merely feeling a sense of togetherness, this tradition serves to foster "sisterhood" among the women. The dress code that is intended to create social capital by instilling "respectable and conservative" dress values then extends its purpose by fostering a lasting network that assists in the creation of social capital among the women. This is fine for students who already have the cultural capital to take comfort in these traditions. However, the students who feel invalidated by the traditions (those who stray from the heteronormative, feminine, and Christian orthodoxy) are likely to compound their lack of cultural capital by being alienated by the traditions meant to develop that very capital in Spelman's students.

Pageants

"Queens" on HBCU campuses occupy a unique role. These women often serve as the incarnation of campus values. While many HBCU campuses have added aspects to their campus pageants that represent a student's cultural heritage, the structure of the pageant largely remains similar to the traditions of historically White pageants. The impact of pageants on the perception of Black women can be ambiguous—while they may inculcate participants with middle-class and heteronormative values and hegemonic femininity, they also can, in certain instances, "provide openings for mending the festering wounds of the racist disparagement of black women's bodies and for celebrating black pride, cultural history, and life-worlds" (Tice, 2012, p. 101). In an effort to counteract the "legacy of disfigurement and violence wrought by white slavery on black womanhood," one participant wrote:

> You will represent every black female on campus. You are the epitome of womanhood, strength, and power. You will let them know that out of the dust of slavery, we have risen... You represent what we have achieved as black women. (p. 108)

Some participants speak of the importance of ownership over their bodies and that they are able to "set our own standards of what black excellence and what black beauty is" (p. 109). Davis (2002) writes, "For black women to reclaim our sexuality, our intimate selves, from all of the people and forces who would seek to expropriate it, regulate it, define it, and confine it, we must first become comfortable speaking about it ourselves" (p. 119). Pageants may offer participants a way to define their own sexuality and present how they choose to be seen. However, "feminine allure often seem[s] to supersede the counter-hegemonic pageant aspirations at black colleges" (p. 112).

Morehouse Miss Maroon and White Pageant: The Heteronormative Ideal Woman

The heteronormative ideal holds that men take the role of the viewers and women, the viewed. One example of this ideal at HBCUs is Morehouse College, an all-male HBCU, and its annual Miss Maroon and White Pageant where, often, a woman from Spelman is chosen as the queen for Morehouse. That an all-male school has a pageant where a woman is chosen to represent their school demonstrates a heteronormative system where there must be a woman on campus to represent the woman that all men should want to marry. To maintain heteronormativity, Miss Maroon and White even greets entering Morehouse freshmen during orientation. She thus epitomizes the woman that each freshman should ideally obtain. Her presence acts as a reminder that men must desire women and also serves to ward off any questions about homosexuality at an all-male institution, while continuing the patriarchal structure by giving men the power to choose the woman who represents them.

Maintaining Patriarchal Structures
In addition to this heteronormative standard, the Miss Maroon and White Pageant also serves to maintain patriarchal practices as it is the men who have the power and the choice to pick any woman they feel represents the ideal image of Black womanhood. Keia Martin, a Spelman alumnae, "argues that although discourse at Spelman supports feminist ideals, the institutional policies and relationship with Morehouse men are heavily rooted in patriarchal ideologies" (Johnson, 2012, p. 84). Many descriptions of pageant contestants illustrate this heteronormative and patriarchal system. The descriptions often go into detail about the women's physical appearance. In the *Morehouse Quarterly*, the author indicates that one contestant "is the vision of which all men dream" (Tice, 2012, p. 113). This statement serves as a microinsult to the woman, as she is being held up as better than other women, indicating that, in general, her sex is not the ideal and that only through extreme efforts has she made herself into what men desire. It also serves as a microinvalidation to men who may not, in fact, be dreaming of women. By placing this heteronormative statement in the school newspaper, the writers are reminding the male student body that it is women they should be "dream[ing]" of and that anything else is unacceptable. At the 2012 Miss Maroon and White Pageant, one male audience member shouts at one contestant, "Marry me!" (Mosely, 2012). Just as the contestant who was dreamt about, this comment serves as a microinsult as it indicates that this woman is somehow better than most women, who are not worthy of his attention. That the audience member would like to marry the contestant also demonstrates that the pageant promotes heteronormative notions of male–female relationships; it assumes that she desires only to marry the audience member.

While Miss Maroon and White may represent the ideal Black woman, she must participate in a pageant judged solely by men. In this contest, all of the judges and the vast majority of the audience are male. In a flier for the pageant, "seven slender contestants" are "wearing low-cut, strapless, or spaghetti-strap black dresses" (Tice, 2012, p. 112). In the flier, each of the women is looking off in a different direction. Not one of the participants is looking directly at the viewer. They stare off into different directions, unwilling or unable to challenge the male gaze. At the 2012 Miss Maroon and White Pageant, as the pageant contestants danced in short tops and short skirts, one could hear men in the audience shouting, "Ah yeah, baby girl!" (Mosely, 2012). This catcalling serves as a microassault and demeans the women dancing. By reducing the women to "baby" girls the viewer is also able to maintain a patriarchal power structure in infantilizing the women on the stage. Audience members felt no compunction about yelling statements that they believed were supportive, but, for the most part, were sexual in nature and served as microassaults. The implication is that the woman is on stage to be viewed as either a potential mate, a sexual being, or less-than the men watching—not as the representative of female strength.

Colorism and Class

The vast majority of the women who participate in the Miss Maroon and White Pageant would pass what Graham (1999) calls the "brown paper bag and the ruler test." This test measures one's skin hue to determine where one falls within the Black class system. If one is lighter than a brown paper bag and/or has hair that when pulled remains as straight as a ruler, then one is generally afforded higher status in Black society. Much like former slaves who were afforded better places on plantations due to their lighter skin color, those with lighter skin are still often viewed as higher class than their darker peers (Graham, 1999). In the flyer for the 2005 Miss Maroon and White Pageant, most, if not all of the women would pass this test. By choosing contestants who are of lighter complexion and who have straighter hair, the stereotypes about colorism and class remain unchallenged at Morehouse. Displaying these women may invalidate women who do not fit this "idealized" lighter version of a Black woman of the middle or upper classes. Due to the tie between color and class, choosing only lighter women microinvalidates both women of a darker complexion and women who may not be of the middle or upper classes.

Although this pageant does not hold a swimsuit competition and often asks women how they would confront issues significant to Blacks, the emphasis on how women look to men remains vital. While ostensibly empowering the women, the fact that these women are put on display and chosen by men demonstrates that they are evaluated in the context of attractiveness to men and ranked according to the men's criteria. The contradictory messages that these pageants promote make it difficult to determine whether or not Black women are being celebrated or demeaned. Participants cite the importance of maintaining traditions and embracing cultural heritage. However, they also cite the importance of "black men seeing us as queens" (Tice, 2012, p. 109). Morehouse's Miss Maroon and White Pageant may crown a woman as a "queen" but that does not mean she is not still viewed through a patriarchal, heteronormative lens that degrades her, and, ultimately, as she is chosen by men, she is only a queen by virtue of being picked by a king.

Miss Spelman Pageant: Rewriting Scripts and Demonstrating Respectability

The Miss Spelman pageant does more to rewrite the narrative of Black women's bodies and their connection to tradition. The pageant spends extensive time—often over two minutes—telling the audience about the accomplishments of each participant and the audience cheers loudest when high GPAs are announced (Jones, 2011a). While keeping with the tradition of pageants on HBCU campuses, Spelman's pageant is unique among women's colleges. One must wonder how this idiosyncratic tradition serves the women of Spelman. It may be that the Miss Spelman pageant serves to reinforce the middle-class feminine ideal in order to uphold notions of Black respectability. Where the White Dress Tradition creates a sense of solidarity by having all of the women wear the same outfit, the Miss Spelman pageant selects one woman to serve as the paragon to which all Spelman women should aspire. While far more dignified than the Miss Maroon and White pageants—the audience does not catcall the contestants and the women are not nearly as sexualized—the women in both pageants serve to create a feminine, middle-class ideal that may be invalidating to those who do not match that example.

Presentation

While the flyer for the Miss Maroon and White Pageant showed women scantily clad, the contestants in the Spelman pageant are presented very differently. On the Spelman website, one day each of the participants graces the home page wearing matching business suits (Spelman Homepage, April 14, 2013). The women present the "professional," "respectable" image that Spelman desires from its students. However, several days later, the website home page features each of the women wearing evening gowns in matching hues (Spelman Homepage, April 19, 2013). In the backdrop for the evening gown photo shoot are easels, making the viewer wonder if the women are on display in a similar fashion to the women who were displayed in the Morehouse flyer. While the women are showing more skin and are wearing outfits very different than their business attire, they do, at least, confront the viewer with direct, penetrating gazes that lend a powerful air to their poses. Their change in attire, however, does illustrate that these women are probably not of the 51% of Spelman students who are on Pell Grants. From a formal dress that matches the other contestants to their unique formal dresses for the pageant, to their talent attire, to their business attire, the women are required to purchase a variety of very expensive outfits in their quest to become Miss Spelman. These articles of clothing confirm to the Spelman community that these women are of middle- to upper-class means and that they represent the values of the institution. The middle- to upper-class presentation that the women must adhere to may invalidate those women who cannot afford to purchase such display and do not come from a background where such displays are valued.

Pagentry

While the judges at the Miss Maroon and White Pageant often chose women of a certain size and color for its pageant, the same look cannot be ascribed to the contestants of the Miss Spelman Pageant. The contestants for the Miss Spelman 2013 Pageant are of various skin tones and there are several that do not conform to the extremely thin body shape that often permeates the world of pageantry. While their appearances do not conform as neatly to the dictates of the "brown paper bag" and "ruler test" to illustrate their status in the middle or upper classes, they still exhibit traits, often through their clothing, their "grace" and their "poise" to assure the audience and judges that they are members of the middle or upper classes. The diversity in the contestants in terms of their skin color and their body type might be validating to the various women at Spelman and illustrate that no matter one's look they could aspire to the position of Miss Spelman; however, there are other ways that the pageant excludes those who do not present themselves as "polished" middle-class women.

"Grace," "Poise," and Class

Campus queens must embark on "class-coded performances" (Tice, 2012, p. 126). The use of certain terms like "grace" and "poise" serve to demonstrate a contestant's membership in the middle or upper classes. Queens are expected to "erase any stigmatizing markers of class disadvantage. They are expected to be self-assured in their etiquette, conduct, and fashion and proficient in casual conversations about food, wine, travel, fashion, academics, shopping, and cultural events as they attend alumni dinners, campus recruitment drives, and fundraising events" (p. 126). The word "poise," in fact, is often a "euphemism for class" (p. 128). The contestants at Spelman, when introduced in the pre-pageant video, are described as "ever graceful, "effervescent," and "elegant" (Whatley, 2012). The video goes on to assure the audience that the seven women have "passed the test" and can "stand tall with poise and grace" (Whatley, 2012). The Miss Spelman pageant, therefore, serves to verify that these women have been molded by the Spelman environment into the ideal middle- to upper-class woman that all of the women on the Spelman campus should aspire to be. Where women in some HBCU pageants work to "enhance their class appeal," the queen at Spelman is already polished and is using her platform to demonstrate to other women what it looks like to be of a certain class (Tice, 2012, p. 128).

Etiquette and Charm Lessons

Etiquette and "personal branding" for the Spelman woman begins at orientation. One of the sessions that students are required to attend is titled, "Successfully Navigating Any Environment: Tools of Etiquette for the Successful Student" ("2012 new student orientation program," 2012, p. 12). It goes on to describe the cultural capital that students will obtain in this etiquette seminar—"Professionalism and appropriate etiquette will invite any number of opportunities. Students will engage in a dialogue on the tools for professional and success in any environment" (p. 12). Beyond institutional etiquette and "personal branding" sessions, often Miss Spelman takes a prominent role in defining appropriate behavior. Queens on HBCU campuses, particularly at Spelman, often serve "as teachers in *My Fair Lady*–style boot camps that aim to refine unruly working-class women through etiquette, life skills, and beauty culture" (Tice, 2012, p. 11). In fact, Miss Spelman 2010–2011, Meighan Parker, made her platform the P.R.E.T.Y. (Positive Representation of Excellence and Talent for Young Women) campaign (Jones, 2011b). Through her platform, Parker embarked on a campaign devoted to "etiquette training and personal branding" for the women at Spelman. Parker takes her role as the epitome of class-conscious "poise" and "grace" and determines that it is her responsibility to instill these values in other women at Spelman. Beyond personal platforms devoted to instilling middle-class values, Miss Spelman also holds a tea every year during homecoming week. Pictures of women from this tea show them wearing white gloves, large hats, fancy dresses as attire befitting their status in the upper classes. This tea is the ultimate culmination of class-conscious endeavors to create respectable ladies out of all women at Spelman and demonstrates that it is Miss Spelman herself, as tea hostess, who serves as the epitome of middle-class aspirations. These practices, however, may invalidate women who do not have the cultural capital to participate in these events. While the institution attempts to instill this capital by holding etiquette lessons and by having the example of Miss Spelman, herself, the very nature of these events may serve as microinvalidations—ignoring the experiential reality of many of the women on campus and implying that their background is not one to take pride in.

Conclusion

From the bonds of slavery to HBCU queen, Black women have been forced to work to reclaim their bodies. Dress codes and beauty pageants, ostensibly, permit these women to rewrite the narratives that slavery and discrimination have placed upon them. However, within these two traditions meant to create cultural and social capital, there are certain aspects that may, in fact, invalidate women. Spelman College serves as a supportive institution intent on fostering the potential of all women there; however, certain traditions at the college may inadvertently serve as microaggressions toward women who do not ascribe to heteronomativity, hegemonic femininity, or are from the lower class. While traditions allow for Black women to create new narratives and the maintenance of traditions is "very important because it keeps us [Black women] attached to our heritage" since Blacks have "been uprooted" (Tice, 2012, p. 107), over time, traditions must be challenged to ensure that they continue to be relevant and validating to the participants. While certain traditions at Spelman, like dress codes, serve to create social capital through the bonds of sisterhood, they must also be examined in an effort to ensure that they promote the values they supposedly espouse. While pageants serve to create connections between HBCU campuses, the sexualized nature of pageants like Miss Maroon and White, and the class-conscious nature of Miss Spelman may invalidate women who do not fit the narrowly prescribed roles defined by these events. Tradition is important, particularly for those who have been forcibly removed from their homeland. However, these traditions must serve to celebrate all Black women and confirm that "out of the dust of slavery [Black women] have risen" so that, through their traditions, Black women can celebrate all that has been achieved (p. 108).

Note

1. While HBCUs primarily served as a vehicle to move lower-income students into the middle class, there was already a small Black middle class consisting of free Blacks and Blacks who were able to establish themselves during Reconstruction who also attended these institutions.

References

2012 New student orientation program (2012). Retrieved on April 25, 2013 from http://www.spelman.edu/admissions/after-acceptance/new-student-orientation.

Bastide, R. (1967). Color, racism, and Christianity. *Deadalus*, *96*(2), 312–327.

Bourdieu, P. (1986). The forms of capital. In J. G. Richardson (Ed.), *Handbook for theory and research in the sociology of education* (pp. 241–358). Westport, CT: Greenwood Press.

Brazzell, J. C. (1992). Bricks without straw: Missionary-sponsored black higher education in the post-emancipation era. *Journal of Higher Education*, *63*(1), 26–49.

Carter, P. L. (February 2003). Black cultural capital, status positioning, and schooling conflicts for low-income African American youth. *Social Problems*, *50*(1), 136–155.

Cassiman, S. A. (2007). Of witches, welfare queens, and the disaster named poverty: The search for a counter-narrative. *Journal of Poverty*, *10*(4), 51–66.

Cooper, A. J. (1892). *A voice from the South*. Xenia, OH: The Aldine Printing House.

Davis, A. (1981). *Women, race, and class*. New York: Random House.

––––––– (2002). Don't let nobody bother yo principle: The sexual economy of American slavery. In S. Harley (Ed.), *Sister circle: Black women and work* (pp. 103–127). New Brunswick, NJ: Rutgers University Press.

Edelman, M. W. (2000). Spelman college: A safe haven for a young black woman. *Journal of Blacks in Higher Education*, *27*, 118–123.

Fallon, (2009, October 23). Yes, I'm a Spelman woman, but do I have to wear a white dress every damn day? Retrieved on April 23, 2013 from http://www.blackyouth-project.com/2009/10/yes-i%E2%80%99m-a-spelman-woman-but-do-i-have-to-wear-a-white-dress-every-damn-day/.

Fleming, J. (1984). *Blacks in college: A comparative study of student success in Black and White institutions*. San Francisco, CA: Jossey-Bass.

Frazier, E. F. (1957). *Black bourgeoisie*. Glencoe, IL: The Free Press.

Gasman, M. (2002). W. E. B. Du Bois and Charles S. Johnson: Differing views on the role of philanthropy in higher education. *History of Education Quarterly*, *42*(4), 493–516.

––––––– (November/December 2009). Historically black colleges and universities during a time of crisis. *Academe*. Retrieved from http://www.aaup.org/article/historically-black-colleges-and-universities-time-economic-crisis#.UT3p3hlM-bN.

Gordon, S. A. (2004). "Boundless possibilities:" Home sewing and the meanings of women's domestic work in the United States, 1890–1930. *Journal of Women's History*, *16*(2), 68–91.

Graham, L. (1999). *Our kind of people: Inside America's Black upper class.* New York: Harper Collins.
Guy-Sheftall, B. (1982). Black women and higher education. Spelman and Bennett colleges revisited. *Journal of Negro Education, 51*(3), 278–287.
Harrison, L. (1997). "It's a nice day for a white wedding": The debutante ball and constructions of femininity. *Feminism & Psychology, 7*(4), 495–516.
Higgenbotham, E. B. (Winter 1992). African-American women's history and the metalanguage of race. *Signs, 17*(2), 251–274.
IPEDS Data Center: Bennett College (2011). Student financial aid. Retrieved on April 22, 2013 from http://nces.ed.gov/ipeds/datacenter/SnapshotX.aspx?unitId=acb4b2b4b4ae.
IPEDS Data Center: Spelman College (2011). Student financial aid. Retrieved on April 22, 2013 from http://nces.ed.gov/ipeds/datacenter/Snapshotx.aspx?unitId=acafacabb1ab.
Johnson, C. (2012). Identity, role, and self-representation The Spelman experience and performing for a gender-specific audience. In J. J. Bickerstaff (Ed.), *The Mellon Mays Undergraduate Fellowship Journal* (pp. 80–86). Cambridge, MA: Harvard University.
Jones, C. (2011a, April 6). *Miss Spelman Pageant 2010.* Retrieved on April 25, 2013 from http://www.youtube.com/watch?v=uo4KcP1_Uw0.
——— (2011b, May 22). *Meighan Parker, Miss Spelman 2010–2011 – Vote for me!* Retrieved on May 4, 2013 from http://www.youtube.com/watch?v=HwrDowkT5CY.
Mosely, R. (2012, April 21). *Morehouse MMW'12—Opening dance.* Retrieved on April 25, 2013 from http://www.youtube.com/watch?v=5tQxDPfQYCU.
New student orientation (n.d.). Retrieved on April 23, 2013 from http://12.13.176.164/students/prospective/newstudents/transpreorientation.shtml.
Perkins, L. M. (1983). The impact of the "cult of true womanhood" on the education of black women. *Journal of Social Issues, 39*(3), 183–190.
Perna, L., Lundy-Wagner, V., Drezner, N. D., Gasman, M., Yoon, S., Bose, E., & Gary, S. (2009). The contributions of HBCUs to the preparation of African American women for STEM careers: A case study. *Research in Higher Education, 50*(1), 1–23.
Shaw, S. J. (1996). *What a woman ought to be and do: Black professional women workers during the Jim Crow Era.* Chicago, IL: University of Chicago Press.
Sue, D. W. (2010). *Microaggressions in everyday life: Race, gender, and sexual orientation.* John Wiley & Sons.
Tice, K. W. (2012). *Queens of academe: Beauty pageantry, student bodies, and college life.* New York: Oxford University Press.
Whatley, J. (2012, April 12). *Ms. Spelman 2012.* Retrieved on May 5, 2013 from http://www.youtube.com/watch?v=0gQiEzTvBzI.
The white dress tradition (n.d.). Retrieved on April 23, 2013 from http://www.spelman.edu/alumnae/alumnae-affairs/the-white-dress-tradition.
Yancy, G. (2008). *Black bodies, White gazes: The continuing significance of race.* Ledham, MD: The Rowman & Littlefield Publishing Group.

CONTRIBUTORS

Ufuoma Abiola is an EdD student in higher education at the University of Pennsylvania. She is also a research assistant at the Penn Center for Minority Serving Institutions.

Jacqueline Amparo is a recent graduate of the higher education master's program at the University of Pennsylvania.

Joseph Barone is a recent graduate of the higher education master's program at the University of Pennsylvania.

Felecia Commodore is a PhD candidate in higher education at the University of Pennsylvania. She is also a research assistant at the Penn Center for Minority Serving Institutions.

Dennis Daly recently graduated from the master's program in higher education at the University of Pennsylvania.

Tiffany N. Decker recently graduated from the master's program in higher education at the University of Pennsylvania.

Christian Edge recently graduated from the master's program at the University of Pennsylvania. He currently works at the University of Pennsylvania.

Paola Esmieu recently graduated from the higher education master's program at the University of Pennsylvania. She currently works at the University of the Sciences.

Yulanda Essoka is a graduate of the higher education master's program at the University of Pennsylvania.

Marybeth Gasman is professor of higher education in the Graduate School of Education at the University of Pennsylvania. She is also the director of the Penn Center for Minority Serving Institutions.

Contributors

Alexandra Iannucci was a student at the University of Pennsylvania. She works at St. Joseph's College.

Brandy Jackson recently graduated from the higher education master's program at the University of Pennsylvania. She is a graduate of Fisk University.

Channing Johnson was a student at the University of Pennsylvania. She is a graduate of Tougaloo College.

Andrew Martinez recently graduated from the higher education master's program at the University of Pennsylvania. He currently works at Cornell University.

Sarah Mullen recently graduated from the higher education master's program at the University of Pennsylvania. She currently works at the University of Pennsylvania.

Matthew Nelson recently graduated from the higher education master's program at the University of Pennsylvania. He is also a graduate of Prairie View A&M University.

Sakinah I. Rahman is a master's student in higher education at the University of Pennsylvania. She currently works at the University of Pennsylvania.

Phillip Scotton is a recent graduate of the higher education program at the University of Pennsylvania.

Atiya Strothers is a PhD. student in higher education at Rutgers State University.

Quinton Stroud recently graduated from the master's program at the University of Pennsylvania. He is also a graduate of Florida A&M University.

Tyree Williams recently graduated from the master's program at the University of Pennsylvania. He is also a graduate of Cheyney University of Pennsylvania.

INDEX

A Different World, 256
Byron Douglass, 258
Cora Catherine Calhoun, 259, 260, 265, 266
Diane Nash, 259, 264, 265, 266
Dwayne Wayne, 256, 257, 259, 262
Jada Pinkett, 257
Jasmine Guy, 259, 260
Jeremiah Gilbert, 257
Judge Mercer Gilbert and socialite Marion Gilbert, 257
Kimberley Reese, 256, 257
Lena Leo Calhoun, 259, 260, 262
Moses Calhoun, 260, 261
Mr. Gaines, 257
Ron Johnson, 256
Whitley Gilbert, 256, 257, 258, 259, 262, 266
Winifred "Freddie" Brooks, 256
Abiola, Ufuoma, 6
academia, 4
access, 4, 5, 6, 19, 57, 58, 60, 65, 77, 93, 98, 111, 115, 116, 120, 141, 152, 160, 161, 175, 191, 203, 211, 242
accreditation, 3, 11
administration, 5
African American presidents, 57, 62, 63, 65, 71, 72
African American students, 5, 7, 22, 69, 70, 146
African American women, 29, 31, 40, 43

Black males, 39–47, 49, 53, 175
black scientists and engineers, 15
Black students, 1, 22, 43, 51, 77, 78, 107, 114–20, 122–4, 134, 137, 141–2, 169, 181, 203–4, 212, 224–5, 229, 276–7
Allen, Walter, 206
alumni, 6, 14, 89–100, 124, 133, 135
American Council on Education (ACE) 2012 report, 62
American College President Study, 63
Amparo, Jacqueline, 6
Anglo-Saxon, 238, 241, 245, 248, 250
Atlanta, GA, 27, 94

Baker, John, 264
Barone, Joseph, 7
Battle and Ashley, 224
Bennett College, 170
Birnbaum and Umbach, 63
Black bourgeoisie, 260, 261, 263, 266
Black Greek Letter Organizations (BGLOs), 204, 205, 206, 212, 213
Alpha Phi Alpha, at Cornell University in 1906, 203
Black Greek Letter Fraternities (BGF), 201, 202, 203, 204, 205, 206, 207, 208, 209, 210, 211, 212, 213
hazing, 15, 16, 18
Black inferiority, 244
Black society, 168
Black Codes, 242

Bouchet, Edward, 58
  Yale University, 58, 170
Bowie State University, 166, 173–6, 178–9
  Krishnasami, Adrian, 173–6, 178–9
Britt, Gerald, 19
Butler, Johnnella, 29, 30
Buttrick, Wallace, 247

Catholic University, 219, 227
Cavalier, 239, 240
  Norman Cavaliers, 239–41
Center for the Study of MSIs, 2
  minority-serving institutions, 63, 82, 86
Champion, Robert, 15, 16, 18
Cheyney University, 51, 89, 181, 189, 190, 191, 192, 193, 194, 196, 197
  Clinton Pettus, 190
  Community College of Philadelphia (CCP), 51
  Dean Tara Kent, 191–2
  Governor Tom Corbett, 190
  The Keystone Honors Academy, 189–94, 197, 198
Christianity, 240, 242
Civil War, 41, 129–31, 235, 239, 242
  Emancipation Proclamation, 41
  Freedman's Bureau, 129
Claflin University, 95
  Fogle, Marcus, 95
  Tisdale, Henry N., 95
Clergy for Marriage Equality, 178
Cole, Johnnetta, 32
Council for the Support and Advancement of Education (CASE), 91
critical race theorists, 13
curriculum, 5, 6

Daley, Dennis, 7
Dallas, 18, 19, 21
Decker, Tiffany, 7
degree attainment, 1, 4
  Bachelor of Arts or Bachelor of Science degrees, 28
  doctoral degree, 57–8, 62, 66
  educational attainment, 59, 68
  Fine Arts, Humanities, Social Sciences, and Natural Sciences, 28
Delaware State University, 79
Dillard University, 14, 43–7, 49, 52
  Dillard chaplain Gall Bowman, 171
diversity, 1, 6–7, 11, 12, 21, 58, 63, 66, 69, 72, 75–6, 78, 82, 85, 86, 116–17, 119, 121–2, 124, 157, 171–4, 188, 211, 223, 225, 256, 262, 290
Douglas, Frederick, 237, 255
Dr. Dre and Jimmy Iovine, 14
  Compton, 14
Du Bois, W. E. B., 262, 263
  Atlanta University, 262, 266
  Clark-Atlanta University, 262, 265

economic crisis, 3
Edge, Christian, 7
endowment, 3, 4, 12
enrollment, 1, 53
  Black male enrollment, 6, 39–43, 45, 47, 51, 53, 171
  undergraduate enrollment, 45
Esmieu, Paola, 6
Essoka, Yulanda, 7
ethnic demographic changes, 5

faculty, 5, 6, 12
  African American faculty, 6, 57, 61–2, 65–6, 70–2
  White faculty, 6, 75–9, 81–6
financial constraints, 3
financial stability, 3
first generation college students, 1, 5, 110, 213
first year attrition rates, 30, 145, 147
  low African American male student persistence, 60
  persistence, 5, 12, 31, 70
  recruitment, 46, 47, 49
  student persistence, 27, 33

Index

Fisk University, 262, 264–5
Florida, 16, 17, 18
Florida A&M University (FAMU), 15–18
Frazier, E. Franklin, 263
funding, 2, 3, 12
　government funding, 3, 4
　performance-based funding, 3
　Title V funding, 119, 120

Gasman and Bowman, 11–13, 15, 23, 91, 96, 98, 100, 135
Harper and Gasman, 172
gender, 5, 223, 224, 228, 229
　gender bias, 222, 226
　gender enrollment gap, 46, 49, 50
　gender expression, 229
　gender gap, 40, 43, 48, 50, 52, 53
　gender identity, 228
　gender makeup, 45, 49
　gender parity, 41–5, 47, 49
　gendered perpetuation of leadership, 45
General Education Board (GEB), 236, 245, 247, 249, 250
generalizations, 11, 12, 13
global education, 4
　international, 5
graduation rates, 2, 5, 28, 30, 48, 68, 183–4, 190, 191, 193–4, 196, 199
Great Migration, 249, 264
Greek Letter Organizations (GLOs), 203
　College of William and Mary, 203
　Greek Letter Organizations (GLOs), 203
　Phi Beta Kappa, 203
　Social Greek Letter Organizations, 203

Hampton and Tuskegee model, 77, 136, 166, 247
Handy, W. C., 131
　Alabama A&M College, 131
　Alabama A&M University, 135

Harper, 50
　anti-deficit achievement framework, 50
　Black Male Achievement Study, 50
Harris, Andrea, 19, 24
Harris-Stowe State College, 79
HBCU graduate and leader of the Coalition of African-American Pastors, 169
　Owens, William, 169
HBCU leaders, 12–15, 20–1, 24, 25, 169
　inequitable funding for HBCUs, 60
　nurturing environments, 5
　prominent Black figures, 15
Helms (1995), 80, 81
　contact, disintegration, reintegration, pseudo-independence, immersion/emersion, and autonomy, 80, 81
　white privilege, 80, 81
higher education, 1, 2, 3, 4, 65, 72, 75–6, 85, 90–2, 107, 108, 110–16, 118–21, 123, 129, 139, 141–2, 146, 150, 161, 170, 183, 186, 205, 212
　American higher education, 11, 57, 89, 139, 203
　equity issues, 57, 58, 65
　higher education community, 2, 3, 4
　inequities in higher education, 39
　Minorities in Higher Education report, 58
　US higher education, 57, 58, 203
　US institution of higher learning, 58, 61
　US postsecondary institutions, 59
Hillman College, 256–9, 263
Hispanic-Serving Institution (HSI), 118–20
Historically White Institutions (HWI), 1, 40, 75–9, 82–6, 93, 107, 108, 111–17, 129, 131, 133, 134, 136, 137, 269
　elite wealthy institutions, 12
　Ivy League Universities, 12, 21
HIV/AIDS, 169–70, 176, 178
honor programs, 181–90, 192–9
　Council of Undergraduate Research, 195

Hooks, Bell, 1994, 113
  native informant, 113
Horne, Lena, 262
Howard University, 83, 84
  moron, martyr, messiah, marginal man, 83, 84
  Warnat, Winifred, 83
Hubei University, 154
  CAPES/HBCU-Brazil Alliance Partnership, 154
  Institute for International Education's International Academic Partnership Program, 154
  President David Wilson, 155
Human Rights Campaign (HRC), 175–6
  Braud, Brandon, 172
  Payne, Donna, 175
Huston-Tillotson, University, 115
  Earvin, Larry, 115

Iannucci, Alexandra, 7
International Training, and the Council on International Educational Exchange (CIEE), 156, 159
internationalization, 159, 160
intersectionality, 167, 173, 219, 221, 223, 224, 279

Jackson, Brandy, 6
Jackson State University, 93
Jim Crow caste system, 236, 239, 244, 245, 248, 264
Johnson, Channing, 7

K-12 system, 58, 62
  K-12 sector, 6
  pipeline, 5, 6
Kimbrough, Walter, 14, 17, 23–5, 39, 43, 46, 47, 48, 49, 50, 52, 98, 169, 170
  Philander Smith College, 169, 170
King, Rodney Riots in Los Angeles, 264

LA Times, 14, 23
Latino, 107, 108, 109, 110, 111, 112, 113, 114, 115, 116, 117, 118, 119, 120, 121, 122, 123, 124, 142
  Afro-Latino, 118, 124
  Chicana, 112
  cultural and familial issues, institution-based issues, and issues of racism, 108
  family ties, 109
  Hispanic, 108, 118, 119, 120
  Hispanic Youth Symposium (HYS), 120
  non-Hispanic Whites, 107
  Pew Hispanic Center, 108
Lawson, James, 265
leadership, 2, 3, 4, 12, 71
Learning Resources Center, 32, 35
LeMoyne-Owen College, 256
LGBT, 5, 7, 165–80, 224, 231
  Black lesbians, 219, 221–5, 227–33
  Lesbian, Gay, Bisexual, and Transgender (LGBT) Centers, 7
  lesbian, gay, bisexual, transgender, and queer (LGBTQ), 219, 221, 224–7, 229–32
  Lesbian, Gay, Bisexual, Transgender, Queer, Intersex and Allies (LGBTQIA), 166, 173, 174, 176
  lesbian identity, 7
  White lesbian, 219, 221–4, 227, 230
Lincoln University in Missouri, 79
Linnaeus, Carolus, 236
Lorde, Audre, 227
lower-income, 1, 20, 120, 139, 143, 145, 147, 160, 269

marching bands, 7
  "Adopt a Band Student Uniform," 135
  Army Captain Drye, Frank, 132
  Army Major Smith, Nathaniel Clark, 132
  Berger, Kenneth, 133
  Black band members, 131, 132
  Black college Battle of the Bands and HBCU Bowls, 133
  first Black band director, 132

Index

The Honda Battle of the Bands (HBOB), 135
Honda Campus All-Star Challenge (HCASC), 135
Marching 100 band, 15
marginalized groups, 6, 107, 116, 220, 221
Margolis and Romero (1998), 67
  hidden curriculum, 67
Martinez, Andrew, 6
Mason Dixon line, 242
media, 7, 11–13, 16–18, 21–5, 89, 91, 100
microaggressions, 221, 277–81, 292
microcultural identity development, 81
  unexamined identity, conformity, resistance and separatism, and integration, 81
Mid-Atlantic University (MAU), 207, 210, 211, 212
  Middle-State University (MSU), 207, 210, 211
  South-Eastern University (SEU), 207, 210, 211, 212
Middlebury College, 41
missionaries, 76, 77
monolithic, 1, 25, 52, 78, 113, 212, 254, 266
Morehouse, 12, 171
  Fluker, Walter Earl, 171
Morgan State University, 153, 154, 155
  Center for Global Studies and Exchange at Morgan State University, 153, 154, 155
  Dr. M'bare N'gom, 153
  Winbush, Ray director of the Institute for Urban Research, 117
Morrill Act of 1890, 59, 91, 130
Mullen, Sarah, 7
multiple identities, 5

National Association for the Advancement of Colored People (NAACP), 266
National Association of Colored Women (NACW), 266
National Black Leadership Commission on AIDS, 170
National Football League, 17
National Science Foundation, 15
  scholarships, 14
NC Institute of Minority Economic Development, 20
Nelson, Matt, 6
New Orleans, 44
  Hurricane Katrina, 48
Norfolk State University, 168
Norman, 238, 240

Obama, Michelle, 255
Office of Civil Rights, 190
Office of Greek Life, 206
  Multicultural Greek Council Advisor, 206
Ogden, Robert C., 247

Patterson, Mary Jane, 59
  first African American female college graduate, 59
  Oberlin College, 59
Paul Quinn College, 18, 93
Peabody, George Foster, 246, 247
Pell Grant recipients, 1, 147, 207
Pennsylvania State System of Higher Education (PASSHE), 184, 189
philanthropists, 3, 15, 77
Price's, Leontyne
  Belafonte, Harry, 255
Puritan, 239, 240, 241, 246, 250
  Anglo-Saxon Cavaliers, 239, 241

Rahman, Sakinah I., 6
Raleigh, NC, 44
Ramirez, Fred (2003), 110
Read, Florence, 31, 35
Reason, Charles Lewis, 61
  New York Central College, McGrawville, 61
recession, 3
  affordable housing, 18
  economic stratification, 20
  inequitable status quo, 19

Index

Reese, James 369th Regiment "Harlem Hellfighters" band, 132
retention rates, 2, 5, 6, 28, 30, 32, 115, 183, 184, 190, 191, 194, 196, 199
Retention strategies, 28, 30, 32, 33
Revolutionary War, 237
Robeson, Paul, 266
Robinson, Larry, 15–18, 24, 25
Robinson and Biran, 228
Rockefeller Sr, John D., 246

Saint Augustine's University, 43, 44, 45, 46, 47, 49, 52
Scotton, Phillip, 6
segregation, 59
    affirmative action, 60, 61, 62, 66, 67, 71, 112
    Brown v. Board of Education, 59, 77, 115, 116, 204
    Civil Rights Movement, 77
    Plessy v. Ferguson in 1896, 59
    racial disparity, 58, 59
    racial segregation in education, 59, 60
shatter complacency, 15, 19
Shaw University, 79
Smith and Borgstedt (1985), 78, 79
Social Darwinism, 244, 245, 248, 250
    Darwin, 244
socioeconomic status (SES), 1, 18, 69
Solórzano and Yosso, 13, 14, 17, 18
Sorrell, Michael J., 18–21, 24, 25, 98
SPEAK, Students Promoting Equal Action and Knowledge, 167
Spelman College, 6, 7, 12, 27–37, 94–5, 97, 153, 155–60, 170, 270, 273, 276–87, 289–92
    Association of Fundraising Professional Collegiate Chapter, 95
    Guy-Sheftall, Beverly, 170
    Moore, Jennifer, 94
    Spelman alumnae, 35–7
    Spelman MILE, 28, 29, 30, 32, 33
    Spelman sisterhood, 35
    The Story of Spelman College, 35
Spencer, Herbert, 244

St. Phillip's College, 119, 120
Steele and Aronson, 22
stereotyping, 3, 11, 13, 17, 21, 113
    stereotype threat, 22
story-telling, 13, 21, 25
    counter-storytelling, 12, 13, 14, 15, 17, 19, 21, 25
Strothers, Atiya, 6
Stroud, Quinton, 6
student affairs, 4
student success, 2, 3, 5, 205
    Black male success, 50
students of color, 5, 6, 139, 141, 142, 145, 147, 151, 165, 166, 171, 172, 173, 203, 207
study abroad, 1, 7, 139, 140, 142, 143, 145, 146, 147, 148, 149, 150, 151, 152, 153, 154, 155, 156, 157, 158, 159, 160, 161, 182, 186
    Council on International Educational Exchange in 1988, 141
    Institute of International Education, 140, 141
Suber, Dianne, 43, 46, 47, 48, 49, 50, 51
Sumner, William Graham, 244
sustainability, 3
Syracuse University, 30

Tatum, Beverly Daniel, 29, 94
Tennessee State Fair, 265
Tennessee State University, 79
The College Board, 27
    College's Strategic Plan Report, 28, 29, 37
The Pew Charitable Trust, 32
The Southern Association of Colleges and School Commission on Colleges, 28
Thompson, 82, 83, 85
    missionary zealot, dedicated professional, young idealistic scholar, and academic reject, 82
Tinto, Vincent, 30
    Tinto's (1993) Model of Institutional Departure, 70

Tougaloo College, 181, 189, 194, 195, 196, 197, 198
  Andrew W. Mellon Foundation, 194
  president Beverly Wade Hogan, 194
Trust's Third Black Colleges Program, 32
Twilight, Alexander, 41

U.S. News & World Report, 28
underrepresentation, 13, 57, 60, 61, 111, 142
United Church of Christ and the United Methodist Church, 44
University of Maine, 183
University of Maryland, Baltimore County, Meyerhoff Program, 187
University of Maryland—College Park, 174, 179
Urban League, 266
US Department of Education in 1996, 76

Van Camp, Barden, Sloan, and Clarke, 225

Wallington, Nehemiah, 246
Washington, Booker T., 132
  Tuskegee Normal School, 132
White Greek Letter Organizations (WGLOs), 204, 205
White Greek Fraternities (WGFs), 202, 204, 208, 211, 212
White students, 6, 112, 213
Williams, Tyree, 7
Wilson, Amanda, 16

Xavier University of Louisiana, 79

Yolanda Watson and Sheila Gregory, 31

GPSR Compliance
The European Union's (EU) General Product Safety Regulation (GPSR) is a set of rules that requires consumer products to be safe and our obligations to ensure this.

If you have any concerns about our products, you can contact us on

ProductSafety@springernature.com

In case Publisher is established outside the EU, the EU authorized representative is:

Springer Nature Customer Service Center GmbH
Europaplatz 3
69115 Heidelberg, Germany

www.ingramcontent.com/pod-product-compliance
Lightning Source LLC
LaVergne TN
LVHW011801060526
838200LV00053B/3647